LIFE OF PYTHAGORAS,

OR

PYTHAGORIC LIFE.

ACCOMPANIED BY

FRAGMENTS OF THE ETHICAL WRITINGS
OF CERTAIN PYTHAGOREANS IN THE DORIC DIALECT;

AND A

COLLECTION OF PYTHAGORIC SENTENCES

FROM STOBÆUS AND OTHERS,

WHICH ARE OMITTED BY GALE IN HIS

OPUSCULA MYTHOLOGICA,

AND HAVE NOT BEEN NOTICED BY ANY EDITOR.

TRANSLATED FROM THE GREEK, BY

THOMAS TAYLOR

———

Approach ye genuine philosophic few,
The Pythagoric Life belongs to you:
But far, far off ye vulgar herd profane;
For Wisdom's voice is heard by you in vain:
And you, Mind's lowest link, and darksome end,
Good Rulers, Customs, Laws, alone can mend.

———

FIRST EDITION, 1818.

RE-PRINTED WITH NEW FORMATTING
AND ADDITIONAL APPENDICES, 2016.

www.kshetrabooks.com

Iamblichus' Life of Pythagoras, or Pythagoric Life.
First Edition, 1818

Re-print of 1st Edition
(with new formatting and additional appendices)

ISBN: 978-1511605250

Contents

Detailed Contents of the Life of Pythagoras

Chapters 1-4: Introduction. Pythagoras's birth, youth, early education. Becomes a student of Thales, etc. Years of learning in Syria, Egypt and Babylon.

Chapters 5-7: Pythagoras returns to Samos. His first student. First attempts to teach widely. Declines political position. Travels to Italy. Builds communities and school at Crotona.

Chapters 8-12: Initial and foundational teachings. On esteem for parents; on temperance; importance of the cultivation of learning; teachings given to politicians, to young boys, to women.

Chapter 13: Taming of wild animals.

Chapter 14: On reincarnation.

Chapters 15-16: Preparation of disciples for erudition. On: Melody; Purifications; Abstentions; Studies; Diet; Exercise. Purifying the dianoetic part of the soul and the divine eye.

Chapters 17-18: Trials and probation for discipleship (initial neglect, quinquennial silence, etc.) Organization of the community. Classes of disciples. General teachings.

Chapter 19: Story of Abaris. The purpose of Pythagoras's Life.

Chapters 20-21: Requirements of discipleship. Daily routine of disciples.

Foreword

The present volume is a verbatim reproduction of Thomas Taylor's translation of Iamblichus's *Life of Pythagoras,* originally published in 1818. Iamblichus's biography does more than simply outline Pythagoras's life, but also provides many insights into the doctrines he taught, his methods of teaching, and perhaps most importantly, the lifestyle he promoted among his students: a lifestyle as applicable today as ever before. Many sound teachings on justice, non-violence, temperance, forebearance, and other virtues are given herein, along with teachings on lifestyle, community, politics and family life.

To aid the reader in seeking out specific doctrines or ideas, we have provided a list of detailed contents for each chapter of the biography. Iamblichus's biography is a text that may be read straight through, or piece by piece, or one selection at a time. Much can be learned from even a basic perusal of the contents of any selected chapter, and many fine quotes on specific topics will be found by using the detailed contents to locate them.

In addition to the *Life of Pythagoras*, Taylor included several other Pythagorean texts in his original publication. We have included these, along with few additional translations which he himself approved as worthy of study.

Texts included in both the 1818 and present volumes are as follows:

1. Taylor's introduction and his translation of the *Life of Pythagoras* along with his Notes and Additional Notes, which shed much light on the subjects dealt with in the biography.

2. His collection of the "Fragments of the Ethical Writings of

Certain Pythagoreans." From the latter has been removed his rendering of the "Sentences of Sextus" (see editor's note in Taylor's introduction).

Additional texts included in the present volume, which have been added as an Appendix, are as follows:

1. Taylor's translation of "The Pythagoric Sentences of Demophilus."
2. Two translations from William Bridgman: "The Similitudes of Demophilus" and "The Golden Sentences of Democrates."
3. William Bridgman's translation of "The Pythagoric Symbols, with the Explanations of Iamblichus," with edits drawn from Taylor's own translation of several of the symbols and explanations, which were included in the original 1818 publication of this *Life of Pythagoras*.

The latter translations being added to the present volume provides the reader with a fine collection of truly *Pythagorean* texts, covering the major themes and topics of their teachings. This ought to give the liberal reader enough to gain a footing into the central doctrines and practices of the Pythagoreans, and these will further aid in a study of the Platonic and Orphic texts, all of which rightly belong together.

———

In this present edition, the formatting of the original has been changed in order to render the text more easily readable. The copious footnotes found in the original have been collected and placed in order at the end of the *Life of Pythagoras*, followed by Taylor's Additional Notes.

In the margins we have added the pagination of the original edition, so that all references made to the original over the intervening centuries may be easily traced in the present volume, despite its altered pagination.

Besides these changes, and minor changes in formatting style, the text has not been altered, except in cases where certain Greek characters were in need of modernization.

Introduction

When it is considered that Pythagoras was the father of philosophy, authentic memoirs of his life cannot fail to be uncommonly interesting to every lover of wisdom, and particularly to those who reverence the doctrines of Plato, the most genuine and the best of all his disciples. And that the following memoirs of Pythagoras by Iamblichus are authentic, is acknowledged by all the critics, as they are for the most part obviously derived from sources of very high antiquity; and where the sources are unknown, there is every reason to believe, from the great worth and respectability of the biographer, that the information is perfectly accurate and true.

Of the biographer, indeed, Iamblichus, it is well known to every tyro in Platonism that he was dignified by all the Platonists that succeeded him with the epithet of *divine;* and after the encomium passed on him by the acute Emperor Julian, that *"he was posterior indeed in time, but not in genius, to Plato,"*[1] all further praise of him would be as unnecessary, as the defamation of him by certain modern critics is contemptible and idle. For these *homonculi* looking solely to his deficiency in point of style, and not to the magnitude of his intellect, perceive only his little blemishes, but have not even a glimpse of his surpassing excellence. They minutely notice the motes that are scattered in the sunbeams of his genius, but they feel not its invigorating warmth, they see not its dazzling radiance.

Of this very extraordinary man there is a life extant by Eunapius, the substance of which I have given in my "History of the Restoration of the Platonic Theology,"[2] and to which I refer the English reader.

At present I shall only select from that work the following biographical particulars respecting our Iamblichus: He was descended of a family equally illustrious, fortunate, and rich. His country was Chalcis, a city of Syria, which was called Cœle. He associated with Anatolius who was the second to Porphyry, but he far excelled him in his attainments, and ascended to the very summit of philosophy. But after he had been for some time connected with Anatolius, and most probably found him insufficient to satisfy the vast desires of his soul, he applied himself to Porphyry, to whom (says Eunapius) he was in nothing inferior, except in the structure and power of composition. For his writings were not so elegant and graceful as those of Porphyry: they were neither agreeable, nor perspicuous; nor free from impurity of diction. And though they were not entirely involved in obscurity, and perfectly faulty; yet as Plato formerly said of Xenocrates, he did not sacrifice to the *Mercurial Graces*. Hence he is far from detaining the reader with delight, who merely regards his diction; but will rather avert and dull his attention, and frustrate his expectation. However, though the surface of his conceptions is not covered with the flowers of elocution, yet the depth of them is admirable, and his genius is truly sublime. And admitting his style to abound in general with those defects, which have been noticed by the critics, yet it appears to me that the decision of the anonymous Greek writer respecting his Answer to the Epistle of Porphyry,[3] is more or less applicable to all his other works. For he says, that "his diction in that Answer is concise and definite, and that his conceptions are full of efficacy, are elegant, and divine."[4]

Iamblichus shared in an eminent degree the favor of divinity, on account of his cultivation of justice; and obtained a numerous multitude of associates and disciples, who came from all parts of the world, for the purpose of participating the streams of wisdom, which so plentifully flowed from the sacred fountain of his wonderful mind. Among these was Sopater the Syrian,[5] who was most skilful both in speaking and writing; Eustathius the Cappadocian; and of the Greeks, Theodorus and Euphrasius. All these were excellent for their virtues and attainments, as well as many other of his disciples, who were not much inferior to the former in eloquence; so that it seems wonderful how Iamblichus could attend to all of them, with such gentleness of manners and benignity of disposition as he continually displayed.

He performed some few particulars relative to the veneration of divinity by himself, without his associates and disciples; but was inseparable from his familiars in most of his operations. He imitated in his diet the frugal simplicity of the most ancient times; and during his repast, exhilarated those who were present by his behaviour, and filled them as with nectar by the sweetness of his discourse.

A celebrated philosopher named Alypius, who was deeply skilled in dialectic, was contemporary with Iamblichus, but was of such a diminutive stature, that he exhibited the appearance of a pigmy. However, his great abilities amply compensated for this trifling defect. For his body might be said to be consumed into soul; just as the great Plato says, that divine bodies, unlike those that are mortal, are situated in souls. Thus also it might be asserted of Alypius, that he had migrated into soul, and that he was contained and governed by a nature superior to man. This Alypius had many followers, but his mode of philosophizing was confined to private conference and disputation, without committing any of his dogmas to writing. Hence his disciples gladly applied themselves to Iamblichus, desirous to draw abundantly from the exuberant streams of his inexhaustible mind. The fame therefore of each continually increasing, they once accidentally met like two refulgent stars, and were surrounded by so great a crowd of auditors, that it resembled some mighty musæum. While Iamblichus on this occasion waited rather to be interrogated, than to propose a question himself, Alypius, contrary to the expectation of every one, relinquishing philosophical discussions, and seeing himself surrounded with a theatre of men, turned to Iamblichus, and said to him:

viii

> "Tell me, O philosopher, is either the rich man unjust, or the heir of the unjust man? For in this case there is no medium."

But Iamblichus hating the acuteness of the question, replied:

> "O most wonderful of all men, this manner of considering, whether some one excels in externals, is foreign from our method of philosophizing; since we inquire whether a man abounds in the virtue which it is proper for him to possess, and which is adapted to a philosopher."

Iamblichus, Life of Pythagoras

After he had said this he departed, and at the same time all the surrounding multitude was immediately dispersed. But Iamblichus, when he was alone, admired the acuteness of the question, and often privately resorted to Alypius, whom he very much applauded for his acumen and sagacity; so that after his decease, he wrote his life. This Alypius was an Alexandrian by birth, and died in his own country, worn out with age: and after him Iamblichus,[6] leaving behind him many roots and fountains of philosophy; which through the cultivation of succeeding Platonists, produced a fair variety of vigorous branches, and copious streams.

For an account of the theological writings of Iamblichus, I refer the reader to my above-mentioned History of the Restoration of the Platonic Theology; and for accurate critical information concerning all his works, to the Bibliotheca Græca of Fabricius.

Of the following work, the life of Pythagoras, it is necessary to observe that the original has been transmitted to us in a very imperfect state, partly from the numerous verbal errors of the text, partly from the want of connexion in the things that are narrated, and partly from many particulars being related in different places, in the very same words; so that the conjecture of Kuster, one of the German editors of this work, is highly probable, that it had not received the last hand of Iamblichus, but that others formed this treatise from the confused materials which they found among his Manuscripts, after his death. Notwithstanding all its defects, however, it is, as I have before observed, a most interesting work; and the benefits are inestimable, which the dissemination of it is calculated to produce. And as two of the most celebrated critics among the Germans, Kuster and Kiessling, have given two splendid editions of this work, it is evident they must have been deeply impressed with a conviction of its value and importance.

As to the Pythagoric Ethical Fragments, all eulogy of them is superfluous, when it is considered that, independently of their being written by very early Pythagoreans, they were some of the sources from which Aristotle himself derived his consummate knowledge of morality, as will be at once evident by comparing his Nicomachean Ethics with these fragments.

With respect to the collection of Pythagoric Sentences in this volume, it is almost needless to observe that they are incomparably excellent; and it is deeply to be regretted that the Greek original of the Sentences of Sextus[7] being lost, the fraudulent Latin version of them by the Presbyter Ruffinus alone remains. I call it a fraudulent version, because Ruffinus, wishing to persuade the reader that these Sentences were written by a bishop of the name of Sixtus, has in many places perverted and contaminated the meaning of the original. In the selection, however, which I have made from the Sentences, I have endeavoured, and I trust not in vain, to give the genuine sense of Sextus, unmingled with the barbarous and polluted interpolations of Ruffinus.

Editor's Note: More has come to light regarding these sentences since Taylor's day, including further copies in Greek, Syriac and Coptic. See the critical edition: *The Sentences of Sextus*, Henry Chadwick, Cambridge University Press, 2003. These sentences, in whichever language one finds them, are much more Christian than Pythagorean. They represent a kind of appropriation of certain Pythagorean ideas and style into Christian thought and cannot be relied upon as purely Pythagorean in nature. For this reason we have not included Taylor's rendition of these sentences in the current volume, and advise the student of Pythagorean doctrine to hold a critical eye while examining them.

If the English reader has my translation of the Sentences of Demophilus, and Mr. Bridgman's translation of the Golden Sentences of Democrates, and the Similitudes of Demophilus,[8] he will then be possessed of all the Pythagoric Sentences that are extant, those alone of Sextus excepted, which I have not translated, in consequence of the very impure and spurious state, in which they at present exist.

I deem it also requisite to observe, that the Pythagoric life which is here delineated, is a specimen of the greatest perfection in virtue and wisdom, which can be obtained by man in the present state. Hence, it exhibits piety unadulterated with folly, moral virtue uncontaminated with vice, science unmingled with sophistry, dignity of mind and manners unaccompanied with pride, a sublime magnificence in   *xi* theory, without any degradation in practice, and a vigor of intellect, which elevates its possessor to the vision of divinity, and thus deifies while it exalts.

Iamblichus'
Life of Pythagoras

Life of Pythagoras, or Pythagoric Life

Chapter I.

Since it is usual with all men of sound understandings, to call on divinity, when entering on any philosophic discussion, it is certainly much more appropriate to do this in the consideration of that philosophy which justly receives its denomination from the divine Pythagoras. For as it derives its origin from the Gods, it cannot be apprehended without their inspiring aid. To which we may also add, that the beauty and magnitude of it so greatly surpasses human power, that it is impossible to survey it by a sudden view; but then alone can any one gradually collect some portion of this philosophy, when, the Gods being his leaders, he quietly approaches to it. On all these accounts, therefore, having invoked the Gods as our leaders, and converting both ourselves and our discussion to them, we shall acquiesce in whatever they may command us to do. We shall not, however, make any apology for this sect having been neglected for a long time, nor for its being concealed by foreign disciplines, and certain arcane symbols, nor for having been obscured by false and spurious writings, nor for many other such-like difficulties by which it has been impeded. For the will of the Gods is sufficient for us, in conjunction with which it is possible to sustain things still more arduous than these. But after the Gods, we shall unite ourselves as to a leader, to the prince and father of this divine philosophy; of whose origin and country we must rise a little higher in our investigation.

Chapter II.

It is said, therefore, that Ancæus who dwelt in Samos in Cephallenia, was begot by Jupiter, whether he derived the fame of such an honorable descent through virtue, or through a certain greatness of soul. He surpassed, however, the rest of the Cephallenians in wisdom and renown. This Ancæus, therefore, was ordered by the Pythian oracle to form a colony from Arcadia and Thessaly; and that besides this, taking with him some of the inhabitants of Athens, Epidaurus, and Chalcis, and placing himself at their head, he should render an island habitable, which from the virtue of the soil and land should be called Melamphyllos;¹ and that he should call the city Samos, on account of Same in Cephallenia. The oracle, therefore, which was given to him, was as follows:

"I order you, Ancæus, to colonise the marine island Samos instead of Same, and to call it Phyllas."

But that a colony was collected from these places, is not only indicated by the honors and sacrifices of the Gods, transferred into those regions together with the inhabitants, but also by the kindred families that dwell there, and the associations of the Samians with each other.

It is said, therefore, that Mnesarchus and Pythaïs, who were the parents of Pythagoras, descended from the family and alliance of this Ancæus, who founded the colony. In consequence, however, of this nobility of birth being celebrated by the citizens, a certain Samian poet says, that Pythagoras was the son of Apollo. For thus he sings:

Pythaïs, fairest of the Samian tribe,
Bore from th' embraces of the God of day
Renown'd Pythagoras, the friend of Jove.

It is worth while, however, to relate how this report became so prevalent. The Pythian oracle then had predicted to this Mnesarchus (who came to Delphi for the purposes of merchandize, with his wife not yet apparently pregnant, and who inquired of the God concerning the event of his voyage to Syria) that his voyage would be lucrative and most conformable to his wishes, but that his wife was now pregnant, and would bring forth a son surpassing in beauty and wisdom all that ever lived, and who would be of the greatest advantage to the human race in every thing pertaining to the life of man. But, when Mnesarchus considered with himself, that the God, without being interrogated concerning his son, had informed him by an oracle, that he would possess an illustrious prerogative, and a gift truly divine, he immediately named his wife Pythaïs, from her son and the Delphic prophet, instead of Parthenis, which was her former appellation; and he called the infant, who was soon after born at Sidon in Phœnicia, Pythagoras; signifying by this appellation, that such an offspring was predicted to him by the Pythian Apollo. For we must not regard the assertions of Epimenides, Eudoxus, and Xenocrates, who suspect that Apollo at that time, becoming connected with Parthenis, and causing her to be pregnant from not being so, had in consequence of this predicted concerning Pythagoras, by the Delphic prophet: for this is by no means to be admitted.[2] Indeed, no one can doubt that the soul of Pythagoras was sent to mankind from the empire of Apollo, either being an attendant on the God, or co-arranged with him in some other more familiar way: for this may be inferred both from his birth, and the all-various wisdom of his soul. And thus much concerning the nativity of Pythagoras.

But after his father Mnesarchus had returned from Syria to Samos, with great wealth, which he had collected from a prosperous navigation, he built a temple to Apollo, with the inscription of Pythius; and took care to have his son nourished with various and the best disciplines, at one time by Creophilus, at another by Pherecydes the Syrian, and at another by almost all those who presided over sacred concerns, to whom he earnestly recommended Pythagoras, that he might be as much as possible sufficiently instructed in divine concerns. He, however, was educated in such a manner, as to be fortunately the most beautiful and godlike of all those that have been celebrated in the annals of history. On the death of his father, likewise, though he was still but a youth, his aspect was most venerable, and his habits most temperate, so that he was even reverenced and honored by elderly men; and converted the attention of all who saw and heard him speak, on himself, and appeared to be an admirable person to every one who beheld him. Hence it was reasonably asserted by many, that he was the son of a God. But he being corroborated by renown of this kind, by the education which he had received from his infancy, and by his natural deiform appearance, in a still greater degree evinced that he deserved his present prerogatives. He was also adorned by piety and disciplines, by a mode of living transcendently good, by firmness of soul, and by a body in due subjection to the mandates of reason. In all his words and actions, he discovered an inimitable quiet and serenity, not being subdued at any time by anger, or laughter, or emulation, or contention, or any other perturbation or precipitation of conduct; but he dwelt at Samos like some beneficent dæmon. Hence, while he was yet a youth, his great renown having reached Thales at Miletus, and Bias at Priene, men illustrious for their wisdom, it also extended to the neighbouring cities. To all which we may add, that the youth was every where celebrated as the *long-haired Samian*, and was reverenced by the multitude as one under the influence of divine inspiration. But after he had attained the eighteenth year of his age, about the period when the tyranny of Policrates first made its appearance, foreseeing that under such a government he might receive some impediment in his studies, which engrossed the whole of his attention, he departed privately by night with one Hermodamas (whose surname was Creophilus, and who was the grandson of him who had formerly been the host, friend, and preceptor in all things of Homer the poet,) to Pherecydes, to Anaximander the natural philosopher, and to Thales at Miletus. He likewise alternately associated with each of these philosophers, in such a manner, that they all loved him, admired his natural endowments, and made him a partaker of their doctrines. Indeed, after Thales had gladly admitted him to his intimate confidence, he admired the great difference between him and other young men, whom Pythagoras left far behind in every accom-plishment. And besides this, Thales increased the reputation Pythagoras had already acquired, by communicating to him such disciplines as he was able to impart: and, apologizing for his old age, and the imbecility of his body, he exhorted him to sail into Egypt, and associate with the Memphian and Diospolitan[3] priests. For he confessed that his own reputation for wisdom, was derived from the instructions of these priests; but that he was neither naturally, nor by exercise, endued with those excellent prerogatives, which were so visibly displayed in the person of Pythagoras. Thales, therefore, gladly announced to him, from all these circumstances, that he would become the wisest and most divine of all men, if he associated with these Egyptian priests.

Chapter. III.

Pythagoras, therefore, having been benefited by Thales in other respects, and especially having learned from him to be sparing of his time; for the sake of this he entirely abstained from wine and animal food, and still prior to these from voracity, and confined himself to such nutriment as was slender and easy of digestion. In consequence of this, his sleep was short, his soul vigilant and pure, and his body confirmed in a state of perfect and invariable health. In possession of such advantages, therefore, he sailed to Sidon, being persuaded that this was his natural country, and also properly conceiving that he might easily pass from thence into Egypt. Here he conversed with the prophets who were the descendants of Mochus the physiologist, and with others, and also with the Phœnician hierophants. He was likewise initiated in all the mysteries of Byblus and Tyre, and in the sacred operations which are performed in many parts of Syria; not engaging in a thing of this kind for the sake of superstition, as some one may be led to suppose, but much rather from a love and desire of contemplation, and from an anxiety that nothing might escape his observation which deserved to be learnt in the arcana or mysteries of the Gods. Having been previously instructed therefore in the mysteries of the Phœnicians, which were derived like a colony and a progeny from the sacred rites in Egypt, and hoping from this circumstance that he should be a partaker of more beautiful, divine, and genuine monuments of erudition in Egypt; joyfully calling to mind also the admonitions of his preceptor Thales, he immediately embarked for Egypt, through the means of some Egyptian sailors, who very opportunely at that time landed on the Phœnician coast under mount Carmelus, in whose temple Pythagoras, separated from all society, for the most part dwelt. But the sailors gladly received him, foreseeing that they should acquire great gain by exposing him to sale. But when, during the voyage, they perceived with what continence and venerable gravity he conducted himself, in conformity to the mode of

living he had adopted, they were more benevolently disposed towards him. Observing, likewise, that there was something greater than what pertains to human nature in the modesty of the youth, they called to mind how unexpectedly he had appeared to them on their landing, when from the summit of mount Carmelus, which they knew was more sacred than other mountains, and inaccessible to the vulgar, he leisurely descended without looking back, or suffering any delay from precipices or opposing stones; and that when he came to the boat, he said nothing more than, "Are you bound for Egypt?" And farther, that on their answering in the affirmative, he ascended the ship and sat silent the whole time of the voyage, in that part of the vessel where he was not likely to incommode the occupations of the sailors. But Pythagoras remained in one and the same unmoved state for two nights and three days, neither partaking of food, nor drink, nor sleep, unless perhaps as he sat in that firm and tranquil condition, he might sleep for a short time unobserved by all the sailors. To which we may add, that when the sailors considered how, contrary to their expectations, their voyage had been continued and uninterrupted, as if some deity had been present; putting all these things together, they concluded that a divine dæmon had in reality passed over with them from Syria into Egypt. Hence, speaking both to Pythagoras and to each other with greater decorum and gentleness than before, they completed, through a most tranquil sea, the remainder of their voyage, and at length happily landed on the Egyptian coast. Here the sailors reverently assisted him in descending from the ship; and after they had placed him on the purest sand, they raised a certain temporary altar before him, and heaping on it from their present abundance the fruits of trees, and presenting him as it were with the first fruits of their freight, they departed from thence, and hastened to their destined port.

But Pythagoras, whose body through such long fasting was become weaker, did not oppose the sailors in assisting him to descend from the ship, and immediately on their departure eat as much of the fruits as was requisite to restore his decayed strength. From thence also he arrived safe at the neighbouring lands, constantly preserving the same tranquillity and modesty of behaviour.

Chapter IV.

But here, while he frequented all the Egyptian temples with the greatest diligence and with accurate investigation, he was both admired and loved by the priests and prophets with whom he associated. And having learnt with the greatest solicitude every particular, he did not neglect to hear of any transaction that was celebrated in his own time, or of any man famous for his wisdom, or any mystery in whatever manner it might be performed; nor did he omit to visit any place in which he thought something more excellent might be found. On this account he went to all the priests, by whom he was furnished with the wisdom which each possessed. He spent therefore two and twenty years in Egypt, in the adyta of temples, astronomizing and geometrizing, and was initiated, not in a superficial or casual manner, in all the mysteries of the Gods, till at length being taken captive by the soldiers of Cambyses, he was brought to Babylon. Here he gladly associated with the Magi, was instructed by them in their venerable knowledge, and learnt from them the most perfect worship of the Gods. Through their assistance likewise, he arrived at the summit of arithmetic, music, and other disciplines; and after associating with them twelve years, he returned to Samos about the fifty-sixth year of his age.

Chapter. V.

On his return to Samos, however, being known by some of the more aged inhabitants, he was not less admired than before. For he appeared to them to be more beautiful and wise, and to possess a divine gracefulness in a more eminent degree. Hence, he was publicly called upon by his country to benefit all men, by imparting to them what he knew. Nor was he averse to this request, but endeavoured to introduce the symbolical mode of teaching, in a way perfectly similar to the documents by which he had been instructed in Egypt; though the Samians did not very much admit this mode of tuition, and did not adhere to him with that according aptitude which was requisite. Though no one therefore attended to him, and no one was genuinely desirous of those disciplines which he endeavoured by all means to introduce among the Greeks, yet he neither despised nor neglected

Samos, because it was his country, and therefore wished to give his fellow-citizens a taste of the sweetness of the mathematical disciplines, though they were unwilling to be instructed in them. With a view to this, therefore, he employed the following method and artifice. Happening to observe a certain youth, who was a great lover of gymnastic and other corporeal exercises, but otherwise poor and in difficult circumstances, playing at ball in the Gymnasium with great aptness and facility, he thought the young man might easily be persuaded to attend to him, if he was sufficiently supplied with the necessaries of life, and freed from the care of procuring them. As soon as the youth, therefore, left the bath, Pythagoras called him to him, and promised that he would furnish him with every thing requisite to the support of his bodily exercise, on condition that he would receive from him gradually and easily, but continually, so that he might not be burdened by receiving them at once, certain disciplines, which he said he had learnt from the Barbarians in his youth, but which now began to desert him through forgetfulness and the incursions of old age. But the young man immediately acceded to the conditions, through the hope of having necessary support. Pythagoras, therefore, endeavoured to instruct him in the disciplines of arithmetic and geometry, forming each of his demonstrations in an abacus, and giving the youth three oboli as a reward for every figure which he learnt. This also he continued to do for a long time, exciting him to the geometrical theory by the desire of honour; diligently and in the best order, giving him (as we have said) three oboli for every figure which he apprehended. But when the wise man observed that the elegance, sweetness, and connexion of these disciplines, to which the youth had been led in a certain orderly path, had so captivated him that he would not neglect their pursuit though he should suffer the extremity of want, he pretended poverty, and an inability of giving him three oboli any longer. But the youth on hearing this replied, "I am able without these to learn and receive your disciplines." Pythagoras then said, "But I have not the means of procuring sufficient nutriment for myself." As it is requisite, therefore, to labour in order to procure daily necessaries and mortal food, it would not be proper that his attention should be distracted by the abacus, and by stupid and vain pursuits. The youth, however, vehemently abhorring the thought of discontinuing his studies, replied: "I will in future provide for you, and repay your kindness in a way resembling that of the stork: for I in my turn will give you three oboli for every figure." And from this time he was so captivated by these disciplines, that he alone, of all the Samians, migrated from his country with Pythagoras, having the same name with him, but being the son of Eratocles.

There are said to be three books of this Samian On Athletics, in which he orders the Athletæ to feed on flesh instead of dry figs; which books are very improperly ascribed by some to Pythagoras the son of Mnesarchus. It is likewise said, that about the same time Pythagoras was admired at Delos, when he approached to the bloodless altar, as it is called, of the father Apollo, and worshipped it. After which he went to all the oracles. He likewise dwelt for some time in Crete and Sparta, for the purpose of becoming acquainted with their laws; and, having been an auditor and learner of all these, he returned home in order to investigate what he had omitted. And in the first place, indeed, he established a school in the city, which is even now called the semicircle of Pythagoras; and in which the Samians now consult about public affairs, conceiving it right to investigate things just and advantageous in that place which he had constructed who paid attention to the welfare of all men. He also formed a cavern out of the city, adapted to his philosophy, in which he spent the greatest part both of the day and night; employing himself in the investigation of things useful in disciplines, framing intellectual conceptions after the same manner as Minos the son of Jupiter. Indeed, he so much surpassed those who afterwards employed his disciplines, that they conceived magnificently of themselves, from the knowledge of theorems of small importance; but Pythagoras gave completion to the science of the celestial orbs, and unfolded the whole of it by arithmetical and geometrical demonstrations. He is, however, to be admired in a still greater degree for what he afterwards accomplished. For when now philosophy had received a great accession, he was admired by all Greece, and the best of those who philosophized came to Samos on his account, in order that they might participate of his erudition. The citizens likewise employed him in all their embassies, and compelled him to unite with them in the administration of public affairs. However, as he easily saw the difficulty of complying

12

13

with the laws of his country, and at the same time remaining at home
and philosophizing, and considered that all philosophers before him
had passed their life in foreign countries, he determined to neglect all
political occupations; induced to this, according to the testimony of
others, by the negligence of the Samians in what relates to education,
and went into Italy, conceiving that place to be his proper country, in
which men well disposed towards learning were to be found in the
greatest abundance. And such was the success of his journey, that on
his arrival at Crotona, which was the noblest city in Italy, he had
many followers, amounting, as it is said, to the number of six
hundred, who were not only excited by his discourses to the study of
philosophy, but also to an amicable division of the goods of life in
common; from whence they acquired the appellation of *Cœnobitæ*.

Chapter. VI.

And these indeed were such as philosophized. But the greatest part
of his disciples consisted of auditors whom they call *Acusmatici*, who
on his first arrival in Italy, according to Nicomachus, being
captivated by one popular oration alone, exceeded two thousand in
number. These, with their wives and children, being collected into
one very large and common auditory, called Homacoïon, and which
for its magnitude resembled a city, founded a place which was
universally called Magna Græcia. This great multitude of people
likewise, receiving laws and mandates from Pythagoras as so many
divine precepts, and without which they engaged in no occupation,
dwelt together with the greatest general concord, celebrated and
ranked by their neighbours among the number of the blessed. At the
same time, as we have already observed, they shared their possessions
in common. Such also was their reverence for Pythagoras, that they
numbered him with the Gods, as a certain beneficent and most
philanthropic dæmon. And some indeed celebrated him as the
Pythian, but others as the Hyperborean Apollo. Some again
considered him as Pæon, but others as one of the dæmons that
inhabit the moon; and others celebrated him as one of the Olympian
Gods,[4] who, in order to benefit and correct the mortal life, appeared
to the men of those times in a human form, in order that he might
extend to them the salutary light of felicity and philosophy. And

indeed a greater good never came, nor ever will come to mankind, than that which was imparted by the Gods through this Pythagoras. Hence, even now the proverb of *the long-haired Samian*, is applied to the most venerable man. But Aristotle relates, in his Treatise On the Pythagoric Philosophy, that such a division as the following was preserved by the Pythagoreans among their principal arcana; *viz.* that of rational animals one kind is a God, another man, and another such as Pythagoras. And indeed they very reasonably apprehended him to be a being of this kind, through whom a right conception and conformable to things themselves was introduced of Gods, heroes, and dæmons; of the world, the all-various motion of the spheres and stars, their oppositions, eclipses, and inequalities, their eccentricities and epicycles; of all the natures contained in the heavens and the earth, together with those that have an intermediate subsistence, whether apparent or occult. Nor was there any thing (in all this variety of information) at all contrary to the phenomena, or the conceptions of intellect. To which we may add, that all such disciplines, theories, and scientific investigations, as truly invigorate the eye of the soul, and purify the intellect from the blindness introduced by studies of a different kind, so as to enable it to perceive the true principles and causes of the universe, were unfolded by Pythagoras to the Greeks. But besides all this, the best polity, popular concord, community of possessions among friends, the worship of the gods, piety to the dead, legislation, erudition, silence, abstinence from animals, continence, temperance, sagacity, divinity, and in one word, whatever is anxiously sought after by the lovers of learning, was brought to light by Pythagoras. On all these accounts, therefore, as I have just now said, he was (every where) so transcendently admired.

Chapter. VII.

It remains therefore after this, that we should relate how he travelled, what places he first visited, what discourses he made, on what subjects, and to whom they were addressed; for thus we shall easily apprehend the nature of his association with the men of that time. It is said then, that as soon as he came to Italy and Sicily, which cities he understood had oppressed each other with slavery, partly at some distant period of past time, and partly at a recent period, he inspired the inhabitants with a love of liberty, and through the means of his auditors, restored to independence and liberated Crotona, Sybaris, Catanes, Rhegium, Himæra, Agrigentum, Tauromenas, and some other cities, for whom also he established laws, through Charondas the Catanæan, and Zaleucus the Locrian, by whom they became flourishing cities, and afforded an example worthy of imitation, for a long time, to the neighbouring kingdoms. He also entirely subverted sedition, discord, and party zeal, not only from his familiars, and their posterity, for many generations, as we are informed by history, but, in short, from all the cities in Italy and Sicily, which were at that time disturbed with intestine and external contentions. For the following apothegm was always employed by him in every place, whether in the company of a multitude or a few, which was similar to the persuasive oracle of a God, and was an epitome and summary as it were of his own opinions; that we should avoid and amputate by every possible artifice, by fire and sword, and all-various contrivances, from the body, disease; from the soul, ignorance; from the belly, luxury; from a city, sedition; from a house, discord; and at the same time, from all things, immoderation: through which, with a most fatherly affection, he reminded each of his disciples of the most excellent dogmas. Such therefore was the common form of his life at that time, both in words and actions. If, however, it be requisite to make a more particular relation of what he did and said, it must be observed, that he came to Italy in the sixty-second Olympiad, at which time Eryxidas of Chalcis conquered in the stadium. But immediately on his arrival he became conspicuous and illustrious, in the same manner as before, when he sailed to Delos. For there, when he performed his adorations at the bloodless altar of the father Apollo, he was admired by the inhabitants of the island.

Chapter VIII.

At that time also, when he was journeying from Sybaris to Crotona, he met near the shore with some fishermen, who were then drawing their nets heavily laden with fishes from the deep, and told them he knew the exact number of the fish they had caught. But the fishermen promising they would perform whatever he should order them to do, if the event corresponded with his prediction, he ordered them, after they had accurately numbered the fish, to return them alive to the sea: and what is yet more wonderful, not one of the fish died while he stood on the shore, though they had been detained from the water a considerable time. Having therefore paid the fishermen the price of their fish, he departed for Crotona. But they every where divulged the fact, and having learnt his name from some children, they told it to all men. Hence those that heard of this affair were desirous of seeing the stranger, and what they desired was easily obtained. But they were astonished on surveying his countenance, and conjectured him to be such a man as he was in reality. A few days also after this, he entered the Gymnasium, and being surrounded with a crowd of young men, he is said to have delivered an oration to them, in which he incited them to pay attention to their elders, evincing that in the world, in life, in cities, and in nature, that which has a precedency is more honorable than that which is consequent in time. As for instance, that the east is more honorable than the west; the morning than the evening; the beginning than the end; and generation than corruption. In a similar manner he observed, that natives were more honorable than strangers, and the leaders of colonies than the builders of cities: and universally Gods than dæmons; dæmons than demigods; and heroes than men. Of these likewise he observed, that the authors of generation are more honorable than their progeny. He said these things, however, for the sake of proving by induction, that children should very much esteem their parents, to whom he asserted they owed as many thanks as a dead man would owe to him who should be able to bring him back again into light. Afterwards, he observed, that it was indeed just to love those above all others, and never to give them pain, who first benefited us, and in the greatest degree. But parents alone benefit their children prior to their birth, and are the causes to their offspring of all their upright conduct; and that when children show themselves to be in no respect inferior to their parents in beneficence towards them, it is not possible for them in this respect to err. For it is reasonable to suppose, that the Gods will pardon those who honor their parents in no less a degree than the divinities themselves; since we learnt from our parents to honor divinity. Hence Homer also added the same appellation to the king of the Gods; for he denominates him the father of Gods and mortals.

18

Many other mythologists also have delivered to us, that the kings of the Gods have been ambitious to vindicate to themselves that excessive love which subsists through marriage, in children towards their parents. And that on this account, they have at the same time introduced the hypothesis of father and mother among the Gods,' the former indeed generating Minerva, but the latter Vulcan, who are of a nature contrary to each other, in order that what is most remote may participate of friendship.

All his auditors likewise having granted that the judgment of the immortals is most valid, he said he would demonstrate to the Crotonians, by the example of Hercules the founder of the colony brought to Crotona, that it is necessary to be voluntarily obedient to the mandates of parents, as they knew from tradition that the God himself had undertaken such great labors in consequence of obeying the commands of one older than himself, and being victorious in what he had undertaken to accomplish, had instituted in honor of his father the Olympic games. He also showed them that they should associate with each other in such a manner, as never to be in a state of hostility to their friends, but to become most rapidly friends to their enemies; and that they should exhibit in modesty of behaviour to their elders, the benevolent disposition of children towards their parents; but in their philanthropy to others, fraternal love and regard.

In the next place, he spoke concerning temperance, and said, that the juvenile age should make trial of its nature, this being the period in which the desires are in the most flourishing state. Afterwards, he exhorted them to consider, that this alone among the virtues was adapted to a boy and a virgin, to a woman, and to the order of those of a more advanced age; and that it was especially accommodated to the younger part of the community. He also added, that this virtue alone comprehended the goods both of body and soul, as it preserved the health and also the desire of the most excellent studies. But this is evident from the opposite. For when the Barbarians and Greeks warred on each other about Troy, each of them fell into the most dreadful calamities, through the incontinence of one man, partly in the war itself, and partly in returning to their native land. And divinity ordained that the punishment of injustice alone should endure for a thousand and ten years, predicting by an oracle the capture of Troy, and ordering that virgins should be annually sent by the Locrians into the temple of Trojan Minerva. Pythagoras also exhorted young men to the cultivation of learning, calling on them to observe how absurd it would be that they should judge the reasoning power to be the most laudable of all things, and should consult about other things through this, and yet bestow no time nor labour in the exercise of it; though the attention which is paid to the body, resembles depraved friends, and rapidly fails; but erudition, like worthy and good men, endures till death, and for some persons procures immortal renown after death. These and other observations of the like kind, were made by Pythagoras, partly from history, and partly from [philosophic] dogmas, in which he showed that erudition is a natural excellence of disposition common to those in each genus, who rank in the first class of human nature. For the discoveries of these, become erudition to others. But this is naturally so worthy of pursuit, that with respect to other laudable objects of attainment, it is not possible to partake of some of them through another person, such as strength, beauty, health, and fortitude; and others are no longer possessed by him who imparts them to another, such as wealth, dominion, and many other things which we shall omit to mention. It is possible, however, for erudition to be received by another, without in the least diminishing that which the giver possesses. In a similar manner also, some goods cannot be possessed by men; but we are capable of being instructed, according to our own proper and deliberate choice. And in the next place, he who being thus instructed, engages in the administration of the affairs of his country, does not do this from impudence, but from erudition. For by education merely men differ from wild beasts, the Greeks from the Barbarians, those that are free from slaves, and philosophers from the vulgar. And in short, those that have erudition possess such a transcendency with respect to those that have not, that seven men have been found from one city, and in one Olympiad, that were swifter than others in the course; and in the whole of the habitable part of the globe, those that excelled in wisdom were also seven in number. But in the following times in which Pythagoras lived, he alone surpassed all others in philosophy. For he called himself by this name [*viz.* a philosopher], instead of a wise man.

Chapter IX.

And this indeed is what he said to the young men in the Gymnasium. But when they had told their parents what they had heard, a thousand men having called Pythagoras into the senate-house, and praised him for what he had said to their sons, desired him, if he had any thing advantageous to say to the Crotonians, to unfold it to those who were the leaders of the administration. He was also the first that advised them to build a temple to the Muses, in order that they might preserve the existing concord. For he observed that all these divinities were called by one common name, [the Muses,] that they subsisted in conjunction with each other, especially rejoiced in common honors, and in short, that there was always one and the same choir of the Muses. He likewise farther observed, that they comprehended in themselves symphony, harmony, rhythm, and all things which procure concord. They also evince that their power does not alone extend to the most beautiful theorems, but likewise to the symphony and harmony of things. In the next place, he said it was necessary they should apprehend that they received their country from the multitude of the citizens, as a common deposit. Hence, it was requisite they should so govern it, that they might faithfully transmit it to their posterity, as an hereditary possession. And that this would firmly be effected, if they were equal in all things to the citizens, and surpassed them in nothing else than justice. For men knowing that every place requires justice, have asserted in fables that Themis has the same order with Jupiter, that Dice, *i.e.* justice, is seated by Pluto, and that Law is established in cities; in order that he who does not act justly in things which his rank in society requires him to perform, may at the same time appear to be unjust towards the whole world. He added, it was proper that the senators should not make use of any of the Gods for the purpose of an oath, but that their language should be such as to render them worthy of belief even without oaths. And likewise, that they should so manage their own domestic affairs, as to make the government of them the object of their deliberate choice. That they should also be genuinely disposed towards their own offspring, as being the only animals that have a sensation of this conception. And that they should so associate with a wife, the companion of life, as to be mindful that other compacts are engraved in tables and pillars, but those with wives are inserted in children. That they should likewise endeavour to be beloved by their offspring, not through nature, of which they were not the causes, but through deliberate choice: for this is voluntary beneficence.

He further observed, that they should be careful not to have connexion with any but their wives, in order that the wives may not bastardize the race through the neglect and vicious conduct of the husbands. That they should also consider, that they received their wives from the Vestal hearth with libations, and brought them home as if they were suppliants, in the presence of the Gods themselves. And that by orderly conduct and temperance, they should become examples both to their own families, and to the city in which they live. That besides this, they should take care to prevent every one from acting viciously, lest offenders not fearing the punishment of the laws, should be concealed; and reverencing beautiful and worthy manners, they should be impelled to justice. He also exhorted them to expel sluggishness from all their actions; for he said that opportunity was the only good in every action. But he defined the divulsion of parents and children from each other, to be the greatest of injuries. And said, that he ought to be considered as the most excellent man, who is able to foresee what will be advantageous to himself; but that he ranks as the next in excellence, who understands what is useful from things which happen to others. But that he is the worst of men who waits for the perception of what is best, till he is himself afflicted. He likewise said, that those who wish to be honored, will not err if they imitate those that are crowned in the course: for these do not injure their antagonists, but are alone desirous that they themselves may obtain the victory. Thus also it is fit that those who engage in the administration of public affairs, should not be offended with those that contradict them, but should benefit such as are obedient to them. He likewise exhorted every one who aspired after true glory, to be such in reality as he wished to appear to be to others: for counsel is not so sacred a thing as praise; since the former is only useful among men, but the latter is for the most part referred to the Gods. And after all this he added, that their city happened to be founded by Hercules, at that time when he drove the oxen through Italy, having been

23

injured by Lacinius; and when giving assistance by night to Croton, he slew him through ignorance, conceiving him to be an enemy. After which, Hercules promised that a city should be built about the sepulchre of Croton, and should be called from him Crotona, when he himself became a partaker of immortality. Hence Pythagoras said, it was fit that they should justly return thanks for the benefit they had received. But the Crotonians, on hearing this, built a temple to the Muses, and dismissed the harlots which they were accustomed to have. They also requested Pythagoras to discourse to the boys in the temple of Pythian Apollo, and to the women in the temple of Juno.

Chapter X.

Pythagoras, therefore, complying with their wish, is said to have given the boys the following advice: That they should neither revile any one, nor take vengeance on those that reviled. He likewise exhorted them to pay diligent attention to learning, which derives its appellation from their age. He added, that it was easy for a modest youth to preserve probity through the whole of life; but that it was difficult for one to accomplish this, who was not naturally well disposed at that age; or rather it is impossible that he who begins his course from a bad impulse, should run well to the end. Besides this, he observed that boys were most dear to divinity, and hence in times of great drought, they were sent by cities to implore rain from the Gods, in consequence of the persuasion that divinity is especially attentive to children; though such as are permitted to be continually conversant with sacred ceremonies, scarcely obtain purification in perfection. From this cause also, the most philanthropic of the Gods, Apollo and Love, are universally represented in pictures as having the age of boys. It is likewise acknowledged, that some of the games in which the conquerors are crowned, were instituted on account of boys; the Pythian, indeed, in consequence of the serpent Python being slain by a boy; but the Nemean and Isthmian, on account of the death of Archemorus and Melicerta. Besides what has been said likewise, while the city of Crotona was building, Apollo promised to the founder, that he would give him a progeny, if he brought a colony into Italy; from which inferring that Apollo providentially attended to the propagation of them, and that all the Gods paid attention to every age, they ought to render themselves worthy of their friendship. He added, that they should exercise themselves in hearing, in order that they may be able to speak. And farther still, that as soon as they have entered into the path in which they intend to proceed to old age, they should follow the steps of those that preceded them, and never contradict those that are older than themselves. For thus hereafter, they will justly think it right that neither should they be injured by their juniors. On account of these exhortations, it must be confessed that he deserved not to be called by his own name, but that all men should denominate him divine.

Chapter XI.

But to the women he is said to have discoursed concerning sacrifices as follows: In the first place indeed, as they would wish that another person who intended to pray for them, should be worthy and good, because the Gods attend to such as these; thus also it is requisite that they should in the highest degree esteem equity and modesty, in order that the Gods may be readily disposed to hear their prayers. In the next place, they should offer to the Gods such things as they have produced with their own hands, and should bring them to the altars without the assistance of servants, such as cakes, honey-combs, and frankincense. But that they should not worship divinity with blood and dead bodies, nor offer many things at one time, as if they never meant to sacrifice again. With respect also to their association with men, he exhorted them to consider that their parents granted to the female nature, that they should love their husbands in a greater degree than those who were the sources of their existence. That in consequence of this, they would do well either not to oppose their husbands, or to think that they have then vanquished, when they submit to them. Farther still, in the same assembly also, Pythagoras is said to have made that celebrated observation, that it is holy for a woman, after having been connected with her husband, to perform sacred rites on the same day; but that this is never holy, after she has been connected with any other man. He also exhorted the women to use words of good omen through the whole of life, and to endeavor that others may predict good things of them. He likewise admonished them not to destroy popular renown, nor to blame the writers of

26

fables, who surveying the justice of women, from their accommodating others with garments and ornaments, without a witness, when it is necessary for some other person to use them, and that neither litigation nor contradiction are produced from this confidence,—have feigned, that three women used but one eye in common, on account of the facility of their communion with each other. He farther observed, that he who is called the wisest of all others, and who gave arrangement to the human voice, and in short, was the inventor of names, whether he was a God or a dæmon, or a certain divine man,[6] perceiving that the genus of women is most adapted to piety, gave to each of their ages the appellation of some God. Hence he called an unmarried woman *Core, i.e.* Proserpine; but a bride, *Nympha;* the woman who has brought forth children, *Mater;* and a grandmother, according to the Doric dialect, *Maia.* In conformity to which also, the oracles in Dodona and at Delphi, are unfolded into light through a woman. But through this praise pertaining to piety, Pythagoras is said to have produced so great a change in female attire, that the women no longer dared to clothe themselves with costly garments, but consecrated many myriads of their vestments in the temple of Juno. The effect also of this discourse is said to have been such, that about the region of the Crotonians the fidelity of the husband to the wife was universally celebrated; [imitating in this respect] Ulysses, who would not receive immortality from Calypso, on condition that he should abandon Penelope. Pythagoras therefore also observed, that it remained for the women to exhibit their probity to their husbands, in order that they might be equally celebrated with Ulysses. In short, it is recorded that through the above-mentioned discourses, Pythagoras obtained no moderate honor and esteem, both in the city of the Crotonians and throughout Italy.

Chapter XII.

It is also said, that Pythagoras was the first who called himself a philosopher; this not being a new name, but previously instructing us in a useful manner in a thing appropriate to the name. For he said that the entrance of men into the present life, resembled the progression of a crowd to some public spectacle. For there men of

every description assemble with different views; one hastening to sell
his wares for the sake of money and gain; but another that he may
acquire renown by exhibiting the strength of his body; and there is
also a third class of men, and those the most liberal, who assemble for
the sake of surveying the places, the beautiful works of art, the
specimens of valor, and the literary productions which are usually
exhibited on such occasions. Thus also in the present life, men of all-
various pursuits are collected together in one and the same place. For
some are influenced by the desire of riches and luxury; others by the
love of power and dominion; and others are possessed with an insane
ambition for glory. But the most pure and unadulterated character, is
that of the man who gives himself to the contemplation of the most
beautiful things, and whom it is proper to call a philosopher.[7] He
adds, that the survey of all heaven, and of the stars that revolve in it, is
indeed beautiful, when the order of them is considered. For they
derive this beauty and order by the participation of the first and the
intelligible essence. But that first essence is the nature of number and
reasons [*i.e.* productive principles,] which pervades through all things,
and according to which all these [celestial bodies] are elegantly
arranged, and fitly adorned. And wisdom indeed, truly so called, is a
certain science which is conversant with the first beautiful objects,[8] and
these divine, undecaying, and possessing an invariable sameness of
subsistence; by the participation of which other things also may be
called beautiful. But philosophy is the appetition of a thing of this kind.
The attention therefore to erudition is likewise beautiful, which
Pythagoras extended, in order to effect the correction of mankind.

29

Chapter XIII.

Moreover, if we may believe in so many ancient and credible
historians as have written concerning him, the words of Pythagoras
contained something of a recalling and admonitory nature, which
extended as far as to irrational animals; by which it may be inferred
that learning predominates in those endued with intellect, since it
tames even wild beasts, and those which are considered to be deprived
of reason. For it is said that Pythagoras detained the Daunian bear
which had most severely injured the inhabitants, and that having
gently stroked it with his hand for a long time, fed it with maize and

acorns, and compelled it by an oath no longer to touch any living thing, he dismissed it. But the bear immediately after hid herself in the mountains and woods, and was never seen from that time to attack any irrational animal. Perceiving likewise an ox at Tarentum feeding in a pasture, and eating among other things green beans, he advised the herdsman to tell the ox to abstain from the beans. The herdsman, however, laughed at him, and said that he did not understand the language of oxen, but if Pythagoras did, it was in vain to advise him to speak to the ox, but fit that he himself should advise the animal to abstain from such food. Pythagoras therefore, approaching to the ear of the ox, and whispering in it for a long time, not only caused him then to refrain from beans, but it is said that he never after tasted them. This ox also lived for a long time at Tarentum near the temple of Juno, where it remained when it was old, and was called the sacred ox of Pythagoras. It was also fed by those that came to it with human food. When likewise he happened to be conversing with his familiars about birds, symbols, and prodigies, and was observing that all these are the messengers of the Gods, sent by them to those men who are truly dear to the Gods, he is said to have brought down an eagle that was flying over Olympia, and after gently stroking, to have dismissed it. Through these things, therefore, and other things similar to these, he demonstrated that he possessed the same dominion as Orpheus, over savage animals, and that he allured and detained them by the power of voice proceeding from the mouth.

Chapter XIV.

With him likewise the best principle originated of a guardian attention to the concerns of men, and which ought to be pre-assumed by those who intend to learn the truth about other things. For he reminded many of his familiars, by most clear and evident indications, of the former life which their soul lived, before it was bound to this body, and demonstrated by indubitable arguments, that he had been Euphorbus the son of Panthus, who conquered Patroclus. And he especially praised the following funeral Homeric verses pertaining to himself, sung them most elegantly to the lyre, and frequently repeated them.

"The shining circlets of his golden hair,
Which ev'n the Graces might be proud to wear,
Instarr'd with gems and gold, bestrow the shore
With dust dishonor'd, and deform'd with gore.
As the young olive in some sylvan scene,
Crown'd by fresh fountains with eternal green,
Lifts the gay head, in snowy flowrets fair,
And plays and dances to the gentle air;
When lo! a whirlwind from high heav'n invades
The tender plant, and withers all its shades;
It lies uprooted from its genial bed,
A lovely ruin now defac'd and dead.
Thus young, thus beautiful, Euphorbus lay,
While the fierce Spartan tore his arms away."[9]

But what is related about the shield of this Phrygian Euphorbus, being dedicated among other Trojan spoils to Argive Juno, we shall omit, as being of a very popular nature. That, however, which he wished to indicate through all these particulars is this, that he knew the former lives which he had lived, and that from hence he commenced his providential attention to others, reminding them of their former life.

Chapter XV.

Conceiving, however, that the first attention which should be paid to men, is that which takes place through the senses; as when some one perceives beautiful figures and forms, or hears beautiful rhythms and melodies, he established that to be the first erudition which subsists through music, and also through certain melodies and rhythms, from which the remedies of human manners and passions are obtained, together with those harmonies of the powers of the soul which it possessed from the first. He likewise devised medicines calculated to repress and expel the diseases both of bodies and souls. And by Jupiter that which deserves to be mentioned above all these particulars is this, that he arranged and adapted for his disciples what are called apparatus and contrectations, divinely contriving mixtures of certain diatonic, chromatic, and euharmonic melodies, through which he easily transferred and circularly led the passions of the soul

into a contrary direction, when they had recently and in an irrational
and clandestine manner been formed; such as sorrow, rage, and pity,
absurd emulation and fear, all-various desires, angers, and appetites,
pride, supineness, and vehemence. For he corrected each of these by the
rule of virtue, attempering them through appropriate melodies, as
through certain salutary medicines. In the evening, likewise, when his
disciples were retiring to sleep, he liberated them by these means from
diurnal perturbations and tumults, and purified their intellective
power from the influxive and effluxive waves of a corporeal nature;
rendered their sleep quiet, and their dreams pleasing and prophetic.
But when they again rose from their bed, he freed them from
nocturnal heaviness, relaxation and torpor, through certain peculiar
songs and modulations, produced either by simply striking the lyre, or
employing the voice. Pythagoras, however, did not procure for himself
a thing of this kind through instruments or the voice, but employing a
certain ineffable divinity, and which it is difficult to apprehend, he
extended his ears, and fixed his intellect in the sublime symphonies of
the world, he alone hearing and understanding, as it appears, the
universal harmony and consonance of the spheres, and the stars that
are moved through them, and which produce a fuller and more
intense melody than any thing effected by mortal sounds.[10] This
melody also was the result of dissimilar and variously differing
sounds, celerities, magnitudes, and intervals, arranged with reference
to each other in a certain most musical ratio, and thus producing a
most gentle, and at the same time variously beautiful motion and
convolution. Being therefore irrigated as it were with this melody,
having the reason of his intellect well arranged through it, and as I
may say, exercised, he determined to exhibit certain images of these
things to his disciples as much as possible, especially producing an
imitation of them through instruments, and through the mere voice
alone. For he conceived that by him alone, of all the inhabitants of
the earth, the mundane sounds were understood and heard, and this
from a natural fountain itself and root. He therefore thought himself
worthy to be taught, and to learn something about the celestial orbs,
and to be assimilated to them by desire and imitation, as being the
only one on the earth adapted to this by the conformation of his
body, through the dæmoniacal power that inspired him. But he

apprehended that other men ought to be satisfied in looking to him, and the gifts he possessed, and in being benefited and corrected through images and examples, in consequence of their inability to comprehend truly the first and genuine archetypes of things. Just, indeed, as to those who are incapable of looking intently at the sun, through the transcendent splendor of his rays, we contrive to exhibit the eclipses of that luminary, either in the profundity of still water, or through melted pitch, or through some darkly-splendid mirror; sparing the imbecility of their eyes, and devising a method of representing a certain repercussive light, though less intense than its archetype, to those who are delighted with a thing of this kind. Empedocles also appears to have obscurely signified this about Pythagoras, and the illustrious and divinely-gifted conformation of his body above that of other men, when he says:

> "There was a man among them [*i.e.* among the Pythagoreans] who was transcendent in knowledge, who possessed the most ample stores of intellectual wealth, and who was in the most eminent degree the adjutor of the works of the wise. For when he extended all the powers of his intellect, he easily beheld every thing, as far as to ten or twenty ages of the human race."

For the words *transcendent*, and *he beheld every thing*, and *the wealth of intellect*, and the like, especially exhibit the illustrious nature of the conformation of his mind and body, and its superior accuracy in seeing, and hearing, and in intellectual perception.

Chapter XVI.

This adaptation therefore of souls was procured by him through music. But another purification of the dianoetic part,[11] and at the same time of the whole soul, through all-various studies, was effected by him as follows: He conceived generally that labor should be employed about disciplines and studies, and ordained like a legislator, trials of the most various nature, punishments, and restraints by fire and sword, for innate intemperance, and an inexhaustible avidity of possessing; which he who is depraved can neither suffer nor sustain. Besides these things also, he ordered his familiars to abstain from all animals, and farther still from certain foods, which are hostile to the reasoning power, and impede its genuine energies. He likewise enjoined them continence of speech, and perfect silence, exercising them for many years in the subjugation of the tongue, and in a strenuous and assiduous investigation and resumption of the most difficult theorems. Hence also, he ordered them to abstain from wine, to be sparing in their food, to sleep little, and to have an unstudied contempt of, and hostility to glory, wealth, and the like: to have an unfeigned reverence of those to whom reverence is due, a genuine similitude and benevolence to those of the same age with themselves, and an attention and incitation towards their juniors, free from all envy. With respect to the amity also which subsists in all things towards all, whether it be that of Gods towards men through piety and scientific theory, or of dogmas towards each other, or universally of the soul towards the body, and of the rational towards the irrational part, through philosophy, and the theory pertaining to it; or whether it be that of men to each other, of citizens indeed through sound legislation, but of strangers through a correct physiology; or of the husband to the wife, or of brothers and kindred, through unperverted communion; or whether, in short, it be of all things towards all, and still farther, of certain irrational animals through justice, and a physical connexion and association; or whether it be the pacification and conciliation of the body which is of itself mortal, and of its latent contrary powers, through health, and a diet and temperance conformable to this, in imitation of the salubrious condition of the mundane elements;—of the appellation of all these, which are summarily comprehended in one and the same name, that of friendship, Pythagoras is acknowledged to have been the inventor and legislator. And, in short, he was the cause to his disciples of the most appropriate converse with the Gods, both when they were awake and when asleep; a thing which never takes place in a soul disturbed by anger, or pain, or pleasure, or, by Jupiter, by any other base desire, or defiled by ignorance, which is more unholy and noxious than all these. By all these inventions, therefore, he divinely healed and purified the soul, resuscitated and saved its divine part, and conducted to the intelligible its divine eye, which, as Plato says, is better worth saving than ten thousand corporeal eyes; for by looking through this alone, when it is strengthened and clarified by appropriate aids, the truth pertaining to all beings is perceived. Referring therefore to this, Pythagoras purified the dianoetic power of the soul. Such also was the form with him of erudition, and these were the things to which he directed his view.

Chapter XVII.

As he therefore thus prepared his disciples for erudition, he did not immediately receive into the number of his associates those who came to him for that purpose, till he had made trial of, and judiciously examined them. Hence in the first place he inquired after what manner they associated with their parents, and the rest of their relatives. In the next place he surveyed their unseasonable laughter, their silence, and their speaking when it was not proper; and farther still, what their desires were, with whom they associated, how they conversed with them, in what they especially employed their leisure time in the day, and what were the subjects of their joy and grief. He likewise surveyed their form, their mode of walking, and the whole motion of their body. Physiognomically also considering the natural indications of their frame, he made them to be manifest signs of the unapparent manners of the soul. When, therefore, he had thus made trial of some one, he suffered him to be neglected for three years, in the mean time observing how he was disposed with respect to stability, and a true love of learning, and if he was sufficiently prepared with reference to glory, so as to despise [popular] honor. After this, he ordered those who came to him to observe a quinquennial silence, in order that he might experimentally know how they were affected as to continence of speech, the subjugation of the tongue being the most difficult of all victories; as those have unfolded to us who instituted the mysteries. During this [probationary] time, however, the property of each was disposed of in common, and was committed to the care of those appointed for this purpose, who were called politicians, economizers, and legislators. And with respect to these probationers, those who appeared to be worthy to participate of his dogmas, from the judgment he had formed of them from their life and the modesty of their behaviour, after the quinquennial silence, then became *Esoterics*, and both heard and saw Pythagoras himself within the veil. For prior to this they participated of his words through the hearing alone, beyond the veil, without at all seeing him, giving for a long time a specimen of their peculiar manners. But if they were rejected they received the double of the wealth which they brought, and a tomb was raised to them as if they were dead by the *homacoï;* for thus all the disciples of the man were called. And if they happened to meet with them afterwards, they behaved to them as if they were other persons, but said that they were dead, whom they had modelled by education, in the expectation that they would become truly good men by the disciplines they would learn. They also were of opinion that those who were more slow in the acquisition of knowledge, were badly organized, and, as I may say, imperfect and barren. If, however, after Pythagoras had physiognomically considered their form, their mode of walking, and every other motion, and the state of their body, and he had conceived good hope respecting them; after likewise the quinquennial silence, and the orgies and initiations from so many disciplines, together with the ablutions of the soul, and so many and such great purifications produced from such various theorems, through which the sagacity and sanctity of the soul is perfectly ingenerated; if, after all this, some one was found to be still sluggish and of a dull intellect, they raised to such a one in the school a certain pillar and monument, (as they are said to have done to Perialus the Thurian, and Cylon the prince of the Sybarites, who were rejected by them) expelled him from the *Homacoion* or auditory, loading him with a great quantity of silver and gold. For these were deposited by them in common, and were committed to the care of certain persons adapted to this purpose, and who were called Economics, from the office which they bore. And if afterwards they happened to meet with such a one, they conceived him to be any other person, than him who according to them was dead. Hence also Lysis, blaming a certain person named Hipparchus, because he had communicated the doctrines of the Pythagoreans to the profane, and to those who acceded to them without disciplines and theory, says as follows:

"It is reported that you philosophize to every one you may happen to meet, and publicly, which Pythagoras did not think fit to do. And these things, indeed, O Hipparchus, you learnt with diligent assiduity, but you have not preserved them; having

39

tasted, O excellent man, of Sicilian delicacies, which you ought
not to have tasted a second time. If, therefore, you abandon
these, I shall rejoice; but if not, you will be dead in my opinion.
For it will be pious to call to mind the divine and human
precepts of Pythagoras, and not to make the goods of wisdom
common to those, who have not even in a dream their soul   *40*
purified. For it is not lawful to extend to every casual person,
things which were obtained with such great labors, and such
diligent assiduity, nor to divulge the mysteries of the Eleusinian
Goddesses to the profane. For those who do either of these, are
equally unjust and impious. But it will be well to consider what a
great length of time we consumed in wiping away the stains
which had insinuated themselves into our breasts, till, after the
lapse of some years, we became fit recipients of the doctrines of
Pythagoras. For as dyers previously purify garments, and then fix
in the colors with which they wish them to be imbued, in order
that the dye may not be washed away, and may never become
evanescent; after the same manner also that divine man prepared
the souls of those that were lovers of philosophy, so that they
might not deceive him in any of those beautiful and good
qualities which he hoped they would possess. For he did not
impart spurious doctrines, nor snares, in which most of the
sophists, who are at leisure for no good purpose, entangle young
men; but he possessed a scientific knowledge of things human
and divine. These men, however, making his doctrine a pretext,
perform many dreadful deeds, ensnaring youth not in a
becoming nor yet in a casual way. Hence they render their
auditors noxious and precipitate. For they infuse theorems and
divine doctrines into confused and turbid manners. Just as if
some one should pour pure and clear water into a deep well full of
mud; for he would disturb the mud, and destroy the clear water.
The same thing likewise takes place between those who teach
and those who are taught after this manner. For dense thickets
and which are full of briars surround the intellect and heart of
those who have not been purely initiated in disciplines, obscure
the mild, tranquil, and reasoning power of the soul, and openly
impede the intellective part from becoming increased and

elevated. It is requisite likewise to call intemperance and avarice the mothers of these thickets; both which are naturally prolific. From intemperance, therefore, unlawful marriages, [unjust] desires, corruptions, intoxication, preternatural pleasures, and certain vehement appetites blossom forth, and which impel their possessors into profundities and precipices. For now desires have compelled some not to abstain either from their mothers or their daughters, and violating law, their country, city, and king, with their hands as it were bound behind them, they are violently dragged along like slaves to extreme destruction. But from avarice germinate rapine, robbery, parricide, sacrilege, sorcery, and such other evils as are the sisters of these. In the first place, therefore, it is necessary to purify the woods in which these passions have fixed their abode, with fire and sword, and all the machines of disciplines; and having liberated the reasoning power from such mighty evils, we may then implant in and deliver to it something useful and good."

So great and so necessary was the attention which, according to Pythagoras, ought to be paid to disciplines prior to philosophy. He likewise ordained that a singular honor, and the most accurate investigation, should be given to the teaching and participation of his dogmas, as he judiciously examined the conceptions of those that came to him, by various documents, and ten thousand forms of scientific theory.

Chapter XVIII.

After this we must narrate how, when he had admitted certain persons to be his disciples, he distributed them into different classes according to their respective merits. For it was not fit that all of them should equally participate of the same things, as they were naturally dissimilar; nor was it indeed right that some should participate of all the most honorable auditions, but others of none, or should not at all partake of them. For this would be uncommunicative and unjust. While therefore he imparted a convenient portion of his discourses to each, he benefited as much as possible all of them, and preserved the proportion of justice, by making each a partaker of the auditions according to his desert. Hence, in conformity to this method, he called some of them Pythagoreans, but others Pythagorists; just as we denominate some men Attics, but others Atticists. Having therefore thus aptly divided their names, some of them he considered to be genuine, but he ordained that others should show themselves to be the emulators of these. He ordered therefore that with the Pythagoreans possessions should be shared in common, and that they should always live together; but that each of the others should possess his own property apart from the rest, and that assembling together in the same place, they should mutually be at leisure for the same pursuits. And thus each of these modes was derived from Pythagoras, and transmitted to his successors. Again, there were also with the Pythagoreans two forms of philosophy; for there were likewise two genera of those that pursued it, the Acusmatici, and the Mathematici. Of these however the Mathematici are acknowledged to be Pythagoreans by the rest; but the Mathematici do not admit that the Acusmatici are so, or that they derived their instruction from Pythagoras, but from Hippasus. And with respect to Hippasus, some say that he was a Crotonian, but others a Metapontine. But the philosophy of the Acusmatici consists in auditions unaccompanied with demonstrations and a reasoning process; because it merely orders a thing to be done in a certain way, and that they should endeavour to preserve such other things as were said by him, as so many divine dogmas. They however profess that they will not speak of them, and that they are not to be spoken of; but they conceive those of their sect to be the best furnished with wisdom, who retained what they had heard more than others. But all these auditions are divided into three species. For some of them indeed signify what a thing is; others what it *especially* is; but others, what ought, or what ought not, to be done. The auditions therefore which signify what a thing is, are such as: What are the islands of the blessed? The sun and moon. What is the oracle at Delphi? The tetractys. What is harmony? That in which the Sirens subsist.[12] But the auditions which signify what a thing *especially* is, are such as, What is the most just thing? To sacrifice. What is the wisest thing? Number.[13] But the next to this in wisdom, is that which gives names to things. What is the wisest of the things that are with us, [*i.e.* which pertain to human concerns]? Medicine. What is the most beautiful? Harmony. What is the most powerful? Mental

43

44 decision. What is the most excellent? Felicity. What is that which is most truly asserted? That men are depraved. Hence they say that Pythagoras praised the Salaminian poet Hippodomas, because he sings:

> Tell, O ye Gods! the source from whence you came,
> Say whence, O men! thus evil you became?

These therefore, and such as these, are the auditions of this kind. For each of these shows what a thing *especially* is. This however is the same with what is called the wisdom of the seven wise men. For they investigated, not what is *simply* good, but what is *especially* so; nor what is difficult, but what is *most* difficult; *viz.* for a man to know himself. Nor did they investigate what is easy, but what is *most* easy; *viz.* to do what you are accustomed to do. For it seems that such auditions as the above, are conformable but posterior in time to such wisdom as that of the seven wise men; since they were prior to Pythagoras. The auditions likewise, respecting what should or should not be done, were such as: That it is necessary to beget children. For it is necessary to leave those that may worship the Gods after us. That it is requisite to put the shoe on the right foot first. That it is not proper to walk in the public ways, nor to dip in a sprinkling vessel, nor to be washed in a bath. For in all these it is immanifest, whether those who use them are pure. Others also of this kind are the following: Do not assist a man in laying a burden down; for it is not proper to be the

45 cause of not laboring; but assist him in taking it up. Do not draw near to a woman for the sake of begetting children, if she has gold. Speak not about Pythagoric[14] concerns without light. Perform libations to the Gods from the handle of the cup, for the sake of an auspicious omen, and in order that you may not drink from the same part [from which you poured out the liquor]. Wear not the image of God in a ring, in order that it may not be defiled. For it is a resemblance which ought to be placed in the house. It is not right to use a woman ill; for she is a suppliant. On this account also we bring her from the Vestal hearth, and take her by the right hand. Nor is it proper to sacrifice a white cock; for this also is a suppliant, and is sacred to the moon. Hence likewise it announces the hours. To him who asks for counsel, give no other advice than that which is the best: for counsel is a sacred

thing. Labors are good; but pleasures are in every respect bad. For as we came into the present life for the purpose of punishment, it is necessary that we should be punished. It is proper to sacrifice, and to enter temples unshod. In going to a temple, it is not proper to turn out of the way; for divinity should not be worshipped in a careless manner. It is good to sustain, and to have wounds in the breast; but it is bad to have them behind. The soul of man alone does not enter into those animals, which it is lawful to kill. Hence it is proper to eat those animals alone which it is fit to slay, but no other animal whatever. And such were the auditions of this kind.

The most extended however were those concerning sacrifices, how they ought to be performed at all other times, and likewise when migrating from the present life; and concerning sepulture, and in what manner it is proper to be buried. Of some of these therefore the reason is to be assigned why they are ordered; such for instance as, it is necessary to beget children, for the sake of leaving another that may worship the Gods instead of yourself. But of others no reason is to be assigned. And of some indeed, the reasons are assumed proximately; but of others, remotely; such as, that bread is not to be broken, because it contributes to the judgment in Hades. The probable reasons however, which are added about things of this kind, are not Pythagoric, but were devised by some who philosophized differently from the Pythagoreans, and who endeavoured to adapt probability to what was said. Thus for instance, with respect to what has been just now mentioned, why bread is not to be broken, some say that it is not proper to dissolve that which congregates. For formerly all those that were friends, assembled in a barbaric manner to one piece of bread. But others say, that it is not proper, in the beginning of an undertaking, to produce an omen of this kind by breaking and diminishing. Moreover, all such precepts as define what is to be done, or what is not to be done, refer to divinity as their end; and every life is coarranged so as to *follow God*. This also is the principle and the doctrine of philosophy. For men act ridiculously in searching for good any where else than from the Gods. And when they do so, it is just as if some one, in a country governed by a king, should reverence one of the citizens who is a magistrate, and neglect him who is the ruler of all of them. For the Pythagoreans thought that such men as we have just mentioned, performed a thing of this kind. For since God is, and is the lord of all things, it is universally acknowledged that good is to be requested of him. For all men impart good to those whom they love, and to those with whom they are delighted; but they give the contrary to good to those to whom they are contrarily disposed. And such indeed is the wisdom of these precepts.

There was, however, a certain person named Hippomedon, an Ægean, a Pythagorean and one of the Acusmatici, who asserted that Pythagoras gave the reasons and demonstrations of all these precepts, but that in consequence of their being delivered to many, and these such as were of a more sluggish genius, the demon-strations were taken away, but the problems themselves were left. Those however of the Pythagoreans that are called *Mathematici*, acknowledge that these reasons and demonstrations were added by Pythagoras, and they say still more than this, and contend that their assertions are true, but affirm that the following circumstance was the cause of the dissimilitude. Pythagoras, say they, came from Ionia and Samos, during the tyranny of Polycrates, Italy being then in a flourishing condition; and the first men in the city became his associates. But, to the more elderly of these, and who were not at leisure [for philosophy], in consequence of being occupied by political affairs, the discourse of Pythagoras was not accompanied with a reasoning process, because it would have been difficult for them to apprehend his meaning through disciplines and demon-strations; and he conceived they would nevertheless be benefited by knowing what ought to be done, though they were destitute of the knowledge of the *why*: just as those who are under the care of physicians, obtain their health, though they do not hear the reason of every thing which is to be done to them. But with the younger part of his associates, and who were able both to act and learn,—with these he conversed through demonstration and disciplines. These therefore are the assertions of the Mathematici, but the former, of the Acusmatici. With respect to Hippasus however especially, they assert that he was one of the Pythagoreans, but that in consequence of having divulged and described the method of forming a sphere from twelve pentagons,[15] he perished in the sea, as an impious person, but obtained the renown of having made the discovery. In reality, however, this as well as every thing else pertaining to geometry, was the invention of that man; for thus without mentioning his name, they denominate Pythagoras. But the Pythagoreans say, that geometry was divulged from the following circumstance: A certain Pythagorean happened to lose the wealth which he possessed; and in consequence of this misfortune, he was permitted to enrich himself from geometry. But geometry was called by Pythagoras *Historia*. And thus much concerning the difference of each mode of philosophizing, and the classes of the auditors of Pythagoras. For those who heard him either within or without the veil, and those who heard him accompanied with seeing, or without seeing him, and who are divided into interior and exterior auditors, were no other than these. And it is requisite to arrange under these, the political, economic and legislative Pythagoreans.

Chapter XIX.

Universally, however, it deserves to be known, that Pythagoras discovered many paths of erudition, and that he delivered an appropriate portion of wisdom conformable to the proper nature and power of each; of which the following is the greatest argument. When Abaris, the Scythian, came from the Hyperboreans, unskilled and uninitiated in the Grecian learning, and was then of an advanced age, Pythagoras did not introduce him to erudition through various theorems, but instead of silence, auscultation for so long a time, and other trials, he immediately considered him adapted to be an auditor of his dogmas, and instructed him in the shortest way in his treatise On Nature, and in another treatise On the Gods. For Abaris came from the Hyperboreans, being a priest of the Apollo who is there worshipped, an elderly man, and most wise in sacred concerns; but at that time he was returning from Greece to his own country, in order that he might consecrate to the God in his temple among the Hyperboreans, the gold which he had collected. Passing therefore through Italy, and seeing Pythagoras, he especially assimilated him to the God of whom he was the priest. And believing that he was no other than the God himself, and that no man resembled him, but that he was truly Apollo, both from the venerable indications which he saw about him, and from those which the priest had known before, he gave Pythagoras a dart which he took with him when he

49

left the temple, as a thing that would be useful to him in the difficulties that would befall him in so long a journey. For he was carried by it, in passing through inaccessible places, such as rivers, lakes, marshes, mountains, and the like, and performed through it, as it is said, lustrations, and expelled pestilence and winds from the cities that requested him to liberate them from these evils. We are informed, therefore, that Lacedæmon, after having been purified by him, was no longer infested with pestilence, though prior to this it had frequently fallen into this evil, through the baneful nature of the place in which it was built, the mountains of Taygetus producing a suffocating heat, by being situated above the city, in the same manner as Cnossus in Crete. And many other similar particulars are related of the power of Abaris. Pythagoras, however, receiving the dart, and neither being astonished at the novelty of the thing, nor asking the reason why it was given to him, but as if he was in reality a God himself, taking Abaris aside, he showed him his golden thigh, as an indication that he was not [wholly] deceived [in the opinion he had formed of him;] and having enumerated to him the several particulars that were deposited in the temple, he gave him sufficient reason to believe that he had not badly conjectured [in assimilating him to Apollo]. Pythagoras also added, that he came [into the regions of mortality] for the purpose of remedying and benefiting the condition of mankind, and that on this account he had assumed a human form, lest men being disturbed by the novelty of his transcendency, should avoid the discipline which he possessed. He likewise exhorted Abaris to remain in that place, and to unite with him in correcting [the lives and manners] of those with whom they might meet; but to share the gold which he had collected, in common with his associates, who were led by reason to confirm by their deeds the dogma, *that the possessions of friends are common.* Thus, therefore, Pythagoras unfolded to Abaris, who remained with him, as we have just now said, physiology and theology in a compendious way; and instead of divination by the entrails of beasts, he delivered to him the art of prognosticating through numbers, conceiving that this was purer, more divine, and more adapted to the celestial numbers of the Gods. He delivered also to Abaris other studies which were adapted to him. That we may return, however, to that for the sake of which the present treatise was written, Pythagoras endeavoured to correct and amend different persons, according to the nature and power of each. All such particulars therefore as these, have neither been transmitted to the knowledge of men, nor is it easy to narrate all that has been transmitted to us concerning him.

Chapter XX.

We shall however exhibit a few specimens, and those the most celebrated, of the Pythagoric discipline, and also the monuments of the studies in which those men engaged. In the first place, therefore, Pythagoras in making trial [of the aptitude of those that came to him] considered whether they could *echemuthein*, *i.e.* whether they were able to refrain from speaking (for this was the word which he used), and surveyed whether they could conceal in silence and preserve what they had learnt and heard. In the next place, he observed whether they were modest. For he was much more anxious that they should be silent than that they should speak. He likewise directed his attention to every other particular; such as whether they were astonished by the energies of any immoderate passion or desire. Nor did he in a superficial manner consider how they were affected with respect to anger or desire, or whether they were contentious or ambitious, or how they were disposed with reference to friendship or strife. And if on his surveying all these particulars accurately, they appeared to him to be endued with worthy manners, then he directed his attention to their facility in learning and their memory. And in the first place, indeed he considered whether they were able to follow what was said, with rapidity and perspicuity; but in the next place, whether a certain love and temperance attended them towards the disciplines which they were taught. For he surveyed how they were naturally disposed with respect to gentleness. But he called this *catartysis*, *i.e. elegance of manners*. And he considered ferocity as hostile to such a mode of education. For impudence, shamelessness, intemperance, slothfulness, slowness in learning, unrestrained licentiousness, disgrace, and the like, are the attendants on savage manners; but the contraries on gentleness and mildness. He considered these things, therefore, in making trial of those that came to him, and in these he exercised the learners. And those that were adapted to receive the goods of the wisdom he possessed, he admitted to be his disciples, and thus endeavoured to elevate them to scientific knowledge. But if he perceived that any one of them was unadapted, he expelled him as one of another tribe, and a stranger.

52   In the next place, I shall speak of the studies which he delivered through the whole of the day to his associates. For those who committed themselves to the guidance of his doctrine, acted in the following manner: they performed their morning walks alone, and in places in which there happened to be an appropriate solitude and quiet, and where there were temples and groves, and other things adapted to give delight. For they thought it was not proper to converse with any one, till they had rendered their own soul sedate, and had co-harmonised the reasoning power. For they apprehended it to be a thing of a turbulent nature to mingle in a crowd as soon as they rose from bed. On this account all the Pythagoreans always selected for themselves the most sacred places. But after their morning walk they associated with each other, and especially in temples, or if this was not possible, in places that resembled them. This time, likewise, they employed in the discussion of doctrines and disciplines, and in the correction of their manners.

Chapter XXI.

After an association of this kind, they turned their attention to the health of the body. Most of them, however, used unction and the course; but a less number employed themselves in wrestling in gardens and groves; others in leaping with leaden weights in their hands, or in pantomime gesticulations, with a view to the strength of the body, studiously selecting for this purpose opposite exercises. Their dinner consisted of bread and honey or the honey-comb; but they did not drink wine during the day. They also employed the time after dinner in the political economy pertaining to strangers and guests, conformably to the mandate of the laws. For they wished to transact

53   all business of this kind in the hours after dinner. But when it was evening they again betook themselves to walking; yet not singly as in the morning walk, but in parties of two or three, calling to mind as they walked, the disciplines they had learnt, and exercising themselves in beautiful studies. After they had walked, they made use

of the bath; and having washed themselves, they assembled in the place where they eat together, and which contained no more than ten who met for this purpose. These, however, being collected together, libations and sacrifices were performed with fumigations and frankincense. After this they went to supper, which they finished before the setting of the sun. But they made use of wine and maize, and bread, and every kind of food that is eaten with bread, and likewise raw and boiled herbs. The flesh also of such animals was placed before them as it was lawful to immolate; but they rarely fed on fish: for this nutriment was not, for certain causes, useful to them. In a similar manner also they were of opinion, that the animal which is not naturally noxious to the human race, should neither be injured nor slain. But after this supper libations were performed, and these were succeeded by readings. It was the custom however with them for the youngest to read, and the eldest ordered what was to be read, and after what manner. But when they were about to depart, the cup-bearer poured out a libation for them; and the libation being performed, the eldest announced to them the following precepts: That a mild and fruitful plant should neither be injured nor corrupted, nor in a similar manner, any animal which is not noxious to the human race. And farther still, that it is necessary to speak piously and form proper conceptions of the divine, dæmoniacal, and heroic genera; and in a similar manner, of parents and benefactors. That it is proper likewise to give assistance to law, and to be hostile to illegality. But these things being said, each departed to his own place *54* of abode. They also wore a white and pure garment. And in a similar manner they lay on pure and white beds, the coverlets of which were made of thread; for they did not use woollen coverlets. With respect to hunting they did not approve of it, and therefore did not employ themselves in an exercise of this kind. Such therefore were the precepts which were daily delivered to the disciples of Pythagoras, with respect to nutriment and their mode of living.

Chapter XXII.

Another mode also of erudition is transmitted to us, which was effected through Pythagoric precepts, and sentences which extended to human life and human opinion; a few of which out of many I shall narrate. One of these therefore contains an exhortation to remove contention and strife from true friendship, and especially from all friendship, if possible. But if this is not possible, at least to expel it from paternal friendship, and universally from that which subsists with elders and benefactors. For to contend pervicaciously with such as these, anger or some other similar passion intervening, is not to preserve, [but destroy] the existing friendship. But they say it is necessary that the smallest lacerations and ulcerations should take place in friendships. And that this will be effected, if both the friends know how to yield and subdue their anger, and especially the younger of the two, and who belongs to some one of the above-mentioned orders. They likewise thought it necessary that the corrections and admonitions which they called *pædartases*, and which the elder employed towards the younger, should be made with much suavity of manners and great caution; and also that much solicitude and appropriation should be exhibited in admonitions. For thus the admonition will become decorous and beneficial. They likewise say that faith should never be separated from friendship, neither seriously nor in jest. For it is no longer easy for the existing friendship to remain in a sane condition, when falsehood once insinuates itself into the manners of those who assert themselves to be friends. And again they say, that friendship is not to be rejected on account of misfortune, or any other imbecility which happens to human life; but that the only laudable rejection of a friend and of friendship, is that which takes place through great and incurable vice. Such therefore was the form of correction with the Pythagoreans through sentences, and which extended to all the virtues, and to the whole of life.

Chapter XXIII.

The mode however of teaching through symbols, was considered by Pythagoras as most necessary. For this form of erudition was cultivated by nearly all the Greeks, as being most ancient. But it was transcendently honored by the Egyptians, and adopted by them in the most diversified manner. Conformably to this, therefore, it will be found, that great attention was paid to it by Pythagoras, if any one clearly unfolds the significations and arcane conceptions of the Pythagoric symbols, and thus develops the great rectitude and truth they contain, and liberates them from their enigmatic form. For they are adapted according to a simple and uniform doctrine, to the great geniuses of these philosophers, and deify in a manner which surpasses human conception. For those who came from this school, and especially the most ancient Pythagoreans, and also those young men who were the disciples of Pythagoras when he was an old man, *viz.* Philolaus[16] and Eurytus, Charondas and Zaleucus, and Brysson, the elder Archytas also, and Aristæus, Lysis and Empedocles, Zanolxis and Epimenides, Milo and Leucippus, Alcmæon, Hippasus and Thymaridas, and all of that age, consisting of a multitude of learned men, and who were above measure excellent,—all these adopted this mode of teaching, in their discourses with each other, and in their commentaries and annotations. Their writings also, and all the books which they published, *most of which have been preserved even to our time,*[17] were not composed by them in a popular and vulgar diction, and in a manner usual with all other writers, so as to be immediately understood, but in such a way as not to be easily apprehended by those that read them. For they adopted that taciturnity which was instituted by Pythagoras as a law, in concealing after an arcane mode, divine mysteries from the uninitiated, and obscuring their writings and conferences with each other. Hence he who selecting these symbols does not unfold their meaning by an apposite exposition, will cause those who may happen to meet with them to consider them as ridiculous and inane, and as full of nugacity and garrulity. When, however, they are unfolded in a way conformable to these symbols, and become obvious and clear even to the multitude, instead of being obscure and dark, then they will be found to be analogous to prophetic sayings, and to the oracles of the Pythian Apollo. They will then also exhibit an admirable meaning, and will produce a divine afflatus in those who unite intellect with erudition. Nor will it be improper to mention a few of them, in order that this mode of discipline may become more perspicuous: Enter not into a temple negligently, nor in short adore carelessly, not even though you should stand at the very doors themselves. Sacrifice and adore unshod. Declining from the public ways, walk in unfrequented paths. Speak not about Pythagoric concerns without light. And such are the outlines of the mode adopted by Pythagoras of teaching through symbols.

56

57

Chapter XXIV.

Since, however, nutriment greatly contributes to the best discipline, when it is properly used, and in an orderly manner, let us consider what Pythagoras also instituted as a law about this. Universally, therefore, he rejected all such food as is flatulent, and the cause of perturbation, but he approved of the nutriment contrary to this, and ordered it to be used, *viz.* such food as composes and compresses the habit of the body. Hence, likewise, he thought that millet was a plant adapted to nutrition. But he altogether rejected such food as is foreign to the Gods; because it withdraws us from familiarity with the Gods. Again, according to another mode also, he ordered his disciples to abstain from such food as is reckoned sacred, as being worthy of honor, and not to be appropriated to common and human utility. He likewise exhorted them to abstain from such things as are an impediment to prophesy, or to the purity and chastity of the soul, or to the habit of temperance, or of virtue. And lastly, he rejected all such things as are adverse to sanctity, and which obscure and disturb the other purities of the soul, and the phantasms which occur in sleep. These things therefore he instituted as laws in common about nutriment.

58 Separately, however, he forbade the most contemplative of philosophers, and who have arrived at the summit of philosophic attainments, the use of superfluous and unjust food, and ordered them never to eat any thing animated, nor in short, to drink wine, nor to sacrifice animals to the Gods, nor by any means to injure animals, but to preserve most solicitously justice towards them. And he himself lived after this manner, abstaining from animal food, and adoring altars undefiled with blood. He was likewise careful in preventing others from destroying animals that are of a kindred nature with us, and rather corrected and instructed savage animals through words and deeds, than injured them through punishment. And farther still, he also enjoined those politicians that were legislators to abstain from animals. For as they wished to act in the highest degree justly, it is certainly necessary that they should not injure any kindred animal. Since, how could they persuade others to act justly, if they themselves were detected in indulging an insatiable avidity by partaking of

animals that are allied to us? For through the communion of life and the same elements, and the mixture subsisting from these, they are as it were conjoined to us by a fraternal alliance. He permitted, however, others whose life was not entirely purified, sacred and philosophic, to eat of certain animals; and for these he appointed a definite time of abstinence. These therefore, he ordered not to eat the heart, nor the brain; and from the eating of these he entirely prohibited all the Pythagoreans. For these parts are of a ruling nature, and are as it were certain ladders and seats of wisdom and life. But other[18] things were considered by him as sacred on account of the nature of a divine reason. Thus he exhorted his disciples to abstain from mallows, because this plant is the first messenger and signal of the sympathy of celestial with terrestrial natures. Thus, too, he ordered them to abstain from the fish melanurus; for it is sacred to the terrestrial Gods. And also not to receive the fish erythinus, through other such like causes. He likewise exhorted them to abstain from beans, on account of many sacred and physical causes, and also such causes as pertain to the soul. And he established as laws other precepts similar to these, beginning through nutriment to lead men to virtue.

Chapter XXV.

Pythagoras was likewise of opinion that music contributed greatly to health, if it was used in an appropriate manner. For he was accustomed to employ a purification of this kind, but not in a careless way. And he called the medicine which is obtained through music by the name of purification. But he employed such a melody as this about the vernal season. For he placed in the middle a certain person who played on the lyre, and seated in a circle round him those who were able to sing. And thus, when the person in the centre struck the lyre, those that surrounded him sung certain pæans, through which they were seen to be delighted, and to become elegant and orderly in their manners. But at another time they used music in the place of medicine. And there are certain melodies devised as remedies against the passions of the soul, and also against despondency and lamentation,[19] which Pythagoras invented as things that afford the greatest assistance in these maladies. And again, he employed other melodies against rage and anger, and against every aberration of the

59

60

soul. There is also another kind of modulation invented as a remedy against desires. He likewise used dancing; but employed the lyre as an instrument for this purpose. For he conceived that the pipe was calculated to excite insolence, was a theatrical instrument, and had by no means a liberal sound.[20] Select verses also of Homer and Hesiod were used by him, for the purpose of correcting the soul. Among the deeds of Pythagoras likewise, it is said, that once through the spondaic song of a piper, he extinguished the rage of a Tauromenian lad, who had been feasting by night, and intended to burn the vestibule of his mistress, in consequence of seeing her coming from the house of his rival. For the lad was inflamed and excited [to this rash attempt] by a Phrygian song; which however Pythagoras most rapidly suppressed. But Pythagoras, as he was astronomizing, happened to meet with the Phrygian piper at an unseasonable time of night, and persuaded him to change his Phrygian for a spondaic song; through which the fury of the lad being immediately repressed, he returned home in an orderly manner, though a little before this, he could not be in the least restrained, nor would in short, bear any admonition; and even stupidly insulted Pythagoras when he met him. When a certain youth also rushed with a drawn sword on Anchitus, the host of Empedocles, because, being a judge, he had publicly condemned his father to death, and would have slain him as a homicide, Empedocles changed the intention of the youth, by singing to his lyre that verse of Homer,

61

> Nepenthe, without gall, o'er every ill
> Oblivion spreads;———[21]

and thus snatched his host Anchitus from death, and the youth from the crime of homicide. It is also related that the youth from that time became the most celebrated of the disciples of Pythagoras. Farther still, the whole Pythagoric school produced by certain appropriate songs, what they called *exartysis* or adaptation, *synarmoge* or elegance of manners, and *epaphe* or contact, usefully conducting the dispositions of the soul to passions contrary to those which it before possessed. For when they went to bed they purified the reasoning power from the perturbations and noises to which it had been exposed during the day, by certain odes and peculiar songs, and by this means procured for themselves tranquil sleep, and few and good dreams. But when they rose from bed, they again liberated themselves from the torpor and heaviness of sleep, by songs of another kind. Sometimes, also, by musical sounds alone, unaccompanied with words, they healed the passions of the soul and certain diseases, enchanting, as they say, in reality. And it is probable that from hence this name *epode*, *i.e.* enchantment, came to be generally used. After this manner, therefore, Pythagoras through music produced the most beneficial correction of human manners and lives.

Chapter XXVI

Since, however, we are narrating the wisdom employed by Pythagoras in instructing his disciples, it will not be inappropriate to relate that which is proximate in a following order to this, *viz.* how 62 he invented the harmonic science, and harmonic ratios. But for this purpose we must begin a little higher. Intently considering once, and reasoning with himself, whether it would be possible to devise a certain instrumental assistance to the hearing, which should be firm and unerring, such as the sight obtains through the compass and the rule, or, by Jupiter, through a dioptric instrument; or such as the touch obtains through the balance, or the contrivance of measures;— thus considering, as he was walking near a brazier's shop, he heard from a certain divine casualty the hammers beating out a piece of iron on an anvil, and producing sounds that accorded with each other, one combination only excepted. But he recognized in those sounds, the diapason, the diapente, and the diatessaron, harmony. He saw, however, that the sound which was between the diatessaron and the diapente was itself by itself dissonant, yet, nevertheless, gave completion to that which was the greater sound among them. Being delighted, therefore, to find that the thing which he was anxious to discover had succeeded to his wishes by divine assistance, he went into the brazier's shop, and found by various experiments, that the difference of sound arose from the magnitude of the hammers, but not from the force of the strokes, nor from the figure of the hammers, nor from the transposition of the iron which was beaten. When, therefore, he had accurately examined the weights and the equal counterpoise of the hammers, he returned home, and fixed one

stake diagonally to the walls, lest if there were many, a certain
difference should arise from this circum-stance, or in short, lest the
peculiar nature of each of the stakes should cause a suspicion of
mutation. Afterwards, from this stake he suspended four chords
consisting of the same materials, and of the same magnitude and
thickness, and likewise equally twisted. To the extremity of each
63 chord also he tied a weight. And when he had so contrived, that the
chords were perfectly equal to each other in length, he afterwards
alternately   struck   two   chords   at   once,   and   found   the
beforementioned symphonies, *viz.* a different symphony in a
different combination. For he discovered that the chord which was
stretched by the greatest weight, produced, when compared with that
which was stretched by the smallest, the symphony diapason. But the
former of these weights was twelve pounds, and the latter six. And,
therefore, being in a duple ratio, it exhibited the consonance
diapason; which the weights themselves rendered apparent. But again,
he found that the chord from which the greatest weight was
suspended compared with that from which the weight next to the
smallest depended, and which weight was eight pounds, produced the
symphony diapente. Hence he discovered that this symphony is in a
sesquialter ratio, in which ratio also the weights were to each other.
And he found that the chord which was stretched by the greatest
weight, produced, when compared with that which was next to it in
weight, and was nine pounds, the symphony diatessaron, analogously
to the weights. This ratio, therefore, he discovered to be sesquitertian;
but that of the chord from which a weight of nine pounds was
suspended, to the chord which had the smallest weight [or six
pounds,] to be sesquialter. For 9 is to 6 in a sesquialter ratio. In like
manner, the chord next to that from which the smallest weight
depended, was to that which had the smallest weight, in a
sesquitertian ratio, [for it was the ratio of 8 to 6,] but to the chord
which had the greatest weight, in a sesquialter ratio [for such is the
ratio of 12 to 8]. Hence, that which is between the diapente and the
diatessaron, and by which the diapente exceeds the diatessaron, is
proved to be in an epogdoan ratio, or that of 9 to 8. But either way it
may be proved that the diapason is a system consisting of the diapente
64 in conjunction with the diatessaron, just as the duple ratio consists of

the sesquialter and sesquitertian, as for instance, 12, 8, and 6; or conversely, of the diatessaron and the diapente, as in the duple ratio of the sesquitertian and sesquialter ratios, as for instance 12, 9, and 6. After this manner, therefore, and in this order, having conformed both his hand and his hearing to the suspended weights, and having established according to them the ratio of the habitudes, he transferred by an easy artifice the common suspension of the chords from the diagonal stake to the limen of the instrument, which he called *chordotonon*. But he produced by the aid of pegs a tension of the chords analogous to that effected by the weights.

Employing this method, therefore, as a basis, and as it were an infallible rule, he afterwards extended the experiment to various instruments; *viz.* to the pulsation of patellæ or pans, to pipes and reeds, to monochords, triangles, and the like. And in all these he found an immutable concord with the ratio of numbers. But he denominated the sound which participates of the number 6 *hypate;* that which participates of the number 8 and is sesquitertian, *mese;* that which participates of the number 9, but is more acute by a tone than mese, he called *paramese*, and *epogdous;* but that which participates of the dodecad, *nete.* Having also filled up the middle spaces with analogous sounds according to the diatonic genus, he formed an octochord from symphonious numbers, *viz.* from the double, the sesquialter, the sesquitertian, and from the difference of these, the epogdous. And thus he discovered the [harmonic] progression, which tends by a certain physical necessity from the most grave [*i.e.* flat] to the most acute sound, according to this diatonic genus. For from the diatonic, he rendered the chromatic and enharmonic genus perspicuous, as we shall some time or other show when we treat of music. This diatonic genus, however, appears to have such physical gradations and progressions as the following; *viz.* a semitone, a tone, and then a tone; and this is the diatessaron, being a system consisting of two tones, and of what is called a semitone. Afterwards, another tone being assumed, *viz.* the one which is intermediate, the diapente is produced, which is a system consisting of three tones and a semitone. In the next place to this is the system of a semitone, a tone, and a tone, forming another diatessaron, *i.e.* another sesquitertian ratio. So that in the more ancient heptachord indeed, all the sounds, from the most grave, which are with respect to each other fourths, produce every where with each other the symphony diatessaron; the semitone receiving by transition, the first, middle, and third place, according to the tetrachord. In the Pythagoric octachord, however, which by conjunction is a system of the tetrachord and pentachord, but if disjoined is a system of two tetrachords separated from each other, the progression is from the most grave sound. Hence all the sounds that are by their distance from each other fifths, produce with each other the symphony diapente; the semitone successively proceeding into four places, *viz.* the first, second, third, and fourth. After this manner, therefore, it is said that music was discovered by Pythagoras. And having reduced it to a system, he delivered it to his disciples as subservient to every thing that is most beautiful.[22]

Chapter XXVII.

Many also of the political actions of his followers are [deservedly] praised. For it is reported that the Crotonians being once impelled to make sumptuous funerals and interments, some one of them said to the people, that he had heard Pythagoras when he was discoursing about divine natures observe, that the Olympian Gods attended to the dispositions of those that sacrificed, and not to the multitude of the sacrifices; but that, on the contrary, the terrestrial Gods, as being allotted the government of things less important, rejoiced in banquets and lamentations, and farther still, in continual libations, in delicacies, and in celebrating funerals with great expense. Whence, on account of his wish to receive, Pluto is called Hades. He suffers, therefore, those that slenderly honor him to remain for a longer time in the upper world; but he always draws down some one of those who are disposed to spend profusely in funeral solemnities, in order that he may obtain the honors which take place in commemoration of the dead. In consequence of this advice, the Crotonians that heard it were of opinion, that if they conducted themselves moderately in misfortunes, they would preserve their own salvation; but that if they were immoderate in their expenses, they would all of them die prematurely. A certain person also having been made an arbitrator in an affair in which there was no witness, led each of the litigants to a

66

certain monument, and said to one of them, the man who is buried in this monument was transcendently equitable; in consequence of which the other litigant prayed that the dead man might obtain much good; but the former said that the defunct was not at all better for the prayers of his opponent. Pythagoras, therefore, condemned what the former litigant said, but asserted that he who praised the dead man for his worth, had done that which would be of no small importance in his claim to belief. At another time, in a cause of great moment, he decided that one of the two who had agreed to settle the affair by arbitration, should pay four talents, but that the other should receive two. Afterwards, he condemned the defendant to pay three talents; and thus he appeared to have given a talent to each of them. Two persons also had fraudulently deposited a garment with a woman who belonged to a court of justice, and told her she was not to give it to either of them unless both were present. Some time after, for the purpose of circumvention, one of them received the common deposit, and said that it was with the consent of the other. But the other, who had not been present [when the garment was returned], acted the part of a sycophant, and related the compact that was made at the beginning, to the magistrates. A certain Pythagorean, however, taking up the affair said, that the woman had acted conformably to the compact, as both parties had been present. Two other persons also appeared to have a strong friendship for each other, but had fallen into a silent suspicion through a flatterer of one of them, who told him that his wife had been corrupted by the other. It so happened, however, that a Pythagorean came into a brazier's shop, where he who conceived himself to be injured, was showing to the artist a sword which he had given him to sharpen, and was indignant with him because it was not sufficiently sharp. The Pythagorean, therefore, suspecting that the sword was intended to be used against him who was accused of adultery, said, This sword is sharper than all things except calumny. This being said, caused the man to consider with himself [what it was he intended to do], and not rashly to sin against his friend who was within, and who had been previously called [by him in order that he might kill him]. A zone also that had golden ornaments having fallen [at the feet] of a certain stranger in the temple of Esculapius, and the laws forbidding any one to take up that

67

which had fallen on the ground, a Pythagorean advised the stranger, who was indignant at this prohibition, to take away the golden ornaments which had not fallen to the ground, but to leave the zone, because this was on the ground.[23] That circumstance, likewise, which by the ignorant is transferred to other places, is said to have happened in Crotona, *viz.* that during a public spectacle, some cranes flew over the theatre, and one of those who had sailed into the port, said to the person who sat near him, Do you see the witnesses? which being heard by a certain Pythagorean, he brought them into the court, consisting of a thousand magistrates, where being examined, it was found that they had thrown certain boys into the sea, and that they called the cranes who flew over the ship [at the time,] witnesses of the deed. When likewise certain persons who had recently become disciples of Pythagoras were at variance with each other, he who was the junior of the two came to the other and said to him, that there was no occasion to refer the affair to a third person, but that it rested with them to commit their anger to oblivion. He, therefore, to whom these words were addressed, replied that he was very much pleased in other respects with what had been said, but that he was ashamed that, being the elder, he had not first said the same thing to the other [who was the junior]. We might here also narrate what is said of Phinthias and Damon,[24] of Plato and Archytas, and likewise of Clinias and Prorus.[25] Omitting, however, these [for the present], we shall mention what is related of Eubulus the Messenian, who when he was sailing homeward, and was taken captive by the Tyrrhenians, was recognized by Nausithus a Tyrrhenian and also a Pythagorean, because he was one of the disciples of Pythagoras, and was taken by him from the pirates, and brought with great safety to Messena. When the Carthaginians, also, were about to send more than five thousand soldiers into a desert island, Miltiades the Carthaginian, perceiving among them the Argive Possiden (both of them being Pythagoreans), went to him, and not manifesting what he intended to do, advised him to return to his native country, with all possible celerity, and having placed him in a ship that was then sailing near the shore, supplied him with what was necessary for his voyage, and thus saved the man from the dangers [to which he was exposed]. In short, he who should relate all that has taken place among the Pythagoreans in their associations with each other, would by the length of his narration exceed the proper quantity and the occasion of his treatise.

I shall therefore rather pass on to show, that some of the Pythagoreans were political characters, and adapted to govern. For they were guardians of the laws, and ruled over certain Italian cities, unfolding to them, and counselling them to adopt the most excellent measures, but abstaining from public revenues. And though they were greatly calumniated, yet at the same time the probity of the Pythagoreans, and the wish of the cities themselves prevailed, so that they were desired by them to administer their political concerns. But at this time the most beautiful of polities appear to have existed in Italy and in Sicily. For Charondas the Catanean, who appears to have been one of the best legislators, was a Pythagorean; as were also the Locrians Zaleucus and Timares, who were celebrated for their legislation. Those also who established the Rheginic polities, that polity which is called Gymnasiarchic, and that which is denominated from Theocles, are said to have been Pythagoreans. Phytius likewise, Theocles, Elecaon, and Aristocrates, excelled among the Pythagoreans in their studies and manners, which also the cities in those places adopted at those times. In short, it is asserted that Pythagoras was the inventor of the whole of political erudition, when he said that nothing is pure among things that have an existence; but that earth participates of fire, fire of air, air of water, and water of spirit. And in a similar manner the beautiful participates of the deformed, the just of the unjust, and other things conformably to these. From this hypothesis, however, the reasoning tends to either part. He also said, that there are two motions of the body and the soul; the one being irrational, but the other the effect of deliberate choice. That three certain lines also constitute polities, the extremes of which mutually touch each other, and produce one right angle; so that one of them has the nature of the sesquitertian; another that of the diapente; and the third is a medium between the other two.[26] But when we consider by a reasoning process the coincidences of the lines with each other, and also of the places under these, we shall find that they represent the best image of a polity. Plato has made the glory of this invention his own; for he clearly says in his Republic, that "the sesquitertian progeny conjoined with the pentad produces two

70

harmonies."[27] It is also said, that Pythagoras cultivated the moderation of the passions, and mediocrity, and that by the conjunction of a certain precedaneous good, he rendered the life of each of his disciples happy. And in short, it is said that he discovered the choice of our good, and of the works adapted to our nature. It is likewise narrated of him, that he withdrew the Crotonians from harlots, and universally from an association with women that were not affianced. For the wives of the Crotonians came to Theano the wife of Brontinus, one of the Pythagoreans, a woman of a wise and excellent soul, (and who was the author of that beautiful and admirable saying, that "it is lawful for a woman to sacrifice on the very day in which she has risen from the embraces of her husband," which some ascribe to Theano the wife of Pythagoras) the Crotonian wives came therefore to her, and entreated her to persuade Pythagoras to discourse to them on the continence which was due from them to their husbands. This she promised to do; and Pythagoras having accordingly made an oration to the Crotonians, which had the desired effect, the incontinence which then prevailed was entirely destroyed. It is further related likewise, that when ambassadors came to the city of the Crotonians from Sybaris, for the purpose of demanding the exiles, Pythagoras beholding one of the ambassadors, who with his own hand had slain one of his friends, made him no answer. But when the man interrogated him, and wished to converse with him, Pythagoras said, that it was not lawful to discourse with homicides. Whence also by certain persons he was thought to be Apollo. All these particulars, therefore, and such as we have a little before mentioned concerning the destruction of tyrants, and the liberation of the cities of Italy and Sicily, and many other circumstances, are indications of the benefits conferred on mankind by Pythagoras in political concerns.

Chapter XXVIII.

That which follows after this, we shall no longer discuss generally, but direct our attention particularly to the works resulting from the virtues of Pythagoras. And we shall begin in the first place from the Gods, as it is usual to do, and indeavour to exhibit his piety, and the admirable works which he performed. Let this, therefore, be one

specimen of his piety, which also we have before mentioned, that he   72
knew what his soul was, and whence it came into the body, and also
its former lives, and that of these things he gave most evident
indications. After this also, let the following be another specimen;
that once passing over the river Nessus with many of his associates, he
spoke to it, and the river in a distinct and clear voice, in the hearing
of all his followers, answered, *Hail Pythagoras!* Farther still, nearly all
historians of his life confidently assert, that in one and the same day
he was present at Metapontum in Italy, and Tauromenium in Sicily,
and discoursed in common with his disciples in both places, though
these cities are separated from each other by many stadia both by land
and sea, and cannot be passed through in a great number of days. The
report, also, is very much disseminated, that he showed his golden
thigh to the Hyperborean Abaris, who said that he resembled the
Apollo among the Hyperboreans, and of whom Abaris was the priest;
and that he did this in order that Abaris might apprehend this to be
true, and that he was not deceived in his opinion. Ten thousand other
more divine and more admirable particulars likewise are uniformly
and unanimously related of *the man:* such as infallible predictions of
earthquakes, rapid expulsions of pestilence and violent winds,
instantaneous cessations of the effusion of hail, and a tranquillization
of the waves of rivers and seas, in order that his disciples might easily
pass over them. Of which things also, Empedocles the Agrigentine,
Epimenides the Cretan, and Abaris the Hyperborean, receiving the
power of effecting, performed certain miracles of this kind in many
places. Their deeds, however, are manifest. To which we may add, that
Empedocles was surnamed *an expeller of winds;* Epimenides, *an
expiator;* and Abaris, *a walker on air;* because being carried on the
dart which was given to him by the Hyperborean Apollo, he passed
over rivers and seas and inaccessible places, like one walking on the
air. Certain persons likewise are of opinion, that Pythagoras did the   73
same thing, when in the same day he discoursed with his disciples at
Metapontum and Tauromenium. It is also said, that he predicted
there would be an earthquake from the water of a well which he had
tasted; and that a ship which was sailing with a prosperous wind,
would be merged in the sea. And let these, indeed, be the indications
of his piety.

Again, however, assuming a more elevated exordium, I am desirous to exhibit the principles of the worship of the Gods, which Pythagoras and his followers established; *viz.* that all such particulars as they define with respect to doing or not doing a thing, have for the mark at which they aim, a consent with divinity. This also is with them the principle, [of piety] and their whole life is arranged with a view *to follow God.* The language, too, of their philosophy is this, that men act ridiculously in exploring good from any other source than the Gods; and that their conduct in this respect resembles that of a man, who in a country governed by a king should reverence one of the magistrates in the city, and neglect him who is the ruler of all of them. For they were of opinion that such was the conduct of mankind. For since God is, and is the Lord of all things, it is universally acknowledged that good is to be requested of him. For all men impart good to those whom they love, and to those with whom they are delighted; but they give the contrary to good, to those to whom they are contrarily disposed. It is evident, therefore, that those things are to be done, in which God delights. It is, however, not easy for a man to know what these are, unless he obtains this knowledge from one who has heard God, or has heard God himself, or procures it through divine art. Hence also, the Pythagoreans were studious of divination. For this alone is an interpretation of the benevolence of the Gods. And in short, he will conceive an employment of this kind
74   to be worthy of regard, who believes that there are Gods; but he who thinks that either of these is folly, will also be of opinion that both are foolish. Many of the mandates, however, of the Pythagoreans were introduced from the mysteries; for they did not conceive them to be the productions of arrogance, but to originate from a certain divinity. And in a similar manner, all the Pythagoreans believe such things as are mythologically related of Aristeas the Proconesian, and Abaris the Hyperborean, and other particulars of a like nature. For they consider every thing of this kind to be credible; and of many [such] things they make trial themselves. They also frequently recollect such-like particulars as appear to be fabulous, as not disbelieving in any thing which may be referred to divinity. A certain person therefore relates, that Eurytus said, that a shepherd feeding his sheep near the tomb of Philolaus, heard some one singing. But the person to whom this was

related, did not at all disbelieve the narration, but asked what kind of harmony it was? Both of them, however, were Pythagoreans, and Eurytus was the disciple of Philolaus. It is, likewise said, that a certain person told Pythagoras, that he appeared to himself once to converse with his father who was dead, and that he asked Pythagoras what this indicated? Pythagoras replied, that it indicated nothing; but that he had in reality conversed with his father. As therefore, said he, nothing is signified by my now discoursing with you, so neither is any thing signified by your conversing with your father. Hence, in all particulars of this kind, they did not think that they were stupid, but those that disbelieved in them. For they did not conceive that some things are possible to the Gods, but others impossible, as those fancy who reason sophistically; but they believed that all things are possible to the Gods. And this very assertion is the beginning of the verses, which they ascribe to Linus, and which are as follow:

> All things may be the objects of our hope,
> Since nothing hopeless any where is found:
> All things with ease Divinity effects,
> And nought can frustrate his almighty power.

75

But they thought that their opinions deserved to be believed, because he who first promulgated them, was not any casual person, but a God. For this was one of their questions: What was Pythagoras? For they say that he was the Hyperborean Apollo; of which this was an indication, that rising up in the Olympic games, he showed his golden thigh; and also that he received the Hyperborean Aoaris as his guest, and was presented by him with the dart on which he rode through the air. But it is said that Abaris came from the Hyperborean regions, in order that he might collect gold for the temple, and that he predicted a pestilence. He also dwelt in temples, and was never seen either to eat or drink. It is likewise said, that rites which purify from evil are performed by the Lacedæmonians, and that on this account Lacedæmon was never infested with pestilence. Pythagoras, therefore, caused this Abaris to acknowledge [that he was more than man,] receiving from him at the same time the golden dart, without which it was not possible for him to find his way. In Metapontum also, certain persons praying that they might obtain what a ship contained that was then sailing into port, Pythagoras said to them, "You will then have a dead body." In Sybaris, too, he caught a deadly serpent and dismissed it. In a similar manner likewise in Tyrrhenia, he caught a small serpent, whose bite was fatal. But in Crotona a white eagle, it is said, suffered Pythagoras to stroke it. A certain person also wishing to hear him discourse, he said that he could not, till some sign appeared. And after this a white bear was seen in Cauconia; the death of which he predicted to one who was about to tell him that it was dead. He likewise reminded Myllias the Crotonian that he had been Midas the son of Gordius. And Myllias passed over to the continent of Asia, in order to perform at the sepulchre [of Midas] those rites which had been enjoined him by Pythagoras. It is likewise said, that the person who bought his house, and who dug up that which had been buried in it, did not dare to tell any one what he saw [on this occasion]. But instead of suffering for this offence, he was seized at Crotona for sacrilege, and put to death. For he took away a golden beard which had fallen from a statue. These things therefore, and others of the like kind, are related by the Pythagoreans, in order to render their opinions worthy of belief. And as these are acknowledged to be true, and it is impossible they should have happened to one man, they consequently think it is clear, that what is related of Pythagoras, should be received as pertaining to a being superior to man, and not to a mere man. This also is the meaning of their enigmatical assertion, that *man, bird, and another third thing, are bipeds.* For the third thing is Pythagoras. Such, therefore, was Pythagoras on account of his piety, and such he was truly thought to be.

With respect to oaths, however, all the Pythagoreans religiously observe them, being mindful of the Pythagoric precept:

> First to th' immortal Gods thy homage pay,
> As they by law are orderly dispos'd;
> And reverence thy oath, but honor next
> Th' illustrious heroes.

Hence a certain Pythagorean, being compelled by law to take an oath, yet in order that he might preserve a Pythagoric dogma, though he would have sworn religiously, chose instead of swearing to pay three talents, this being the fine which he was condemned to pay to the defendant. That Pythagoras however thought that nothing was from chance and fortune, but that all events happened conformably to divine providence, and especially to good and pious men, is confirmed by what is related by Androcydes in his treatise on Pythagoric Symbols, of Thymaridas the Tarentine, and a Pythagorean. For when through a certain circumstance he was about to sail from his own country, and his friends who were present were embracing him, and bidding him farewell, some one said to him, when he had now ascended into the ship, "May such things happen to you from the Gods, O Thymaridas, as are conformable to your wishes!" But he replied, "predict better things; for I should rather wish that such things may happen to me as are conformable to the will of the Gods." For he thought it was more scientific and equitable, not to resist or be indignant with divine providence. If, therefore, any one wishes to learn what were the sources whence these men derived so much piety, it must be said, that a perspicuous paradigm of the Pythagoric theology according to numbers, is in a certain respect to be found in the writings of Orpheus. Nor is it to be doubted, that Pythagoras receiving auxiliaries from Orpheus, composed his treatise Concerning the Gods, which on this account also he inscribed the Sacred Discourse, because it contains the flower of the most mystical place in Orpheus; whether this work was in reality written by Pythagoras, as by most authors it is said to have been, or as some of the Pythagoric school who are both learned and worthy of belief assert, was composed by Telauges; being taken by him from the commentaries which were left by Pythagoras himself to his daughter Damo, the sister of Telauges, and which it is said after her death were given to Bitale the daughter of Damo, and to Telauges the son of Pythagoras, and the husband of Bitale, when he was of a mature age. For when Pythagoras died, he was left very young with his mother Theano. In this Sacred Discourse also, or treatise concerning the Gods (for it has both these inscriptions), who it was that delivered to Pythagoras what is there said concerning the Gods, is rendered manifest. For it says that:

> "*Pythagoras the son of Mnesarchus was instructed in what pertains to the Gods, when he celebrated orgies in the Thracian Libethra, being initiated in them by Aglaophemus; and that*

77

78

*Orpheus the son of Calliope, having learnt wisdom from his
mother in the mountain Pangæus, said, that the eternal essence of
number is the most providential principle of the universe, of
heaven and earth, and the intermediate nature; and farther still,
that it is the root of the permanency of divine natures, of Gods
and dæmons.*"[28]

79   From these things, therefore, it is evident that he learnt from the
Orphic writers that the essence of the Gods is defined by number.
*Through the same numbers also, he produced an admirable fore-
knowledge and worship of the Gods, both which are especially most
allied to numbers.* This, however, may be known from hence; for it is
necessary to adduce a certain fact, in order to procure belief of what is
said. When Abaris performed sacred rites in his accustomed manner,
he procured a fore-knowledge of future events, which is studiously
cultivated by all the Barbarians, through sacrificing animals, and
especially birds; for they are of opinion that the viscera of such
animals are subservient to a more accurate inspection. Pythagoras,
therefore, not wishing to suppress his ardent pursuit of truth, but to
impart it to him through a certain safer way, and without blood and
slaughter, and also because he thought that a cock was sacred to the
sun, furnished him with a consummate knowledge of all truth, as it is
said, through the arithmetical science. He also obtained from piety,
faith concerning the Gods. For Pythagoras always proclaimed, that
nothing admirable pertaining to the Gods or divine dogmas should
be disbelieved, because the Gods are able to accomplish all things.
And the divine dogmas in which it is requisite to believe, are those
which Pythagoras delivered. Thus, therefore, the Pythagoreans
believed in, and assumed the things about which they dogmatized,
because they were not the progeny of false opinion. Hence Eurytus the
Crotonian, the auditor of Philolaus said, that a shepherd feeding his
sheep near the tomb of Philolaus, heard some one singing. But the
person to whom this was related, did not at all disbelieve the
narration, but asked what kind of harmony it was. Pythagoras
himself, also, being asked by a certain person what was indicated by
seeming in sleep to converse with his father who was dead, answered
that it indicated nothing. For neither, said he, is any thing portended
by your speaking with me.

Pythagoras likewise used pure and white garments, and in a similar 80 manner white and pure coverlids; for he did not use those that were made of wool. And this custom he also delivered to his auditors. In speaking also of the natures superior to man, he employed honorable appellations, and words of good omen, and upon every occasion made mention of and reverenced the Gods; so that while at supper, he performed libations to the divinities, and ordered his disciples to celebrate with hymns the beings that are above us, every day. He paid attention likewise to rumors and omens, prophecies, and lots, and in short, to all casual circumstances. Moreover, he sacrificed to the Gods with millet, cakes, honey-combs, and other fumigations. But he did not sacrifice animals, nor did any one of the contemplative philosophers. His other disciples, however, *viz.* the acusmatici, and the politici, were ordered by him to sacrifice animals, such as a cock, or a lamb, or some other animal recently born, but not frequently. At the same time they were prohibited from sacrificing oxen. This also is an indication of the honor which he paid to the Gods, that he exhorted his disciples never to employ the names of the Gods uselessly in swearing. On which account also Syllus, one of the Pythagoreans in Crotona, paid a fine for not swearing, though he could have sworn without violating truth. An oath too such as the following is ascribed to the Pythagoreans, as they were unwilling, through reverence, to name Pythagoras; just as they very much abstained from using the names of the Gods. But they manifested the man through the invention of the tetractys.

> I swear by him who the tetractys found,
> Whence all our wisdom springs, and which contains
> Perennial Nature's fountain, cause, and root.

And, in short, it is said that Pythagoras was emulous of the Orphic mode of writing and [piety of] disposition; and that he honored the Gods in a way similar to that of Orpheus, placing them in images and 81 in brass, not conjoined to our forms, but to divine receptacles;[29] because they comprehend and provide for all things, and have a nature and morphe similar to the universe. He also promulgated purifications, and initiations as they are called, which contain the most accurate knowledge of the Gods. And farther still, it is said, that

he was the author of a compound divine philosophy and worship of
the Gods; having learnt indeed some things from the followers of
Orpheus, but others from the Egyptian priests; some from the
Chaldæans and Magi; some from the mysteries performed in Eleusis,
in Imbrus, Samothracia, and Delos; and some also from those which
are performed by the Celtæ, and in Iberia. It is also said that the
Sacred Discourse of Pythagoras is extant among the Latins, and is
read not to all, nor by all of them, but by those who are promptly
disposed to learn what is excellent, and apply themselves to nothing
base. He likewise ordained that men should make libations thrice,
and observed that Apollo delivered oracles from the tripod, because
the triad is the first number. That sacrifices also should be made to
Venus on the sixth day, because this number is the first that partakes
of every number, and, when divided in every possible way, receives the
power of the numbers subtracted and of those that remain. But that it
is necessary to sacrifice to Hercules on the eighth day of the month
from the beginning, looking in so doing to his being born in the
seventh month. He further asserted, that it was necessary that he who
entered a temple should be clothed with a pure garment, and in
which no one had slept; because sleep in the same manner as the black
and the brown, is an indication of sluggishness; but purity is a sign of
equality and justice in reasoning. He also ordered, that if blood should
be found involuntarily spilt in a temple, a lustration should be made,
either in a golden vessel, or with the water of the sea; the former of
these [*i.e.* gold] being the most beautiful of things, and a measure by
which the price of all things is regulated; but the latter as he
conceived being the progeny of a moist nature, and the nutriment of
the first and more common matter. He likewise said, that it was not
proper to bring forth children in a temple; because it is not holy that
in a temple the divine part of the soul should be bound to the body.
He further ordained, that on a festive day neither the hair should be
cut, nor the nails pared; not thinking it fit that we should leave the
service of the Gods for the purpose of increasing our good. He also
said, that a louse ought not to be killed in a temple; conceiving that a
divine power ought not to participate of any thing superfluous and
corruptible. But that the Gods should be honored with cedar, laurel,
cypress, oak, and myrtle; and that the body should not be purified

with these, nor should any of them be divided by the teeth. He likewise ordained, that what is boiled should not be roasted; signifying by this that mildness is not in want of anger. But he would not suffer the bodies of the dead to be burned; following in this the Magi, being unwilling that any thing divine should communicate with a mortal nature. He likewise thought it was holy for the dead to be carried out in white garments; obscurely signifying by this the simple and first nature, according to number and the principle of all *83* things. But above all things he ordained, that an oath should be taken religiously; since that which is behind is long.[30] And he said, that it is much more holy to be injured than to kill a man: for judgment is deposited in Hades, where the soul and its essence, and the first nature of things are [properly] estimated. Farther still, he ordered that sepulchral chests [*i.e.* biers] should not be made of cypress, because the sceptre of Jupiter was made of this wood, or for some other mystic reason. He likewise ordained that libations should be performed before the table of Jupiter the Saviour, and of Hercules and the Dioscuri; in so doing celebrating Jupiter as the presiding cause and leader of this nutriment; Hercules, as the power of nature; and the Dioscuri, as the symphony of all things. But he said, that libations should not be offered with closed eyes. For he did not think it fit, that any thing beautiful should be undertaken with shame and bashfulness. Moreover, when it thundered, he ordained that the earth should be touched, in remembrance of the generation of things. But he ordered that temples should be entered from places on the right hand, and that they should be departed out of from the left hand. For he asserted that the right hand is the principle of what is called the odd number, and is divine; but that the left hand is a symbol of the even number, and of that which is dissolved. And such is the mode which he is said to have adopted in the cultivation of piety. But other particulars which we have omitted concerning it, may be conjectured from what has been said. So that I shall cease to speak further on this subject.

Chapter XXIX.

84

Of his wisdom, however, the commentaries written by the Pythagoreans afford, in short, the greatest indication; for they adhere to truth in every thing, and are more concise than all other compositions, so that they savour of the ancient elegance of style, and the conclusions are exquisitely deduced with divine science. They are also replete with the most condensed conceptions, and are in other respects various and diversified both in the form and the matter. At one and the same time likewise, they are transcendently excellent, and without any deficiency in the diction, and are in an eminent degree full of clear and indubitable arguments, accompanied with scientific demonstration, and as it is said, the most perfect syllogism; as he will find to be the case, who, proceeding in such paths as are fit, does not negligently peruse them. This science, therefore, concerning intelligible natures and the Gods, Pythagoras delivers in his writings from a supernal origin. Afterwards, he teaches the whole of physics, and unfolds completely ethical philosophy and logic. He likewise delivers all-various disciplines, and the most excellent sciences. And in short there is nothing pertaining to human knowledge which is not accurately discussed in these writings. If therefore it is acknowledged, that of the [Pythagoric] writings which are now in circulation, some were written by Pythagoras himself, but others consist of what he was heard to say, and on this account are anonymous, but are referred to Pythagoras as their author;—if this be the case, it is evident that he was abundantly skilled in all wisdom. But it is said that he very much applied himself to geometry among the Egyptians. For with the Egyptians there are many geometrical problems; since it is necessary that from remote periods, and from the time of the Gods themselves,[31] on account of the increments and decrements of the Nile, those that were skilful should have measured all the Egyptian land which they cultivated. Hence also geometry derived its name. Neither did they negligently investigate the theory of the celestial orbs, in which likewise Pythagoras was skilled. Moreover, all the theorems about lines appear to have been derived from thence. For it is said that what pertains to computation and numbers, was discovered in Phœnicia. For some persons refer the theorems about the celestial bodies to the Egyptians and Chaldeans in common. It is said therefore, that Pythagoras having received and increased all these [theories,] imparted the sciences, and at the same time demonstrated them to his auditors with perspicuity and elegance. And he was the first indeed that denominated philosophy, and said that it was the desire, and as it were love of wisdom. But he defined wisdom to be the science of the truth which is in beings. And he said that beings are immaterial and eternal natures, and alone possess an efficacious power, such as incorporeal essences. But that the rest of things are only homonymously beings, and are so denominated through the participation of real beings, and such are corporeal and material forms, which are generated and corrupted, and never truly are. And that wisdom is the science of things which are properly beings, but not of such as are homonymously so. For corporeal natures are neither the objects of science nor admit of a stable knowledge, since they are infinite and incomprehensible by science, and are as it were non-beings, when compared with universals, and are incapable of being properly circumscribed by definition. It is impossible however to conceive that there should be science of things which are not naturally the objects of science. Hence it is not probable that there will be a desire of science which has no subsistence, but rather that desire will be extended to things which are properly beings, which exist with invariable permanency, and are always consubsistent with a true appellation. For it happens that the perception of things which are homonymously beings, and which are never truly what they seem to be, follows the apprehension of real beings; just as the knowledge of particulars follows the science of universals. For he who knows universals properly, says Archytas, will also have a clear perception of the nature of particulars. Hence things which have an existence are not alone, nor only-begotten, nor simple, but they are seen to be various and multiform. For some of them are intelligible and incorporeal natures, and which are denominated beings; but others are corporeal and fall under the perception of sense, and by participation communicate with that which has a real existence. Concerning all these therefore, he delivered the most appropriate sciences, and left nothing [pertaining to them] uninvestigated. *He likewise unfolded to men those sciences which are common [to all disciplines,]* as for instance the demonstrative, the definitive, and that which consists in dividing, as may be known from the Pythagoric commentaries. He was also accustomed to pour forth sentences resembling oracles to his familiars in a symbolical manner, and

86

which in the greatest brevity of words contained the most abundant and multifarious meaning, like the Pythian Apollo through certain oracles, or like nature herself through seeds small in bulk, the former exhibiting conceptions, and the latter effects, innumerable in multitude, and difficult to be understood. Of this kind is the sentence, *The beginning is the half of the whole*, which is an apothegm of Pythagoras himself. But not only in the present hemistich, but in others of a similar nature, the most divine Pythagoras has concealed the sparks of truth; depositing as in a treasury for those who are capable of being enkindled by them, and with a certain brevity of diction, an extension of theory most ample and difficult to be comprehended, as in the following hemistich:

87

All things accord in number:

which he very frequently uttered to all his disciples. Or again, *Friendship is equality; equality is friendship*. Or in the word *cosmos*, *i.e.* the world; or by Jupiter, in the word *philosophy*, or in the so much celebrated word *tetractys*. All these and many other inventions of the like kind, were devised by Pythagoras for the benefit and amendment of his associates; and they were considered by those that understood them to be so venerable, and so much the progeny of divine inspiration, that the following was adopted as an oath by those that dwelt together in the common auditory:

I swear by him who the tetractys found,
And to our race reveal'd; the cause and root,
And fount of ever-flowing Nature.

This therefore was the form of his wisdom which is so admirable.

It is also said, that of the sciences which the Pythagoreans honored, music, medicine and divination, were not among the least. But they were habitually silent and prompt to hear, and he who was able to hear [in a proper manner] was praised by them. Of medicine, however, they especially embraced the diretetic species, and in the exercise of this were most accurate. And in the first place, indeed, they endeavoured to learn the indications of symmetry, of labor, food, and repose. In the next place, with respect to the preparation of food, they were nearly the first who attempted to employ themselves in it, and to define the mode in which it should be performed. The Pythagoreans likewise employed cataplasms more frequently than their predecessors; but they in a less degree approved of medicated ointments. These however they principally used in the cure of ulcerations. But incisions and burnings they admitted the least of all things. Some diseases also they cured by incantations. Pythagoras, however, thought that music greatly contributed to health, if it was used in a proper manner. The Pythagoreans likewise employed select sentences of Homer and Hesiod for the amendment of souls. But they thought it was necessary to retain and preserve in the memory things which they had learnt and heard; and that it was requisite to be furnished with disciplines and auditions, to as great an extent as there was an ability of learning and remembering; the former of these being the power by which knowledge is obtained, but the latter, the power by which it is preserved. Hence, they very much honored the memory, abundantly exercised, and paid great attention to it. In learning too, they did not dismiss what they were taught, till they had firmly comprehended the first rudiments of it; and they recalled to their memory what they had daily heard, after the following manner: A Pythagorean never rose from his bed till he had first recollected the transactions of the former day; and he accomplished this by endeavouring to remember what he first said, or heard, or ordered his domestics to do when he was rising, or what was the second and third thing which he said, heard, or commanded to be done. And the same method was adopted with respect to the remainder of the day. For again, he endeavoured to recollect who was the first person that he met, on leaving his house, or who was the second; and with whom he in the first, or second, or third place discoursed. And after the same manner he proceeded in other things. For he endeavoured to resume in his memory all the events of the whole day, and in the very same order in which each of them happened to take place. But if they had sufficient leisure after rising from sleep, they tried after the same manner to recollect the events of the third preceding day. And thus they endeavoured to exercise the memory to a great extent. For there is not any thing which is of greater importance with respect to science, experience and wisdom, than the ability of remembering. From these studies therefore it happened that all Italy was filled with philosophers, and this place, which before was unknown, was

88

89

afterwards on account of Pythagoras called Magna Græcia. Hence also it contained many philosophers, poets, and legislators. For the rhetorical arts, demonstrative reasonings, and the laws written by them, were transferred from Italy to Greece. Those likewise who make mention of physics, adduce as the principal physiologists Empedocles and the Elean Parmenides. Those too, who wish to cite sentences, pertaining to the conduct of human life, adduce for this purpose the conceptions of Epicharmus. And nearly all philosophers make use of these. Thus much therefore concerning the wisdom of Pythagoras, how in a certain respect he very much impelled all his auditors to the pursuit of it, as far as they were adapted to its participation, and how perfectly it was delivered by him.

Chapter XXX.

With respect to justice, however, we shall learn in the best manner, how he cultivated and delivered it to mankind, if we survey it from its first principle, and from what first causes it germinates, and also direct our attention to the first cause of injustice. For thus we shall discover how he avoided the latter, and what methods he adopted in order that the former might be properly ingenerated in the soul. The principle of justice therefore, is the common and the equal, through which, in a way most nearly approximating to one body and one soul, all men may be co-passive, and may call the same thing mine and thine; as is also testified by Plato, who learnt this from the Pythagoreans. This therefore, Pythagoras effected in the best manner, exterminating every thing private in manners, but increasing that which is common as far as to ultimate possessions, which are the causes of sedition and tumult. For all things [with his disciples] were common and the same to all, and no one possessed any thing private. And he indeed, who approved of this communion, used common possessions in the most just manner; but he who did not, received his own property, which he brought to the common stock, with an addition to it, and departed. And thus he established justice in the best manner, from the first principle of it.

In the next place, therefore, association with men introduces justice; but alienation, and a contempt of the common genus, produce injustice. Wishing therefore to insert this familiarity from afar in men, he also ordained that his disciples should extend it to animals of the same genus, and commanded them to consider these as their familiars and friends; so as neither to injure, nor slay, nor eat any one of them. He therefore who associates men with animals, because they consist of the same elements as we do, and participate with us of a more common life, will in a much greater degree establish fellowship with those who partake of a soul of the same species, and also of a rational soul. From this also it is evident that he introduced justice produced from the most proper principle. Since likewise the want of riches, sometimes compels many to do something contrary to justice, he well foresaw that this would be the case, and through economy procured for himself liberal expenses, and what was just in sufficient abundance. For again, a just arrangement of domestic concerns is the principle of all good order in cities. For cities are constituted from houses. It is said therefore, that Pythagoras himself was the heir of the property of Alcæus, who died after performing an embassy to the Lacedæmonians, but that notwithstanding this, he was no less admired for his economy than for his philosophy. When also he was married, he so educated the daughter that was born to him, and who was afterwards married to Meno the Crotonian, that when she was a virgin she was the leader of choirs, but when a wife she held the first place among those that approached to altars. It is likewise said, that the Metapontines preserving the remembrance of Pythagoras after his time, made his house a temple of Ceres, but the street in which he lived a museum.

Because also insolence, luxury, and a contempt of the laws, frequently impel men to injustice, on this account he daily exhorted his disciples to give assistance to law, and to be hostile to illegality. Hence he made such a division as the following: that what is called luxury, is the first evil that usually glides into houses and cities; that the second is insolence; and the third destruction. That hence luxury should by all possible means be excluded and expelled [from every house and city,] and that men should be accustomed from their birth to a temperate and manly life. He farther added, that it is requisite to be purified from all malediction, whether it be that which is lamentable, or that which excites hostility, and whether it be of a reviling, or insolent, or scurrilous nature.

91

Besides these, likewise, he established another most beautiful species of justice, *viz.* the legislative; which orders indeed what ought to be done; but forbids what ought not to be done. This species, however, is more excellent than the judicial form of justice. For it resembles medicine which heals those that are diseased. It differs from it however in this, that it does not suffer disease to commence, but pays attention from afar to the health of the soul. This therefore being the case, the best of all legislators came from the school of Pythagoras: in the first place, indeed, Charondas the Catanæan; and in the next

92 place, Zaleucus and Timaratus, who wrote laws for the Locrians. Besides these likewise there were Theætetus and Helicaon, Aristocrates, and Phytius, who became the legislators of the Rhegini. All these likewise obtained from their citizens honors similar to those of the Gods. For Pythagoras did not act like Heraclitus, who said that he would write laws for the Ephesians, and also petulantly[32] said, that in those laws he would order the citizens to hang themselves. But Pythagoras endeavoured to establish laws, with great benevolence and political science. Why however is it requisite to admire these men? For Zamolxis being a Thracian, and the slave of Pythagoras, after he had heard the discourses of Pythagoras, having obtained his liberty, and returned to the Getæ, gave laws to them, as we have before observed in the beginning of this work, and exhorted the citizens to fortitude, *having persuaded them that the soul is immortal. Hence even at present, all the Galatæ, and Trallians, and many others of the Barbarians, persuade their children that the soul cannot be destroyed; but that it remains after death, and that death is not to be feared, but danger is to be encountered with a firm and manly mind.* Having therefore instructed the Getæ in these things, and written laws for them, he was considered by them as the greatest of the Gods.

Farther still, he apprehended that the dominion of the Gods was most efficacious to the establishment of justice, and supernally from this he constituted a polity and laws, and also justice. It will not however be foreign to the purpose, to add particularly the manner in which he thought we ought to conceive of divinity; *viz.* that we should conceive that he exists, and that he is so disposed towards the

93 human race, that he inspects and does not neglect it. And this conception which the Pythagoreans derived from Pythagoras, they

apprehended to be of great utility. For we require an inspection of this kind, which we do not in any thing think fit to resist. But such as this is the inspective government of divinity. For if a divine nature is a thing of this kind, it deserves to have the empire of the universe. For it was rightly said by the Pythagoreans, that man is an animal [so far as pertains to his irrational part,] naturally insolent, and various, according to impulses, desires, and the rest of the passions. He requires therefore a transcendent inspection and government of this kind, from which a certain castigation and order may be derived. Hence they thought that every one being conscious of the variety of his nature, should never be forgetful of piety towards, and the worship of divinity; but should always place him before the eye of the mind, as inspecting and diligently observing the conduct of mankind. But after divinity and the dæmoniacal nature, they thought that every one should pay the greatest attention to his parents and the laws, and should be obedient to them, not feignedly, but faithfully. And universally, they thought it necessary to believe, that nothing is a greater evil than anarchy; since the human race is not naturally adapted to be saved, when no one rules over it.

These men also thought it right to adhere to the customs and legal institutes of their ancestors, even though they should be somewhat inferior to other customs and laws. For to fly from the existing laws, and to be studious of innovation, is by no means profitable and salutary. Pythagoras therefore gave many other specimens of piety to the Gods, evincing that his life was conformable to his doctrines. Nor will it be foreign to the purpose to mention one of them, which may serve to elucidate the rest. But I will relate what Pythagoras said and did relative to the embassy from Sybaris to Crotona, about demanding the return of the exiles. For some of his associates were slain by order of the ambassadors, one of whom slew a part of them with his own hands; but another was the son of one of those who had excited the sedition, and who died through disease. When the Crotonians therefore were deliberating how they should act in this affair, Pythagoras said to his disciples, that he was not willing the Crotonians should be so greatly discordant in this affair, and that in his opinion, the ambassadors should not even lead victims to the altars, much less ought they to drag suppliants [*i.e.* the exiles] from

94

them. But when the Sybarites came to him with their complaints, and the man who had slain some of his associates with his own hands, was defending his conduct, Pythagoras said, that he should not answer [an homicide]. Hence, some persons accused him of asserting that he was Apollo, because prior to this some one having asked him about a certain object of inquiry, why the thing was so; he in his turn asked the interrogator, if he would think fit to inquire of Apollo when he was delivering oracles to him, why he delivered them? But to another of the ambassadors who appeared to him to deride his school, in which he taught the return of souls to the supernal realms, and who said that he would give him an epistle to his father, as he was about to descend into Hades, and exhorted him to bring another letter in answer, from his father, when he returned; Pythagoras replied, that he was not about to descend into the abode of the impious, where he clearly knew that murderers were punished. But the ambassadors reviling him, he proceeded to the sea, many persons following him, and there sprinkled himself with marine water. Some one however of the Crotonian counsellors, after reviling the rest of the ambassadors, observed that he understood they had defamed Pythagoras, whom not even a brute would dare to blaspheme, though all animals should again utter the same voice as men, which fables report they did in the beginning of things.

Pythagoras likewise discovered another method of restraining men from injustice, through the judgment of souls, truly knowing indeed that this method may be taught, and also knowing that it is useful to the suppression of justice through fear. He asserted therefore, that it is much better to be injured than to kill a man; for that judgment is deposited in Hades, where the soul, and its essence, and the first nature of beings, are properly estimated. Being desirous, however, to exhibit in things unequal, without symmetry and infinite, a definite, equal, and commensurate justice, and to show how it ought to be exercised, he said, that justice resembles that figure, which is the only one among geometrical diagrams, that having indeed infinite compositions of figures, but dissimilarly disposed with reference to each other, yet has equal demonstrations of power.[33] Since also there is a certain justice in making use of another person, such a mode of it as the following, is said to have been delivered by the Pythagoreans: Of associations with others, one kind is seasonable, but another is unseasonable. These likewise are distinguished from each other by difference of age, desert, the familiarity of alliance, and of beneficence, and whatever else there may be of the like kind in the different associations of men with each other. For there is a species of association, *viz.* of a younger with a younger person, which does not appear to be unseasonable; but that of a younger with an elderly person is unseasonable. For no species of anger, or threatening, or boldness, is becoming in a younger towards an elderly man, but all unseasonable conduct of this kind should be cautiously avoided. A similar reasoning likewise should be adopted with respect to desert. For it is neither decorous, nor seasonable, to use an unrestrained freedom of speech, or to adopt any of the above-mentioned modes of conduct, towards a man who has arrived at the true dignity of consummate virtue. Conformably to this also, was what he said respecting the association with parents, and likewise with benefactors. He added, that there is a certain various and multiform use of an opportune time. For of those that are enraged and angry, some are so seasonably, but others unseasonably. And again, of those that aspire after, desire, and are impelled to any thing appetible, an opportune time is the attendant on some, and an unseasonable time on others. And the same thing may be said concerning other passions and actions, dispositions, associations, and meetings. He further observed, that an opportune time is *to a certain extent* to be taught, and also, that what happens contrary to expectation, is capable of receiving an artificial discussion; but that when it is considered universally and simply, none of the above-mentioned particulars pertain to it. Nearly, however, such things are the attendants on it, as follow the nature of opportune time, *viz.* what is called the florid, the becoming, the adapted, and whatever else there may be homogeneous to these. He likewise asserted, that principle [or the beginning] is in the universe unity, and is the most honorable of things; and that in a similar manner it is so in science, in experience, and in generation. And again, that the number two is most honorable in a house, in a city, in a camp, and in all such like systems. But that the nature of principle is difficult to be surveyed and apprehended in all the above-mentioned particulars. For in sciences, it is not the province of any casual understanding to learn and judge, by well surveying the parts of things, what the nature is of the principle of these. He added, that it makes a great difference, and that there is danger with respect to the knowledge of the whole of things, when principle is not rightly assumed. For none, in short, of the consequent conclusions can be sane, when the true principle is unknown. The same thing may also be said respecting a principle of another kind. For neither can a house, nor a city, be well instituted, unless each has a true ruler, who governs those that voluntarily submit to him. For it is necessary that in both these the governor should be willing to rule, and the governed to obey. Just as with respect to disciplines, when they are taught with proper effect, it is necessary that there should be a concurrence in the will both of the teacher and learner. For if there is a resistance on the part of either, the proposed work will never be accomplished in a proper manner. Thus therefore, he proved, that it was beautiful to be persuaded by rulers, and to be obedient to preceptors. But he exhibited the following as the greatest argument through deeds, of the truth of his observations. He went from Italy to Delos, to Pherecydes the Syrian, who had been his preceptor, in order that he might afford him some assistance, as he was then afflicted with what is called the morbus pedicularis, and he carefully attended him to the time of his death, and piously performed whatever rites were due to his dead preceptor. So diligent was he in the discharge of his duties to him from whom he had received instruction.

Moreover, with respect to compacts and the veracity pertaining to them, Pythagoras so prepared his disciples for the observance of them, that, as it is said, Lysis having once performed his adorations in the temple of Juno, met, as he was departing from it, about the vestibules with Euryphamus the Syracusan, who was one of his fellow disciples, and was then entering into the temple. Euryphamus therefore desiring Lysis to wait for him, till he also had adored the Goddess, Lysis sat down on a stone seat which was placed there. Euryphamus however having finished his adoration, and becoming absorbed in certain profound conceptions, forgot his appointment, and went out of the temple through another gate. But Lysis waited for him without quitting his seat, the remainder of that day and the following night, and also the greater part of the next day. And perhaps he would have

98

stayed there for a still longer time, unless Euryphamus on the following day, had heard in the auditory, that Lysis was wanted by his associates. Recollecting therefore his compact, he came to Lysis, and liberated him from his engagement, at the same time telling him the cause of his forgetfulness, and added, "Some God produced in me this oblivion, as a trial of your firmness in preserving your compacts." Pythagoras likewise ordained abstinence from animal food, for many other reasons, and likewise because it is productive of peace. For those who are accustomed to abominate the slaughter of animals as iniquitous and preternatural, will think it to be much more unlawful to kill a man, or engage in war. But war is the leader and legislator of slaughter. For by this it is increased, and becomes strong and powerful. Not to step also above the beam of the balance, is an exhortation to justice, announcing, that whatever is just should be cultivated, as will be shown when we discuss the Pythagoric symbols. It appears therefore, through all these particulars, that Pythagoras paid great attention to the exercise of justice, and to the delivery of it to mankind, both in deeds and in words.

Chapter XXXI.

It follows, in the next place, that we should speak of temperance, and show how it was cultivated by Pythagoras, and how he delivered it to his associates. We have already therefore narrated the common precepts concerning it, in which it is said that every thing incommensurate should be cut off with fire and sword. The abstinence also from animal food, is a precept of the same species; and likewise from certain foods calculated to produce intemperance, and impeding the vigilance and genuine energies of the reasoning power. Farther still, to this species the precept belongs, that sumptuous food should indeed be introduced in banquets, but should [shortly after] be sent away, and given to the servants, being placed on the table merely for the sake of punishing the desires. Likewise, that no liberal and ingenuous woman should wear gold, but only harlots. And again, the exercise of taciturnity, and perfect silence, for the purpose of governing the tongue. Likewise a strenuous and assiduous resumption and investigation of the most difficult theorems. But on account of all these, we must refer to the same virtue [*i.e.* to temperance,] abstinence

from wine; paucity of food and sleep; an inartificial contempt of
renown, wealth, and the like; a sincere reverence towards those to
whom reverence is due, but an unfeigned similitude of behaviour and
benevolence towards those of the same age; an animadversion and
exhortation of those that are younger, without envy; and every thing
else of the like kind.

The temperance also of those men, and how Pythagoras taught this
virtue, may be learnt from what Hippobotus and Neanthes narrate of
Myllias and Timycha who were Pythagoreans. For they say that
Dionysius the tyrant could not obtain the friendship of any one of the
Pythagoreans, though he did every thing to accomplish his purpose;
for they had observed, and carefully avoided his monarchical
disposition. He sent therefore to the Pythagoreans, a troop of thirty
soldiers, under the command of Eurymenes the Syracusan, who was
the brother of Dion, in order that by treachery their accustomed
migration from Tarentum to Metapontum, might be opportunately
effected for his purpose. For it was usual with them to change their
abode at different seasons of the year, and they chose such places as
were adapted to this migration. In Phalæ therefore, a craggy part of
Tarentum, through which the Pythagoreans must necessarily pass in
their journey, Eurymenes insidiously concealed his troop, and when
the Pythagoreans, expecting no such thing, came to that place about
the middle of the day, the soldiers rushed upon them with shouts,
after the manner of robbers. But the Pythagoreans being disturbed
and terrified at an attack so unexpected, and at the superior number
of their enemies (for the whole number of the Pythagoreans was but
ten), and considering also that they must be taken captive, as they
were without arms, and had to contend with men who were variously
armed,—they found that their only safety was in flight, and they did
not conceive that this was foreign to virtue. For they knew that
fortitude, according to the decision of right reason, is the science of
things which are to be avoided and endured. And this they now
obtained. For those who were with Eurymenes, being heavy-armed,
would have abandoned the pursuit of the Pythagoreans, if the latter in
their flight had not arrived at a certain field sown with beans, and
which were in a sufficiently flourishing condition. Not being willing
therefore to violate the dogma which ordered them not to touch

beans, they stood still, and from necessity attacked their pursuers with stones and sticks, and whatever else they happened to meet with, till they had slain some, and wounded many of them. All the Pythagoreans however, were at length slain by the spearmen, nor would any one of them suffer himself to be taken captive, but preferred death to this, conformably to the mandates of their sect.

Eurymenes therefore, and his soldiers, were beyond measure disturbed on finding that they should not be able to bring one of the Pythagoreans alive to Dionysius, though they were sent by him for this purpose alone. Hence, having piled earth on the slain, and buried them in that place in a common sepulchre, they turned their steps homeward. As they were returning, however, they happened to meet with Myllias the Crotonian, and his wife Timycha the Lacedemonian, whom the other Pythagoreans had left behind, because Timycha being pregnant, was now in her sixth[34] month, and on this account walked leisurely. These therefore, the soldiers gladly made captive, and led them to the tyrant, paying every attention to them, in order that they might be brought to him safe. But the tyrant having learnt what had happened, was greatly dejected, and said to the two Pythagoreans, "You shall obtain from me honors transcending all others in dignity, if you will consent to reign in conjunction with me." All his offers however being rejected by Myllias and Timycha; "If then," said he, "you will only teach me one thing, I will dismiss you with a sufficiently safe guard." Myllias therefore asking him what it was he wished to learn; Dionysius replied, "It is this, why your companions chose rather to die, than to tread on beans?" But Myllias immediately answered, "My companions indeed submitted to death, in order that they might not tread upon beans, but I would rather tread on them, than tell you the cause of this." Dionysius therefore, being astonished at this answer, ordered him to be forcibly taken away, but commanded Timycha to be tortured: for he thought, that as she was a woman, pregnant, and deprived of her husband, she would easily tell him what he wanted to know, through fear of the torments. The heroic woman, however, grinding her tongue with her teeth, bit it off, and spit it at the tyrant; evincing by this, that though her sex being vanquished by the torments might be compelled to disclose something which ought to be concealed in silence, yet the

101

102

member subservient to the development of it, should be entirely cut off. So much difficulty did they make in admitting foreign friendships, even though they should happen to be royal.

Similar to these also, were the precepts concerning silence, and which tended to the exercise of temperance. For the subjugation of the tongue, is of all other continence the most difficult. The persuading likewise the Crotonians to abstain from the profane and spurious association with harlots, pertains to the same virtue. And besides this, the correction through music, by means of which Pythagoras restored a young man to temperance, who had become furious through love. The exhortation also, which leads from lascivious insolence, must be referred to the same virtue. And these things Pythagoras delivered to the Pythagoreans, he himself being the cause of them. For they so attended to their bodies, that they might always remain in the same condition, and not at one time be lean, but at another, abounding in flesh. For they considered this to be an indication of an anomalous life. In a similar manner also with respect to the mind, they were careful that they might not be at one time cheerful, and at another sad, but that they might be mildly joyful with uniformity. But they expelled rage, despondency, and perturbation. *And it was a precept with them, that no human casualties ought to be unexpected by those who are endued with intellect, but that they should expect every thing may happen which it is not in their power to prevent.* But if at any time they were in a rage, or oppressed with sorrow, or any thing else of this kind, they separated themselves from the rest of their associates, and each by himself alone endeavoured to digest and heal the passion.

103

This also is said of the Pythagoreans, that no one of them when angry, either punished a servant, or admonished any free man, but each of them waited till his mind was restored to its former [tranquil] condition. But they called *to admonish, pædartan.* For they accomplished this waiting by employing silence and quiet. Hence Spintharus relates of Archytas the Tarentine, that returning after a certain time from the war which the city of Tarentum waged against the Messenians, to inspect some land which belonged to him, and finding that the bailiff and the other servants, had not paid proper attention to the cultivation of it, but had greatly neglected it, being

enraged, he was so indignant, that he told his servants it was well for
them he was angry; since, if this had not happened, they would not
have escaped the punishment due to so great an offence. Spintharus
likewise says that a similar thing is related of Clinias. For he also
deferred all admonitions and punishments, till his mind was restored
to tranquillity.

It is farther related of the Pythagoreans, that they expelled from
themselves lamentation, weeping, and every thing else of this kind;
and that neither gain, nor desire, nor anger, nor ambition, nor any
thing of a similar nature, became the cause of dissention among
them; but that all the Pythagoreans were so disposed towards each
other, as a worthy father is towards his offspring. This also is a
beautiful circumstance, that they referred every thing to Pythagoras,
and called it by his name, and that they did not ascribe to themselves
the glory of their own inventions, except very rarely. For there are
very few whose works are acknowledged to be their own. The accuracy   104
too, with which they preserved their writings is admirable. For in so
many ages, no one appears to have met with any of the commentaries
of the Pythagoreans, prior to the time of Philolaus. But he first
published those three celebrated books, which Dion the Syracusan is
said to have bought, at the request of Plato, for a hundred mina. For
Philolaus had fallen into a certain great and severe poverty; and from
his alliance to the Pythagoreans, was a partaker of their writings.

With respect also to opinion,[35] it is related that they spoke of it as
follows: That it is the province of a stupid man to pay attention to the
opinion of every one, and especially to that of the multitude. For it
belongs to a few only to apprehend and opine rightly; since it is
evident that this pertains to the intelligent alone. But they are few. It
is manifest therefore, that a power of this kind does not extend itself
to the multitude. But it is also stupid to despise the opinion of every
one. For it will happen that he who is so disposed will be unlearned
and incorrigible. It is however necessary that he who is destitute of
science should learn those things of which he is ignorant, and has no
scientific knowledge. And it is likewise necessary that the learner
should pay attention to the opinion of him who possesses science, and
is able to teach. And universally, it is necessary that those young men
who wish to be saved, should attend to the opinion of their elders, and

of those who have lived well. But in the whole of human life there are certain ages (denominated by them as it is said *endedasmenæ*) which it is not in the power of any casual person to connect with each other. For they are expelled by each other, unless some one conducts a man from his birth, in a beautiful and upright manner. It is necessary therefore, when a child is educated well, and is formed to temperance and fortitude, that a great part of his education should be given to the age of adolescence [which is that of a lad]. In a similar manner also, when a lad is formed to temperance and fortitude, it is necessary that a great part of his education should be transferred to the age of manhood. For that which happens to the multitude is absurd and ridiculous. For they fancy it is requisite that boys should be orderly and temperate, and should abstain from every thing which appears to be troublesome and indecorous; but that when they have arrived at adolescency, they may for the most part do whatever they please. Hence there is nearly a conflux of both kinds of errors into this age. For lads commit many faults which are both puerile and virile. For, in short, to avoid every kind of sedulity and order, and to pursue every species of sport, and puerile intemperance and insolence, are most adapted to the age of a boy. Such a disposition therefore as this, is derived from the puerile into the following age. But the genus of strong desires, and of different species of ambition, and in a similar manner the remaining impulses and dispositions, when they are of a severe and turbulent nature, are derived from the virile age into that of adolescency. Hence this of all the ages demands the greatest attention. And universally, no man ought to be suffered to do whatever he pleases, but it is always necessary that there should be a certain inspection, and a legal and elegantly-formed government, to which each of the citizens is obedient. For the animal, when left to itself and neglected, rapidly degenerates into vice and depravity.

It is likewise said, that the Pythagoreans frequently inquired and doubted why we accustom boys to take their food in an orderly and commensurate manner, and show them that order and symmetry are beautiful; but that the contraries to these, disorder and incommensuration, are base; and that he who is given to wine and is insatiable, is held in great disgrace. For if no one of these is useful to us when we have arrived at the age of virility, it was in vain that we were accustomed, when boys, to an order of this kind. And there is also the same reason concerning the other manners [to which we are accustomed when boys]. This, therefore, is not seen to happen in other animals which are disciplined by men; but immediately from the first, a whelp and a colt are accustomed to, and learn those things which it is requisite for them to do when they have arrived at the perfection of their nature. And universally, it is said that the Pythagoreans exhorted both those they happened to meet, and their familiars, to avoid pleasure as a thing that required the greatest caution. For nothing so much deceives us, or precipitates us into error, as this passion. In short, as it seems, they contended that we should never do any thing with a view to pleasure as the end. For this scope is, for the most part, indecorous and noxious. *But they asserted, that especially looking to the beautiful and decorous, we should do whatever is to be done.*[36] And that in the second place we should look to the advantageous and the useful. These things, however, require no casual judgment.

With respect to what is called desire, these men are said to have asserted as follows: That *desire indeed, itself, is a certain tendency, impulse, and appetite of the soul, in order to be filled with something, or to enjoy something present, or to be disposed according to some sensitive energy;* but that there is also a desire of the contraries to these, and this is a desire of the evacuation and absence, and of having no sensible perception of certain things. That this passion likewise is various, and is nearly the most multifarious of all those that pertain to man. But that many human desires are adscititious, and procured by men themselves. Hence this passion requires the greatest attention, and no casual care and corporeal exercise. For that the body when empty should desire food, is natural: and again, it is also natural, that when filled, it should desire an appropriate evacuation. But to desire superfluous nutriment, or superfluous and luxurious garments or coverlids, or habitations, is adscititious. They also reasoned in the same manner concerning furniture, vessels, servants, and cattle subservient to food. And universally, with respect to human passions, they are nearly things of such a kind, as to be nowhere permanent, but to proceed to infinity. Hence attention should be paid to youth from the earliest period, in order that they may aspire after such

107

things as are proper, may avoid vain and superfluous desires, and thus
be undisturbed by, and purified from, such-like appetites, and may
despise those who are objects of contempt, because they are bound to
[all-various] desires. But it must be especially observed, that vain,
noxious, superfluous, and insolent desires subsist with those who have
the greatest power. For there is not any thing so absurd, which the
soul of such boys, men, and women, does not incite them to perform.
In short, the variety of food which is assumed, is most manifold. For
there are an infinite number of fruits, and an infinite multitude of
roots, which the human race uses for food. It likewise uses all-various
kinds of flesh; and it is difficult to find any terrestrial, aerial, or
aquatic animal, which it does not taste. It also employs all-various
contrivances in the preparation of these, and manifold mixtures of
juices. Hence it properly follows that the human tribe is insane and
multiform, according to the motion of the soul. For each kind of
108   food that is introduced into the body, becomes the cause of a certain
peculiar disposition.

We however perceive that some things become immediately the
cause of a great change in quality, as is evident in wine. For when it is
drank abundantly, it makes men at first more cheerful, but afterwards
more insane and indecorous. But men are ignorant of those things
which do not exhibit a power of this kind; though every thing that is
eaten is the cause of a certain peculiar disposition. Hence it requires
great wisdom, to be able to know and perceive, what kind and what
quantity of food ought to be used. This science, however, was at first
unfolded by Apollo and Pæon; but afterwards by Esculapius and his
followers.

With respect to generation also, the Pythagoreans are said to have
made the following observations. In the first place, they thought it
necessary to guard against what is called untimely [offspring]. For
neither untimely plants, nor animals, are good; but prior to their
bearing fruit, it is necessary that a certain time should intervene, in
order that seeds and fruit may be produced from strong and perfect
bodies. It is requisite, therefore, that boys and virgins should be
accustomed to labors and exercises, and appropriate endurance, and
that food should be given to them adapted to a life of labor,
temperance, and endurance. But there are many things of this kind in

human life, which it is better to learn at a late period, and among these is the use of venery. It is necessary, therefore, that a boy should be so educated, as not to seek after such a connexion as this, within the twentieth year of his age. But when he arrives at this age, he should use venery rarely. This however will be the case, if he thinks that a good habit of body is an honorable and beautiful thing. For intemperance and a good habit of body, are not very much adapted to subsist together in the same person. It is also said, that those laws were praised by the Pythagoreans, which existed prior to their time in *109* Grecian cities, and which prohibited the having connexion with a woman who is a mother, or a daughter, or a sister, either in a temple, or in a public place. For it is beautiful and advantageous that there should be numerous impediments to this energy. These men also apprehended, as it seems, that preternatural generations, and those which are effected in conjunction with wanton insolence, should be entirely prevented from taking place; but that those should be suffered to remain, which are according to nature, and subsist with temperance, and which take place in the chaste and legal procreation of children.

They likewise were of opinion that great providential attention should be paid by those who beget children, to the future progeny. The first, therefore, and the greatest care which should be taken by him who applies himself to the procreation of children is, that he lives temperately and healthfully, that he neither fills himself with food unseasonably, nor uses such aliments as may render the habits of the body worse than they were, and above all things, that he avoids intoxication. For they thought that depraved seed was produced from a bad, discordant, and turbid temperament. And universally they were of opinion, that none but an indolent and inconsiderate person would attempt to produce an animal, and lead it into existence, without providing with all possible diligence that its ingress into being and life might be most elegant and pleasing. For those that are lovers of dogs, pay every possible attention to the generation of whelps, in order that they may be produced from such things as are proper, and when it is proper, and in such a way as is proper, and thus may become a good offspring. The same attention also is paid by those who are lovers of birds. And it is evident that others also who are studious about the procreation of generous animals, endeavour by all possible means, that the generation of them may not be in vain. It would be absurd therefore that men should pay no attention to their own offspring, but should both beget them casually and with perfect carelessness, and, after they are begotten, nourish and educate them with extreme negligence. For this is the most powerful and most manifest cause of the vice and depravity of the greater part of mankind. For with the multitude the procreation of children is undertaken in a beastly and rash manner. And such were the assertions, and such the doctrine of these men, which they verified both in words and deeds, respecting temperance; these precepts having been originally received by them from Pythagoras himself, like certain oracles delivered by the Pythian Apollo.

Chapter XXXII.

With respect to fortitude, however, many of the particulars which have been already related, appropriately pertain to it; such as the admirable deeds of Timycha, and of those Pythagoreans who chose to die rather than transgress the decisions of Pythagoras concerning beans, and other things conformable to such-like pursuits. Such also are the deeds which Pythagoras himself generously accomplished, when he travelled everywhere alone, and underwent immense labors and dangers, choosing to leave his country, and dwell among strangers. Likewise, when he dissolved tyrannies, gave an orderly arrangement to confused polities, and emancipated cities. When also he caused illegality to cease, and impeded the operations of insolent and tyrannical men; exhibiting himself a benignant leader to the just and mild, but expelling savage and licentious men from his association, and refusing even to give them an answer; gladly, indeed, giving assistance to the former, but with all his might resisting the latter. Many instances therefore of these things might be adduced, and of upright actions frequently performed by him. But the greatest of all these, is what he said and did to Phalaris, with an invincible freedom of speech. For when he was detained in captivity by Phalaris, the most cruel of tyrants, a wise man of the Hyperborean race, whose name was Abaris, was his associate, who came to him for the sake of conversing with him, and asked him many questions, and especially such as were of a sacred nature, respecting statues and the most holy worship, the providence of the Gods, celestial and terrestrial natures, and many other things of a similar kind. But Pythagoras, being under the influence of divine inspiration, answered Abaris vehemently, and with all truth and persuasion, so as to convince those that heard him. Then, however, Phalaris was inflamed with anger against Abaris, because he praised Pythagoras, and was ferociously disposed towards Pythagoras himself. He also dared to utter blasphemies against the Gods themselves, and such as he was accustomed to pour forth. But Abaris gave Pythagoras thanks for what he said; and after this, learnt from him that *all things are suspended from and governed by the heavens; which he evinced to be the case from many other things, and also from the energy of sacred rites.* And Abaris was so far from thinking that Pythagoras, who taught these things, was an enchanter, that he beyond measure admired him as if he had been a God. To these things, however, Phalaris replied by endeavouring to subvert divination, and openly denying the efficacy of the things which are performed in sacred rites. But Abaris transferred the discourse from these particulars to such as are clearly apparent to all men; and endeavoured to persuade him that there is a divine providence, from those circumstances which transcend all human hope and power, whether they are immense wars, or incurable diseases, or the corruption of fruits, or the incursions of pestilence, or certain other things of the like kind, which are most difficult to be borne, and deplorable, arising from the beneficent energies of certain dæmoniacal and divine powers.[37]

Phalaris, however, shamelessly and audaciously opposed what was said. Again therefore Pythagoras, suspecting that Phalaris intended to put him to death, but at the same time knowing that he was not destined to die by Phalaris, began to address him with great freedom of speech. For looking to Abaris he said, that a transition was naturally adapted to take place from the heavens to aerial and terrestrial beings. And again, he showed that all things follow the heavens, from instances most known to all men. He likewise indubitably demonstrated, that the [deliberative] power of the soul possesses freedom of will. And proceeding still farther, he amply discussed the perfect energy of reason and intellect. Afterwards also,

112

with his [usual] freedom of speech, he spoke concerning tyranny, and all the prerogatives of fortune, and concerning injustice and human avarice, and solidly taught him that all these are of no worth. In the next place, he gave him a divine admonition concerning the most excellent life, and earnestly entered on a comparison of it with the most depraved life. He likewise most clearly unfolded to him, how the soul, and its powers and passions, subsist; *and, what is the most beautiful thing of all, demonstrated to him that the Gods are not the causes of evils, and that diseases, and such things as are the calamities of the body, are the seeds of intemperance;* reprehending at the same time mythologists and poets for what they have badly said in fables [on this subject]. Confuting Phalaris also, he admonished him, and exhibited to him through works what the power of heaven is, and the magnitude of that power; and proved to him by many arguments, that legal punishment is reasonably established. He likewise clearly showed him what the difference is between men and other animals; and scientifically discussed internal and external speech. He also perfectly demonstrated the nature of intellect, and of the knowledge which descends from it; together with many other ethical dogmas consequent to these things.

Farther still, he instructed him in what is most beneficial among the things that are useful in life; and in the mildest manner adapted admonitions harmonizing with these; adding at the same time prohibitions of what ought not to be done. And that which is the greatest of all, he unfolded to him the distinction between the productions of fate, and those of intellect, and also the difference between what is done by destiny, and what is done by fate. He likewise wisely discussed many things concerning dæmons, and the immortality of the soul. These things however pertain to another treatise. But those particulars are more appropriate to our present purpose which belong to the cultivation of fortitude. For if, when situated in the midst of dreadful circumstances, Pythagoras appears to have philosophized with firmness of decision, if on all sides he resisted and repelled fortune, and strenuously endured its attacks, and if he employed the greatest freedom of speech towards him who brought his life into danger, it is evident that he perfectly despised those things which are thought to be dreadful, and that he considered them

113

as undeserving of notice. If also, when he expected according to appearances to be put to death, he entirely despised this, and was not moved by the expectation of it, it is evident that he was perfectly free from the dread of death.[38]

He performed however what is still more generous than this, by effecting the dissolution of tyranny, restraining the tyrant when he was about to bring the most deplorable calamities on mankind; and liberating Sicily from the most cruel and imperious power. But that it was Pythagoras who accomplished this, is evident from the oracles of Apollo, in which it is predicted that the domination of Phalaris would then be dissolved, when those that were governed by him should become better men, and be more concordant with each other; such as they then became, when Pythagoras was present with them, through the doctrines and instruction which he imparted to them. A greater proof however of the truth of this, is derived from the time in which it happened. For on the very same day in which Phalaris put Pythagoras and Abaris in danger of death, he himself was slain by stratagem. That also which happened to Epimenides may be an argument of the truth of these things. For as he, who was the disciple of Pythagoras, when certain persons intended to destroy him, invoked the Furies, and the avenging Gods, and by so doing caused all those that attempted his life, to destroy each other;—thus also Pythagoras, who gave assistance to mankind, after the manner and with the fortitude of Hercules, for the benefit of men, punished and occasioned the death of him who had acted in an insolent and disorderly manner towards others; and this through the oracles themselves of Apollo, to the series of which divinity both he and Epimenides spontaneously belonged from their very birth. And thus far, indeed, we have thought it requisite to mention this admirable and strenuous deed, the effect of his fortitude.

We shall however adduce another example of it, *viz.* the salvation of legitimate opinion; for, preserving this, he performed that which appeared to him to be just, and which was dictated by right reason, not being diverted from his intention either by pleasure, or labor, or any other passion, or danger. His disciples also chose to die rather than transgress his mandates. And when they were exposed to all-various fortunes, they preserved invariably the same manners. When also they were involved in ten thousand calamities, they never deviated from his precepts. But it was a never-failing exhortation with them, always to give assistance to law, but to be hostile to illegality, and to be accustomed from their birth to a life of temperance and fortitude, in order to restrain and repel luxury. They had also certain melodies which were devised by them, as remedies against the passions of the soul, and likewise against despondency and lamentation, which Pythagoras invented, as affording the greatest assistance in these maladies. And again, they employed other melodies against rage and anger, through which they gave intension and remission to these passions, till they reduced them to moderation, and rendered them commensurate with fortitude. *That, however, which afforded them the greatest support in generous endurance, was the persuasion that no human casualties ought to be unexpected by men who are in the possession of intellect, but that all things ought to be expected by them, over which they have no absolute power.*

Moreover, if at any time they happened to be angry, or sorrowful, they immediately separated themselves from the rest of their associates, and each by himself alone strenuously endeavoured to digest and heal the passion [by which he was oppressed]. They also conceived generally, that labor should be employed about disciplines and studies, and that they should be severely exercised in trials of the most various nature, in punishments and restraints by fire and sword, in order to be liberated from innate intemperance, and an inexhaustible avidity of possessing; and that for this purpose, no labors, nor any endurance should be spared. In order to accomplish this likewise, they generously exercised abstinence from all animals, and besides this, from certain other kinds of food. Hence also arose their detention of speech, and their perfect silence as preparatory to the subjugation of the tongue; in which for many years they exercised their fortitude. To which also may be added, their strenuous and assiduous investigation and resumption of the most difficult theorems; and on account of these things, their abstinence from wine, their paucity of food and sleep, and their contempt of glory, wealth, and the like. And in conjunction with all these particulars, they extended themselves to fortitude.

It is likewise said, that these men expelled lamentations and tears, and every thing else of this kind. They also abstained from entreaty, from supplication, and from all such illiberal adulation, as being effeminate and abject.[39] To the same conception likewise the peculiarity of their manners must be referred, and that all of them perpetually preserved among their arcana, the most principal dogmas in which their discipline was chiefly contained, keeping them with the greatest silence from being divulged to strangers, committing them unwritten to the memory, and transmitting them orally to their successors, as if they were the mysteries of the Gods. Hence it happened, that nothing of their philosophy worth mentioning, was made public, and that though for a long time it had been taught and learnt, it was alone known within their walls. But to those out of their walls, and as I may say, to the profane, if they happened to be present, these men spoke obscurely to each other through symbols, of which the celebrated precepts that are now in circulation retain a vestige; such as, Dig not fire with a sword, and other symbols of the like kind, *117* which, taken literally, resemble the tales of old women; but when unfolded, impart a certain admirable and venerable benefit to those that receive them.

The precept, however, which is of the greatest efficacy of all others to the attainment of fortitude, is that which has for its most principal scope the being defended and liberated from those bonds which detain the intellect in captivity from infancy, and without which no one can learn or perceive any thing sane or true, through whatever sense he may energize. For according to the Pythagoreans,

'Tis mind that all things sees and hears;
What else exists is deaf and blind.

But the precept which is next to this in efficacy is that which exhorts to be beyond measure studious of purifying the intellect, and by various methods adapting it through mathematical orgies to receive something divinely beneficial, so as neither to fear a separation from body, nor, when led to incorporeal natures, to be forced to turn away the eyes, through their most refulgent splendor,[40] nor to be converted to those passions which nail and fasten the soul to the body. And, in short, which urges the soul to be untamed by all those passions which are the progeny of the realms of generation, and which draw it to an inferior condition of being. For the exercise and ascent through all these, is the study of the most perfect fortitude. And such are the instances adduced by us of the fortitude of Pythagoras, and the Pythagoreans.

Chapter XXXIII.

With respect to the amity, however, which subsists in all things towards all, Pythagoras delivered it in the clearest manner. And, the amity of the Gods indeed towards men, he unfolded through piety and scientific cultivation; but that of dogmas towards each other, and universally of the soul towards the body, and of the rational towards the species of the irrational part, through philosophy, and the theory pertaining to it. With respect to the amity of men also towards each other; that of citizens he delivered through sane legislation, but that of strangers through a correct physiology; and that between man and wife, or children, or brothers, and kindred, through unperverted communion. In short, he unfolded the friendship of all things towards all, and still farther, of certain irrational animals, through justice and a physical connexion and association. But the pacification and conciliation of the body, which is of itself mortal, and of its latent contrary powers, he unfolded through health, and a diet and temperance conformable to this, in imitation of the salubrious condition of the mundane elements. In all these, however, Pythagoras is acknowledged to have been the inventor and legislator of the summary comprehension of them in one and the same name, which is that of friendship. And indeed he delivered such an admirable friendship to his associates, that even now those who are benevolent in the extreme towards each other, are said to belong to the Pythagoreans. It is necessary therefore to narrate the discipline of Pythagoras respecting these things, and the precepts which he used towards his disciples.

These men, then, exhorted others to remove from true friendship, contest and contention, and if possible, indeed, from all friendship; but if not, at least from that which is parental, and universally from that which pertains to seniors and benefactors. For to strive or contend with such as these, in consequence of anger intervening, or some other such-like passion, is not the salvation of the existing

118

friendship. But they said it is requisite that there should be the least possible scars and ulcers in friendships; and that this will be the case, if *119* those that are friends know how to soften and subdue anger. If both indeed know this, or rather the younger of the two, and who ranks in some one of the above-mentioned orders [their friendship will be more easily preserved]. They also were of opinion, that corrections and admonitions, which they called *pædartases*, should take place from the elder to the younger with much suavity and caution; and likewise, that much sedulous and appropriate attention should be manifested in admonitions. For thus they will be decorous and beneficial. They also said, that confidence should never be separated from friendship, neither seriously nor even in jest. For it is no longer easy for the existing friendship to be in a sane condition, when falsehood once insinuates itself into the manners of those that acknowledge themselves to be friends. Again, according to them, friendship should not be abandoned on account of misfortune, or any other imbecility to which human life is incident; but they said, that the only approvable rejection of a friend and friendship, is that which arises from great and incorrigible vice. Likewise, that hatred should not be voluntarily entertained against those who are not perfectly bad; but that if it is once formed, it should be generously and strenuously retained, unless the object of it changes his manners, so as to become a better man. That the hostility also should not consist in words, but in deeds. And that this war is legitimate and holy, when it is conducted in such a way as it becomes one man to contend with another.

They likewise said, that we should never, to the utmost of our power, become the cause of dissension; but that we should as much as possible avoid the source of it. That in the friendship also, which is intended to be pure, the greater part of the things pertaining to it ought to be definite and legitimate. And that these should be properly distinguished, and should not be casual; and moreover, that we should *120* be careful that our conversation may never be negligently and casually performed, but with modesty, benevolence, and good order. Also, that no passion, such as desire, or anger, be rashly excited, and in a bad and erroneous manner. And the same thing must be said of the remaining passions and dispositions.

Moreover, that they did not decline foreign friendships carelessly, but that they avoided and guarded against them, with the greatest sedulity; and also, that they rigidly preserved friendship towards each other for many ages, may be inferred from what Aristoxenus in his treatise *On the Pythagoric Life*, says he heard from Dionysius, the tyrant of Sicily, when having fallen from monarchy he taught grammar at Corinth. For Aristoxenus says as follows:

"These men as much as possible prohibited lamentations and tears, and every thing of this kind; and in a similar manner adulation, entreaty, supplication, and the like. Dionysius, therefore, having fallen from his tyranny and come to Corinth, narrated to us the particulars concerning Phintias and Damon the Pythagoreans; and these were respecting the one being sponsor for the death of the other. But the mode of the suretyship was as follows: He said that certain persons, who were familiar with him, had frequently made mention of the Pythagoreans, defaming and reviling them, calling them arrogant, and asserting that their gravity, their pretended fidelity, and apathy would be laid aside, if any one should cause them to fall into [some great] calamity. Certain persons however contradicting this, and contention arising on the subject, recourse was had to artifice, and one of the accusers of Phintias said before him, that he evidently conspired with certain others against the life of Dionysius. This also was testified by some that were present, and the charges against Phintias appeared to be very probable. Phintias therefore was astonished at the accusation. But when Dionysius had unequivocally said, that he had accurately explored all these particulars, and that it was necessary that he should die, Phintias replied, that if it appeared requisite to him that this should take place, he requested that he would grant him the remainder of the day, in order that he might settle his own affairs, and also those of Damon. For those men lived together, and had all things in common. Phintias, however, being the elder, the management of the domestic concerns was for the most part undertaken by him. He requested therefore, that Dionysius would suffer him to depart for this purpose, and he would appoint Damon for his surety. Dionysius therefore said

121

that he wondered at the request, and that he asked him whether there was any man who was willing to become security for the death of another. But Phintias asserting that there was, Damon was sent for, who, on hearing what had happened, said that he would become the sponsor, and that he would remain there till Phintias returned. Dionysius therefore said, that he was immediately astonished at these circumstances; but that they who at first introduced the experiment, derided Damon as one who would be caught, and said sneeringly that he would be the vicarious stag. When therefore it was near sunset, Phintias came to die; at which all that were present were astonished and subdued. But Dionysius said, that having embraced and kissed the men, he requested that they would receive him as the third into their friendship. They however would by no means consent to a thing of this kind, though he entreated them to comply with his request."

And these things are related by Aristoxenus, who received them from Dionysius himself.

It is also said, that the Pythagoreans endeavoured to perform the offices of friendship to those of their sect, though they were unknown to, and had never been seen by each other, when they had received a certain indication of the participation of the same doctrines; so that *122* from such friendly offices the assertion may be credited, that worthy men, even though they should dwell in the most remote parts of the earth, are mutually friends, and this before they become known to and salute each other. It is said therefore, that a certain Pythagorean, travelling through a long and solitary road on foot, came to an inn; and there, from labor and other all-various causes, fell into a long and severe disease, so as to be at length in want of the necessaries of life. The inn-keeper, however, whether from commiseration of the man, or from benevolence, supplied him with every thing that was requisite, neither sparing for this purpose any assistance or expense. But the Pythagorean falling a victim to the disease, wrote a certain symbol, before he died, in a table, and desired the inn-keeper, if he should happen to die, to suspend the table near the road, and observe whether any passenger read the symbol. For that person, said he, will repay you what you have spent on me, and will also thank you for your kindness. The inn-keeper, therefore, after the death of the Pythagorean, having buried, and paid the requisite attention to his body, had neither any hopes of being repaid, nor of receiving any recompense from some one who might read the table. At the same time, however, being surprised at the request of the Pythagorean, he was induced to expose the writing in the public road. A long time after, therefore, a certain Pythagorean passing that way, having understood the symbol, and learnt who it was that placed the table there, and having also investigated every particular, paid the inn-keeper a much greater sum of money than he had disbursed.

It is likewise related of Clinias the Tarentine, that when he had learnt that Prorus the Cyrenrean, who was zealously addicted to the Pythagorean doctrines, was in danger of losing all his property, he sailed to Cyrene, after having collected a sum of money, and restored the affairs of Prorus to a better condition, not only incurring, in so doing, a diminution of his own property, but despising the peril which he was exposed to in the voyage. After the same manner also, Thestor Posidoniates, having learnt from report alone, that Thymaridas Parius the Pythagorean had fallen into poverty, from the possession of great wealth, is said to have sailed to Parus, after having collected a large sum of money, and thus reinstated Thymaridas in property. These therefore are beautiful instances of friendship. *The decisions, however, of the Pythagoreans respecting the communion of divine goods, the concord of intellect, and things pertaining to a divine soul, are much more admirable than the above examples. For they perpetually exhorted each other, not to divulse the God within them. Hence all the endeavour of their friendship both in deeds and words, was directed to a certain divine mixture, to a union with divinity, and to a communion with intellect and a divine soul.* But it is not possible to find any thing better than this, either in what is uttered by words, or performed by deeds. For I am of opinion, that all the goods of friendship are comprehended in this. Hence, as we have collected in this, as in a summit, all the prerogatives of the Pythagoric friendship, we shall omit to say any thing further about it.

Chapter XXXIV.

Since, however, we have thus generally, and with arrangement, discussed what pertains to Pythagoras and the Pythagoreans; let us after this narrate such scattered particulars relative to this subject, as do not fall under the above-mentioned order. It is said, therefore, that each of the Greeks who joined himself to this community of the Pythagoreans, was ordered to use his native language. For they did not approve of the use of a foreign tongue. Foreigners also united themselves to the Pythagoric sect, *viz*. the Messenians, the Lucani, Picentini, and the Romans. And Metrodorus the son of Thyrsus who was the father of Epicharmus,[41] and who transferred the greater part of his doctrine to medicine, says in explaining the writings of his father to his brother, that Epicharmus, and prior to him Pythagoras, conceived that the best dialect, as well as the best harmony of music, is the Doric; that the Ionic and the Æolic participate of the chromatic harmony; but that the Attic dialect is replete with this in a still greater degree. They were also of opinion, that the Doric dialect, which consists of vocal letters, is enharmonic.

Fables likewise bear testimony to the antiquity of this dialect. For in these it is said that Nereus married Doris the daughter of Ocean; by whom he had fifty daughters, one of which was the mother of Achilles. Metrodorus also says, that according to some, Hellen was the offspring of Deucalion, who was the son of Prometheus and Pyrrha the daughter of Epimetheus; and that from him came Dorus, and Æolus. He farther observes, that he learnt from the sacred rites of the Babylonians, that Hellen was the offspring of Jupiter, and that the sons of Hellen were Dorus, Xuthus, and Æolus; with which narrations Herodotus also accords. It is difficult, however, for those in more recent times to know accurately, in particulars so ancient, which of these narrations is to be preferred. But it may be collected from each of these histories, that the Doric dialect is acknowledged to be the most ancient; that the Æolic is next to this, which received its name from Æolus; and that the Ionic ranks as the third, which derived its appellation from Ion the son of Xuthus. The Attic is the fourth, which was denominated from Creusa, the daughter of Erectheus, and is posterior to the former dialects by three generations, as it existed about the time of the Thracians, and the rape of Orithyia, as is evident from the testimony of most histories. Orpheus also, who is the most ancient of the poets, used the Doric dialect.

Of medicine, however, they especially embraced the diætetic species, and in the exercise of this were most accurate. And in the first place, indeed, they endeavoured to learn the indications of symmetry, of labor, food, and repose. In the next place, with respect to the preparation of food, they were nearly the first who attempted to employ themselves in it, and to define the mode in which it should be performed. The Pythagoreans likewise employed cataplasms, more frequently than their predecessors; but they in a less degree approved of medicated ointments. These, however, they principally used in the cure of ulcerations. But incisions and burnings they admitted the least of all things. Some diseases also they cured by incantations. But they are said to have objected to those who expose disciplines to sale; who open their souls like the gates of an inn to every man that approaches to them; and who, if they do not thus find buyers, diffuse themselves through cities, and, in short, hire gymnasia and require a reward from young men for those things which are without price. Pythagoras, however, concealed the meaning of much that was said by him, in order that those who were genuinely instructed might clearly be partakers of it; but that others, as Homer says of Tantalus, might be pained in the midst of what they heard, in consequence of receiving no delight from thence.

I think also, it was said by the Pythagoreans, respecting those who teach for the sake of reward, that they show themselves to be worse than statuaries, or those artists who perform their work sitting. For these, when some one orders them to make a statue of Hermes, search for wood adapted to the reception of the proper form; but those pretend that they can readily produce the works of virtue from every nature.[42] The Pythagoreans likewise said, that it is more necessary to pay attention to philosophy, than to parents and agriculture; for it is owing to the latter, indeed, that we live; but philosophers and preceptors are the causes of our living well, and becoming wise, in consequence of having discovered the right mode of discipline and instruction. Nor did they think fit either to speak or write in such a way, that their conceptions might be obvious to any casual persons;

but Pythagoras is said to have taught this in the first place to those that came to him, that, being purified from all incontinence, they should preserve in silence the doctrines they had heard. It is said, therefore, that he who first divulged the theory of commensurable and incommensurable quantities, to those who were unworthy to receive it, was so hated by the Pythagoreans that they not only expelled him from their common association, and from living with them, but also constructed a tomb for him, as one who had migrated from the human and passed into another life. Others also say, that the Divine Power was indignant with those who divulged the dogmas of Pythagoras: for that he perished in the sea, as an impious person, who rendered manifest the composition of the *icostagonus; viz.* who delivered the method of inscribing in a sphere the dodecredron, which is one of what are called the five solid figures. But according to others, this happened to him who unfolded the doctrine of irrational and incommensurable quantities.[43] Moreover, all the Pythagoric discipline was symbolic, and resembled enigmas and riddles, consisting of apothegms, in consequence of imitating antiquity in its character; just as the truly divine and Pythian oracles appear to be in a certain respect difficult to be understood and explained, to those who carelessly receive the answers which they give. Such therefore, and so many are the indications respecting Pythagoras and the Pythagoreans, which may be collected from what is disseminated about them.

127

Chapter XXXV.

There were, however, certain persons who were hostile to these men, and rose against them. That stratagems therefore were employed to destroy them, during the absence of Pythagoras, is universally acknowledged; but those that have written on this subject, differ in their account of the journey which he then undertook. For some say that he went to Pherecydes the Syrian, but others to Metapontum. Many causes, however, of the stratagems are enumerated. And one of them, which is said to have originated from the men called Cylonians, was as follows: Cylon the Crotonian held the first place among the citizens for birth, renown, and wealth; but otherwise, he was a severe, violent, and turbulent man, and of tyrannical manners. He had, however, the greatest desire of being made a partaker of the Pythagoric life, and having applied himself to Pythagoras, who was now an elderly man,[44] for this purpose, was *128* rejected by him on account of the above-mentioned causes. In consequence of this, therefore, he and his friends exercised violent hostilities against Pythagoras and his disciples. So vehement likewise and immoderate[45] was the ambition of Cylon, and of those who arranged themselves on his side, that it extended itself to the very last of the Pythagoreans. Pythagoras, therefore, for this cause went to Metapontum, and there is said to have terminated his life. But those who were called the Cylonians continued to form stratagems against the Pythagoreans, and to exhibit indications of all possible malevolence. Nevertheless, for a certain time the probity of the Pythagoreans subdued [this enmity,] and also the decision of the cities themselves, so that they were willing that their political concerns should be managed by the Pythagoreans [alone]. At length, however, the Cylonians became so hostile to the men,[46] that setting fire to the house of Milo in which the Pythagoreans were seated, and were consulting about warlike concerns; they burnt all the men except two, Archippus and Lysis. For these being in perfect vigour, and most robust, escaped out of the house. But this taking place, and no mention being made by the multitude of the calamity which had happened, the Pythagoreans ceased to pay any further attention to the affairs of government. This however happened through two causes, through the negligence of the cities (for they were not at all affected by so great a calamity taking place) and through the loss of those men who were most qualified to govern. But of the two Pythagoreans that were saved, and both of whom were Tarentines, Archippus indeed returned to Tarentum; but Lysis hating the negligence [of the cities] went into Greece, and dwelt in the Achaia of Peloponnesus. *129* Afterwards, he migrated to Thebes, being stimulated by a certain ardent desire [of retreating thither]; and *there he had for his auditor Epaminondas, who called Lysis his father.* There also Lysis terminated his life. But the rest of the Pythagoreans, except Archytas of Tarentum, departed from Italy, and being collected together in Rhegium, there dwelt with each other. The most celebrated of them, however, were Phanto, Echecrates, Polymnastus, and Diocles, who were Phlyasians; and Xenophilus Chalcidensis of Thrace. But in the course of time, when the administration of public affairs proceeded into a worse condition, these Pythagoreans nevertheless preserved their pristine manners and disciplines, though the sect began to fail, till it generously perished. These things, therefore, are narrated by Aristoxenus.

Nicomachus, however, in other respects accords with Aristoxenus, but as to the journey of Pythagoras, he says that this stratagem took place, while Pythagoras was at Delos. For he went there, in order to give assistance to his preceptor Pherecydes the Syrian who was then afflicted with the morbus pedicularis, and when he died, performed the necessary funeral rites. Then, therefore, those who had been rejected by the Pythagoreans, and to whom monuments had been raised, as if they were dead, attacked them, and committed all of them to the flames. Afterwards, they were overwhelmed by the Italians with stones, and thrown out of the house unburied. At that time, therefore, it happened that science failed together with those who possessed scientific knowledge, because till that period, it was preserved by them in their breasts as something arcane and ineffable. But such things only as were difficult to be understood, and which were not unfolded, were preserved in the memory of those who did not belong to the Pythagorean sect; a few things excepted, which certain Pythagoreans, who happened at that time to be in foreign lands, preserved as certain sparks of science very obscure and of difficult investigation. These also, being left by themselves, and not moderately dejected by the calamity, were scattered in different places, and no longer endured to have any communion with the rest of mankind. But they lived alone in solitary places, wherever they happened to meet with them; and each greatly preferred an association with himself to that with any other person.

Fearing, however, lest the name of philosophy should be entirely exterminated from mankind, and that they should on this account incur the indignation of the Gods, by suffering so great a gift of theirs to perish, they made an arrangement of certain commentaries and symbols, and likewise, collected together the writings of the more ancient Pythagoreans, and of such things as they remembered. These, each left at his death to his son, or daughter, or wife, with a strict injunction not to give them to any one out of the family. This mandate therefore, was for a long time observed, and was transmitted in succession to their posterity.

Since, however, Apollonius dissents in a certain place respecting these particulars, and adds many things which we have not mentioned, we shall also insert his narration of the stratagem employed against the Pythagoreans. He says, therefore, that the envy of others attended Pythagoras from his childhood. For as long as he conversed with all that came to him, he was pleasing to them; but when he associated with his disciples alone, the favourable opinion which the multitude entertained of him was diminished. And they permitted him indeed, to pay more attention to strangers than to themselves; but they were indignant at his preferring some of their fellow-citizens before others, and they apprehended that his disciples assembled together with intentions hostile to them. In the next place, as the young men that were indignant with him were of high rank, and surpassed others in wealth, and when they arrived at a proper age, not only held the first honors in their own families, but also managed the affairs of the city in common, they formed a large body of men (for they were more than three hundred in number) and in consequence of this there was but a small part of the city, which was not conversant with the same manners and the same pursuits as they were.

Moreover, as long as the Crotonians continued in their own country, and Pythagoras dwelt with them, that form of government remained which had been established when the city was founded, but which was not pleasing to the people, and therefore induced them to seek an occasion of producing a change. When therefore Sybaris was captured, and the land taken in the war was not divided by lot, according to the desire of the multitude, their silent hatred of the Pythagoreans burst forth, and the populace separated themselves from them. But the leaders of this dissension were those that were most near to the Pythagoreans, both by alliance and familiarity. The cause however of the discord was this, that many of the actions of the Pythagoreans offended these leaders, as well as casual persons, because these actions had something peculiar in them when compared with those of others. But in the greatest of these actions they conceived that disgrace befel themselves alone.

Farther still, no one of the Pythagoreans called Pythagoras by his name, but while he was alive, when they wished to denote him, they called him *divine;* and after his death they denominated him *that man;* just as Homer represents Eumæus when he makes mention of Ulysses, saying,

Him, tho' he's absent, yet I fear, O guest,
To name; such is the greatness of my love and care.

Conformably likewise to the precepts of their master, the Pythagoreans always rose from bed before the rising of the sun; and never wore a ring in which the image of God was engraved. They also carefully observed to adore the rising sun, and avoided wearing a ring of the above mentioned description, lest they should have it about them at funerals, or in some impure place. In a similar manner, they were attentive to the mandate of Pythagoras, not to do any thing without previous deliberation and disquisition; but to form a plan in the morning of what ought to be done [in the course of the day,] and at night to call to mind the actions of the day, by this means at one and the same time exploring their conduct, and exercising their memory. Thus too, they observed the precept, that if any one of their associates appointed to meet them at a certain place, they should stay there till he came, through the day and the night; in this again, the Pythagoreans being accustomed to remember what was said, and not to speak casually. In short Pythagoras ordered them to be attentive to order and method as long as they lived, and not to blaspheme at the time of death, but to die with propitious words, such as are used by those who are sailing out of port into the Adriatic sea.[47]

The kindred of the Pythagoreans however, were indignant that the Pythagoreans gave their right hand to those of their own sect alone, their parents excepted; and that they shared their possessions with each other in common, but excluded their relations from this fellowship, as if they were strangers. These, therefore, becoming the sources of the dissension, the rest readily fell into hostility against the Pythagoreans. Hippasus, also, Diodorus and Theages said at the same time, that every citizen ought to be a partaker of the magistracy and the assembly, and that the rulers should give an account of their conduct, to those who were elected by lot for this purpose from the

132

133 multitude. But the Pythagoreans, Alcimachus, Dimachus, Meton and Democedes opposed this, and persevered in prohibiting the dissolution of the polity derived from their ancestors. Those however, who patronized the multitude, subdued the other party. The multitude therefore, being assembled together, Cylon and Ninon who were rhetoricians accused the Pythagoreans. And of these, one belonged to the class of the rich, but the other was a plebeian. They also divided their harangues between themselves. But of these harangues, the longer being delivered by Cylon, Ninon concluded, pretending that he had explored the arcana of the Pythagoreans, and that he had connected and committed to writing such particulars as were especially calculated to criminate the Pythagoreans, and giving a book to ascribe, he ordered him to read it. But the book was inscribed *the Sacred Discourse*. And the following is a specimen of what it contained: Friends are to be venerated in the same manner as the Gods; but others are to be treated as brutes. This very sentence also is ascribed to Pythagoras by his disciples, and is by them expressed in verse as follows:

> He like the blessed Gods his friends rever'd,
> But reckon'd other men of no account.

Homer, too, especially deserves to be praised for calling a king *the shepherd of the people*. For being a friend to that government in which the rulers are few, he evinced by this epithet that the rest of men are cattle. To beans it is requisite to be hostile, as being the leaders of decision by lot; for by these men were allotted the administration of affairs. Again, empire should be the object of desire: for they proclaim that it is better to be one day a bull, than to be an ox for ever. That the legal institutes of others are laudable; but that they should be exhorted to use those which are known to themselves. In one word, Ninon showed that their philosophy was a conspiracy against the multitude, and therefore exhorted them not to hear the *133* counsellors, but to consider that they would never have been admitted into the assembly, if the council of the Pythagoreans had been approved by the session of a thousand men; so that it was not fit to suffer those to speak, who prevented to the utmost of their power others from being heard. He observed, therefore, that they should consider the right hand which was rejected by the Pythagoreans, as hostile to them, when they gave their suffrages by an extension of the hands, or calculated the number of the votes. That they should also consider it to be a disgraceful circumstance, that they who conquered thirty myriads of men at the river Tracis, should be vanquished by a thousandth part of the same number through sedition in the city itself. In short Ninon so exasperated his hearers by his calumnies, that in a few days after, a great multitude assembled together intending to attack the Pythagoreans as they were sacrificing to the Muses in a house near to the temple of Apollo. The Pythagoreans, however, foreseeing that this would take place, fled to an inn; but Democedes, with those that had arrived at puberty, withdrew to Platea. And those that had dissolved the laws made a decree in which they accused Democedes of compelling the younger part of the community to the possession of empire, and proclaimed by a cryer that thirty talents should be given to any one who destroyed him. An engagement also taking place, and Theages having vanquished Democedes in that contest, they distributed to him the thirty talents which the city had promised. But as the city, and the whole region were involved in many evils, the exiles were brought to judgment, and the power of decision being given to three cities, *viz.* to the Tarentines, Metapontines, and the Caulonians, those that were sent by them to determine the cause were corrupted by money, as we learn from the chronicles of the Crotonians. Hence the Crotonians condemned by their own decision those that were accused, to exile. In consequence, too, of this decision, and the authority which it conferred on them, they expelled all those from the city, who were dissatisfied with the existing state of affairs, and at the same time banished all their families, asserting that it was not fit to be impious, and that children ought not to be divulsed from their parents. They likewise abolished loans, and made the land to be undivided.[48]

Many years after this, when Dinarchus and his associates were slain in another battle, and Litagus also was dead, who had been the greatest leader of the seditious, a certain pity and repentance induced the citizens to recall those Pythagoreans that were left, from exile. For this purpose, they sent ambassadors from Achaia, and through them became amicable with the exiles, and consecrated their oaths at

Delphi. But the Pythagoreans who returned from exile were about sixty in number, except those who were of a more advanced age, among which were some who applied themselves to medicine, and restored health to those that were sick by a certain diet; of which method of cure they were themselves the authors. It happened however, that those Pythagoreans who were saved, and who were particularly celebrated by the multitude, at that time in which it was said to the lawless, *This is not the condition of things which was under Ninon;*—these same Pythagoreans having left the city in order to procure assistance against the Thurians who invaded the country, perished in battle, mutually defending each other.   But the city was so changed into a contrary opinion [of the Pythagoreans,] that besides the praise which it bestowed on them, it apprehended that it would gratify the Muses in a still greater degree, if it performed a public sacrifice in the temple of the Muses, which at the request of the Pythagoreans, they had before constructed in honor of those Goddesses. And thus much concerning the attack which was made on the Pythagoreans.

136

Chapter XXXVI.

The successor, however, of Pythagoras, is acknowledged by all men to have been Aristæus, the son of Damophon the Crotonian, who existing at the same time as Pythagoras, was seven ages prior to Plato. Aristæus likewise, was not only thought worthy to succeed Pythagoras in his school, but also to educate his children, and marry his wife Theano, because he was eminently skilled in the Pythagoric dogmas. For Pythagoras himself is said to have taught in his school, forty years wanting one, and to have lived nearly one hundred years. But Aristæus, when much advanced in years, relinquished the school; and after him Mnesarchus succeeded, who was the son of Pythagoras. Bulagoras succeeded Mnesarchus, in whose time it happened that the city of the Crotonians was plundered. Gartydas the Crotonian succeeded Bulagoras, on his return from a journey which he had undertaken prior to the war. Nevertheless on account of the calamity of his country, he suffered so much anxiety, as to die prematurely through grief. But it was the custom with the rest of the Pythagoreans, when they became very old, to liberate themselves from the body as from a prison.

Moreover, some time after, Aresas Lucanus, being saved through certain strangers, undertook the management of the school; and to him came Diodorus Aspendius, who was received into the school, on account of the paucity of the Pythagoreans it contained. And in Heraclea, indeed, were Clinias and Philolaus; but at Metapontum, Theorides and Eurytus; and at Tarentum Archytas. It is also said that Epicharmus was one of the foreign auditors; but that he was not one of the school. Having however arrived at Syracuse, he abstained from philosophizing openly, on account of the tyranny of Hiero. But he inserted the conceptions of the men in metre, and published in comedies the occult dogmas of Pythagoras.

137

Of all the Pythagoreans, however, it is probable that many are unknown and anonymous. But the following are the names of those that are known and celebrated:

Of the Crotonians, Hippostratus, Dymas, Ægon, Æmon, Sillus, Cleosthenes, Agelas, Episylus, Phyciadas, Ecphantus, Timæus, Buthius, Eratus, Itmæus, Rhodippus, Bryas, Evandrus, Myllias, Antimedon, Ageas, Leophron, Agylus, Onatus, Hipposthenes, Cleophron, Alcmæon, Damocles, Milon, Menon.

Of the Metapontines, Brontinus, Parmiseus, Orestadas, Leon, Damarmenus, Æneas, Chilas, Melisias, Aristeas, Laphion, Evandrus, Agesidamus, Xenocades, Euryphemus, Aristomenes, Agesarchus, Alceas, Xenophantes, Thraseus, Arytus, Epiphron, Eiriscus, Megistias, Leocydes, Thrasymedes, Euphemus, Procles, Antimenes, Lacritus, Damotages, Pyrrho, Rhexibius, Alopecus, Astylus, Dacidas, Aliochus, Lacrates, Glycinus.

Of the Agrigentines, Empedocles.

Of the Eleatæ, Parmenides.

Of the Tarentines, Philolaus, Eurytus, Archytas, Theodorus, Aristippus, Lycon, Hestireus, Polemarchus, Asteas, Clinias, Cleon, Eurymedon, Arceas, Clinagoras, Archippus, Zopyrus, Euthynus, Dicæarchus, Philonidas, Phrontidas, Lysis, Lysibius, Dinocrates, Echecrates, Paction, Acusiladas, Icmus, Pisicrates, Clearatus.

Of the Leontines, Phrynichus, Smichias, Aristoclidas, Clinias, Ahroteles, Pisyrrhydus, Bryas, Evandrus, Archemachus, Mimnomachus, Achmonidas, Dicas, Carophantidas.

Of the Sybarites, Metopus, Hippasus Proxenus, Evanor, Deanax, Menestor, Diocles, Empedus, Timasius, Polemæus, Evæus, Tyrsenus.

Of the Carthaginians, Miltiades, Anthen, Odius, Leocritus.

138   Of the Parians, Ætius, Phænecles, Dexitheus, Alcimachus, Dinarchus, Meton, Timæus, Timesianax, Amærus, Thymaridas.

Of the Locrians, Gyptius, Xenon, Philodamus, Evetes, Adieus, Sthenonidas, Sosistratus, Euthynus, Zaleucus, Timares.

Of the Posidonians, Athamas, Simus, Proxenus, Cranous, Myes, Bathylaus, Phædon.

Of the Lucani, Ocellus and Occillus who were brothers, Oresandrus, Cerambus, Dardaneus, Malion.

Of the Ægeans, Hippomedon, Timosthenes, Euelthon, Thrasydamus, Crito, Polyetor.

Of the Lacones, Autocharidas, Cleanor, Eurycrates.

Of the Hyperboreans, Abaris.

Of the Rheginenses, Aristides, Demosthenes, Aristocrates, Phytius, Helicaon, Mnesibulus, Hipparchides, Athosion, Euthycles, Opsimus.

Of the Selinuntians, Calais.

Of the Syracusans, Leptines, Phintias, Damon.

Of the Samians, Melissus, Lacon, Archippus, Glorippus, Heloris, Rippon.

Of the Caulonienses, Callibrotus, Dicon, Nastas, Drymon, Xentas.

Of the Phliasians, Diocles, Echecrates, Polymnastus, Phanton.

Of the Sicyonians, Poliades, Demon, Sostratius, Sosthenes.

Of the Cyrenæans, Prorus, Melanippus, Aristangelus, Theodorus.

Of the Cyziceni, Pythodorus, Hipposthenes, Butherus, Xenophilus.

Of the Catanæi, Charondas, Lysiades.

Of the Corinthians, Chrysippus.

Of the Tyrrhenians, Nausitheus.

Of the Athenians, Neocritus.

And of Pontus, Lyramnus.

In all, two hundred and eighteen. [And these, indeed, are not all the Pythagoreans, but of all of them they are the most famous.[49]]

But the most illustrious Pythagorean women are Timycha, the wife of Myllias the Crotonian. Philtis, the daughter of Theophrius the Crotonian. Byndacis, the sister of Ocellus and Occillus, Lucanians. Chilonis, the daughter of Chilon the Lacedæmonian. Cratesiclea the

Lacedæmonian, the wife of Cleanor the Lacedæmonian. Theano, the wife of Brontinus of Metapontum. Mya, the wife of Milon the Crotonian. Lasthenia the Arcadian. Abrotelia, the daughter of Abroteles the Tarentine. Echecratia the Phliasian. Tyrsenis, the Sybarite. Pisirrhonde, the Tarentine. Nisleadusa, the Lacedæmonian. Bryo, the Argive. Babelyma, the Argive. And Cleæchma, the sister of Autocharidas the Lacedæmonian. In all seventeen.

139

Fragments of the Ethical Writings
of Certain Pythagoreans.

FROM

HIPPODAMUS, THE THURIAN,

IN HIS TREATISE

ON FELICITY.

Of animals, some are the recipients of felicity, but others are incapable of receiving it. And those animals, indeed, are receptive of it that have reason. For felicity cannot subsist without virtue; and virtue is first ingenerated in that which possesses reason. But those animals are incapable of receiving felicity, that are destitute of reason. For neither can that which is deprived of sight, receive the work or the virtue of sight; nor can that which is destitute of reason, be the recipient of the work, or the virtue of that which possesses reason. With respect to felicity, however, and virtue, the former is as a work, but the latter as a certain art, to that which possesses reason. But of animals which possess reason, some are self-perfect, and these are such as are perfect through themselves, and are indigent of nothing external, either to their existence, or to their existing well and beautifully. And such, indeed, is God. Those animals, however, are not self-perfect, which are not perfect through themselves, but are in want of external causes to their perfection. And man is an animal of this kind. Of animals, therefore, which are not self-perfect, some

109

indeed are perfect, but others are not perfect. And those indeed are perfect which derive their subsistence both from their own [proper] causes, and from external causes. And they derive it indeed from their own causes, because they obtain from thence both an excellent nature and deliberate choice; but from external causes, because they receive from thence equitable legislation and good rulers. But the animals which are not perfect, are either such as participate of neither of these, or of some one of these, or whose souls are entirely depraved. And such will the man be who is of a description different from the above.

Moreover, of perfect men there are two differences. For some of them are naturally perfect; but others are perfect according to life. And those indeed alone that are good, are naturally perfect. But these are such as possess virtue. For the virtue of the nature of every thing is a summit and perfection. Thus the virtue of the eye is the summit and perfection of the nature of the eye. But the virtue of man is the summit and perfection of the nature of man. Those also are perfect according to life, who are not only good, but happy. For felicity, indeed, is the perfection of human life. But human life is a system of actions: and felicity gives completion to the actions. Virtue also and fortune give completion to actions; virtue, indeed, according to use; but good fortune according to prosperity. God therefore is neither good through learning virtue from any one, nor is he happy through being attended by good fortune. For he is good by nature, and happy by nature, and always was and will be, and will never cease to be, such; since he is incorruptible, and naturally good. But man is neither happy nor good by nature, but requires discipline and providential care. And in order to become good, indeed, he requires virtue; but in order to become happy, good fortune. On this account, human felicity summarily consists of these two things, *viz.* of praise, and the predication of beatitude. Of praise indeed, from virtue; but of the predication of beatitude, from prosperity. It possesses virtue therefore, through a divine destiny, but prosperity through a mortal allotment. But mortal are suspended from divine concerns, and terrestrial from such as are celestial. Things subordinate, also, are suspended from such as are more excellent. And on this account, the good man who follows the Gods is happy; but he who follows mortal natures is miserable. For to him who possesses wisdom, prosperity is good and useful. It is good, indeed, through his knowledge of the use of it; but it is useful, through his co-operating with actions. It is beautiful, therefore, when prosperity is present with intellect, and when sailing as it were with a prosperous wind, actions are performed looking to virtue; just as a pilot looks to the motions of the stars. For thus, he who does this will not only follow God, but will also co-arrange human with divine good.

This also is evident, that [human] life becomes different from disposition and action. But it is necessary that the disposition should be either worthy or depraved; and that action should be attended either with felicity or misery. And a worthy disposition, indeed, participates of virtue; but a bad one of vice. With respect to actions, also, those that are prosperous are attended with felicity; (for they derive their completion through looking to reason) but those that are unfortunate, are attended with misery; for they are frustrated of the end. Hence, it is not only necessary to learn virtue, but also to possess and use it, either for security, or increase, [of property when it is too little] or, which is the greatest thing of all, for the emendation of families and cities. For it is not only necessary to have the possession of things beautiful, but also the use of them. All these things, however, will take place, when a man lives in a city that uses equitable laws. And these, indeed, I say, are what is called the horn of Amalthea. For all things are contained in equitable legislation. And without this, the greatest good of human nature can neither be effected, nor, when effected, be increased and become permanent. For this comprehends in itself virtue, and the tendency to virtue; because excellent natures are generated according to it. Manners, likewise, studies, and laws, subsist through this in the most excellent condition; and besides these, rightly-deciding reason, and piety and sanctity towards the most honorable natures. So that it is necessary that he who is to be happy, and whose life is to be prosperous, should live and die in a country governed by equitable laws, relinquishing all illegality. At the same time what has been said is attended with necessity. For man is a part of society, and hence from the same reasoning, will become entire and perfect, if he not only associates with others, but associates in a becoming manner. For some things are naturally adapted to subsist in many things, and not in one thing;

146

others in one thing, and not in many; but others both in many, and
in one thing, and on this account in one thing, because in many. For
harmony, indeed, and symphony and number, are naturally adapted
to be ingenerated in many things. For nothing which makes a whole
from these parts, is sufficient to itself.[1] But acuteness of seeing and
hearing, and swiftness of feet, subsist in one thing alone. Felicity,
however, and the virtue of soul, subsist both in one thing and in
many, in a whole, and in the universe. And on this account they
subsist in one thing, because they also subsist in many: and they
subsist in many, because they are inherent in a whole and in the
universe. For the orderly distribution of the whole nature of things
methodically arranges each particular. And the orderly distribution of
particulars gives completion to the whole of things and to the
universe. But this follows from the whole being naturally prior to the
part, and not the part to the whole. For if the world was not, neither
the sun nor the moon would exist, nor the planets, nor the fixed stars.
But the world existing, each of these also exists.

The truth of this also may be seen in the nature itself of animals.
For if animal had no existence, there would neither be eye, nor
mouth, nor ear. But animal existing, each of these likewise exists. As
the whole, however, is to the part, so is the virtue of the whole to the
virtue of the part. For harmony not existing, and a divine inspection
of mundane affairs, things which are adorned would no longer be
able to remain in an excellent condition. And equitable legislation
not existing in a city, it is not possible for a citizen to be good or
happy. Health, likewise, not existing in the animal, it is not possible
for the foot or the hand to be strong and healthy. For harmony
indeed is the virtue of the world; equitable legislation is the virtue of a
city; and health and strength are the virtue of the body. Each of the
parts likewise in these things is co-arranged on account of the whole
and the universe. For the eyes see on account of the whole body. And
the other parts and members are co-arranged for the sake of the
whole [body] and the universe.

147

EURYPHAMUS,

IN HIS TREATISE

CONCERNING HUMAN LIFE.

———————

The perfect life of man falls short indeed of the life of God, because it is not self-perfect, but surpasses that of irrational animals, because it participates of virtue and felicity. For neither is God in want of external causes; since being naturally good and happy, he is perfect from himself; nor any irrational animal. For brutes being destitute of reason, they are also destitute of the sciences pertaining to actions. But the nature of man partly consists of his own proper deliberate choice, and partly is in want of the assistance derived from divinity. For that which is capable of being fashioned by reason, which has an intellectual perception of things beautiful and base, can erectly extend itself from earth, and look to heaven, and can perceive with the eye of intellect the highest Gods,—that which is capable of all this, participates likewise of assistance from the Gods. But in consequence of possessing will, deliberate choice, and a principle of such a kind in itself as enables it to study virtue, and to be agitated by the storms of vice, to follow, and also to apostatize from the Gods,—it is likewise able to be moved by itself. Hence it is a partaker of praise and blame, honor and ignominy, partly from the Gods and partly from men, according as it zealously applies itself either to virtue or vice. For the whole reason of the thing is as follows: Divinity introduced man into

149 the world as a most exquisite animal, to be reciprocally honored with himself, and *as the eye of the orderly distribution of things.* Hence also man gave names to things, becoming himself the character of them. He likewise invented letters, procuring through these a treasury of memory. And he imitated the established order of the universe, co-harmonizing by judicial proceedings and laws the communion of cities. For no work is performed by men more decorous to the world, or more worthy of the notice of the Gods, than the apt constitution of a city governed by good laws, and an orderly distribution of laws and a polity. For though each man himself by himself is nothing, and is not himself by himself sufficient to lead a life conformable to the common concord, and apt composition of a polity, yet he is well adapted to the whole and to the perfect system of society. For the life of man is the image of a lyre accurately [harmonized,] and in every respect perfect. For every lyre requires these three things, apparatus, apt composition, and a certain musical contrectation. And apparatus indeed, is a preparation of all the appropriate parts; *viz.* of the chords, and of the instruments which co-operate with the well-sounding and striking of the lyre. But the apt composition of the commixture of the sounds with each other. And the musical contrectation is the motion of these conformably to the apt composition. Thus also human life requires these same three things. Apparatus, indeed, which is the completion of the parts of life. But the parts of life are the goods of the body, of riches, renown, and friends. The apt composition is the co-arrangement of these according to virtue and the laws. And the musical contrectation is the commixture of these conformably to virtue and the laws; virtue sailing with a prosperous wind, and having nothing externally resisting it. For felicity does not consist in being driven from the purpose of voluntary intentions, but in obtaining

150 them; nor in virtue being without attendants and ministrant aids; but in completely possessing its own proper powers which are adapted to actions. For man is not self-perfect, but imperfect. And he becomes perfect, partly from himself, and partly from an external cause. He is likewise perfect, either according to nature, or according to life. And he is perfect indeed according to nature, if he becomes a good man. For the virtue of each thing is the summit and perfection of the nature of that thing. Thus the virtue[2] of the eyes is the summit and perfection of the nature of the eyes; and this is also true of the virtue of the ears. Thus too, the virtue of man is the summit and perfection of the nature of man. But man is perfect according to life, when he becomes happy. For felicity is the perfection and completion of human goods. Hence, again, virtue and prosperity become the parts of the life of man. And virtue, indeed, is a part of him so far as he is soul, but prosperity so far as he is connected with body. But both are parts of him so far as he is an animal. For it is the province of virtue to use in a becoming manner the goods which are conformable to nature; but of prosperity to impart the use of them. And the former, indeed, imparts deliberate choice and right reason; but the latter, energies and actions. For to wish what is beautiful in conduct and to endure things of a dreadful nature, is the proper business of virtue. But it is the work of prosperity to render deliberate choice successful, and to cause actions to arrive at the [desired] end. For the general conquers in conjunction with virtue and good fortune. The pilot sails well in conjunction with art and prosperous winds. The eye sees well in conjunction with acuteness of vision[3] and light. And the life of man becomes most excellent through virtue itself, and prosperity.

FROM

HIPPARCHUS,

IN HIS TREATISE

ON TRANQUILLITY.

Since men live but for a very short period, if their life is compared with the whole of time, they will make a most beautiful journey as it were, if they pass through life with tranquillity. This however they will possess in the most eminent degree, if they accurately and scientifically know themselves, *viz.* if they know that they are mortal and of a fleshly nature, and that they have a body which is corruptible and can be easily injured, and which is exposed to every thing most grievous and severe, even to their latest breath. And in the first place, let us direct our attention to those things which happen to the body; and these are pleurisy, inflammation of the lungs, phrensy, gout, stranguary, dysentery, lethargy, epilepsy, putrid ulcers, and ten thousand other diseases. But the diseases which happen to the soul are much greater and more dire than these. For all the iniquitous, evil, illegal, and impious conduct in the life of man, originates from the passions of the soul. For through preternatural immoderate desires many have become subject to unrestrained impulses, and have not refrained from the most unholy pleasures, arising from being connected with daughters or even mothers. Many also have been induced to destroy their fathers, and their own offspring. But what occasion is there to be prolix in narrating externally impending evils,

152 such as excessive rain, drought, violent heat and cold; so that frequently from the anomalous state of the air, pestilence and famine are produced, and all-various calamities, and whole cities become desolate? Since therefore many such-like calamities are impendent, we should neither be elevated by the possession of corporeal goods, which may rapidly be consumed by the incursions of a small fever, nor with what are conceived to be prosperous external circumstances, which frequently in their own nature perish more rapidly than they accede. For all these are uncertain and unstable, and are found to have their existence in many and various mutations; and no one of them is permanent, or immutable, or stable, or indivisible. Hence well considering these things, and also being persuaded, that if what is present and is imparted to us, is able to remain for the smallest portion of time, it is as much as we ought to expect; we shall then live in tranquillity and with hilarity, generously bearing whatever may befal us.

Now, however, many previously conceiving in imagination, that all that is present with, and imparted to them by nature and fortune, is better than it is, and not thinking it to be such as it is in reality, but such as it is able to become when it has arrived at the summit of excellence, they burden the soul with many great, nefarious, and stupid evils, when they are suddenly deprived of [these evanescent goods]. And thus it happens to them that they lead a most bitter and miserable life. But this takes place in the loss of riches, or the death of friends or children, or in the privation of certain other things, which are conceived by them to be most honorable possessions. Afterwards, weeping and lamenting, they assert of themselves, that they alone are most unfortunate and miserable, not remembering that these things have happened, and even now happen, to many others; nor are they able to understand the life of those that are now in existence, and of those that have lived in former times, nor to see in what great 153 calamities and waves of evils, many of the present time are, and of the past have been involved. Considering with ourselves therefore, that many having lost their property, have afterwards on account of this very loss been saved, since hereafter they might either have fallen into the hands of robbers, or into the power of a tyrant; that many also who have loved certain persons, and have been benevolently disposed towards them in the extreme, have afterwards greatly hated them;—considering all these things, which have been delivered to us by history, and likewise learning that many have been destroyed by their children, and by those that they have most dearly loved; and comparing our own life with that of those who have been more unhappy than we have been, and taking into account human casualties [in general] and not only such as happen to ourselves, we shall pass through life with greater tranquillity. For it is not lawful that he who is himself a man, should think the calamities of others easy to be borne, and not his own, since he sees that the whole of life is naturally exposed to many calamities. Those however, that weep and lament, besides not being able to recover what they have lost, or recal to life those that are dead, impel the soul to greater perturbations, in consequence of its being filled with much depravity. It is requisite therefore, that, being washed and purified, we should by all possible contrivances wipe away our inveterate stains by the reasonings of philosophy. But we shall accomplish this by adhering to prudence and temperance, being satisfied with our present circumstances, and not aspiring after many things. For men who procure for themselves a great abundance [of external goods], do not consider that the enjoyment of them terminates with the present life. We ought therefore to use the goods that are present; and by the assistance of the beautiful and venerable things of which philosophy is the source, we shall be liberated from the insatiable desire of depraved possessions.

FROM

ARCHYTAS,

IN HIS TREATISE CONCERNING

THE GOOD AND HAPPY MAN.

In the first place, it is requisite to know this, that the good man is not immediately happy from necessity; but that this is the case with the man who is both happy and good. For the happy man obtains both praise and the predication of blessedness; but the good man [so far as he is good] obtains praise alone. The praise also arises from virtue; but the predication of blessedness from good fortune. And the worthy man, indeed, becomes such from the goods which he possesses; but the happy man is sometimes deprived of his felicity. For the power of virtue is perfectly free, but that of felicity is subject to restraint. For long-continued diseases of the body, and depri-vations of the senses, cause the flourishing condition of felicity to waste away. God, however, differs from a good man in this, that God indeed not only possesses virtue genuine and purified from every mortal passion, but his power also is unwearied and unrestrained, as being adapted to the most venerable and magnificent production of eternal works. Man indeed, by the mortal condition of his nature, not only enjoys this power and this virtue in a less degree; but sometimes through the want of symmetry[4] in the goods which he possesses, or through powerful custom, or a depraved nature, or through many other causes, he is unable to possess in the extreme a good which is perfectly true.

155   Since therefore of goods, some are eligible for their own sakes, and not for the sake of another thing; but others are eligible for the sake of something else, and not on their own account; there is also a certain third species of goods, which is eligible both on its own account, and for the sake of another thing. What, therefore, is the good which is eligible on its own account, and not for the sake of something else? It is evident that it is felicity. For we aspire after other things for the sake of this, but we do not desire this for the sake of any thing else. Again, what are those goods which we desire indeed for the sake of something else, but which we do not desire on their own account? It is evident they are such things as are useful, and pre-eligible goods, which become the causes of our obtaining things which are eligible [on their own account]; such as corporeal labors, exercise, and frictions which are employed for the sake of a good habit of body; and also reading, meditation, and study, which are undertaken for the sake of things beautiful and virtue. But what are the things which are eligible on their own account, and also for the sake of something else? They are such things as the virtues, and the habits of them, deliberate choice and actions, and whatever adheres to that which is really beautiful. Hence, that indeed which is eligible on its own account, and not on account of something else, is a solitary good and one. But that which is eligible for its own sake, and for the sake of another thing, is triply divided. For one part of it indeed subsists about the soul; another about the body; and another pertains to externals. And that which is about the soul, consists of the virtues of the soul; that which is about the body, of the virtues of the body; and that which pertains to externals, consists of friends, glory, honor, and wealth. There is likewise a similar reasoning with respect to that which is eligible on account of something else. For one part of it

156   indeed is effective of the goods of the soul; another part of it, of the goods of the body; and that which pertains to externals is the cause of wealth, glory, honor, and friendship.

That virtue however happens to be eligible for its own sake, is evident from the following considerations. For if things which are naturally subordinate, I mean the goods of the body, are eligible for their own sakes, but the soul is better than the body, it is evident that we love the goods of the soul on their own account, and not for the sake of the consequences with which they are attended.

There are likewise three definite times of human life; one of prosperity; another of adversity; and a third subsisting between these. Since therefore, he is a good man who possesses and uses virtue; but he uses it according to three seasons; for he uses it either in adversity, or in prosperity, or in the time between these; and in adversity indeed he is unhappy, but in prosperity happy, and in the middle condition, he is not happy [though he is not miserable];—this being the case, it is evident that felicity is nothing else than the use of virtue in prosperity. We now speak, however, of the felicity of man. But man is not soul alone, but is likewise body. For the animal which consists of both, and that which is constituted from things of this kind is man. For though the body is naturally adapted to be the instrument of the soul, yet this as well as the soul is a part of man [so far as he is an animal.⁵] Hence of goods also, some are the goods of man, but others, of the parts of man. And the good of man, indeed, is felicity. But of the parts of man, the good of the soul is prudence, fortitude, justice, and 157 temperance. And the good of the body is beauty, health, a good corporeal habit, and excellence of sensation. With respect to externals however, wealth, glory, honor, and nobility, are naturally adapted to be attendant on man, and to follow precedaneous goods. The less, also, are ministrant to the greater goods. Thus friendship, glory, and wealth, are ministrant both to the body and the soul; but health, strength, and excellence of sensation, are subservient to the soul; and prudence [*i.e.* wisdom] and justice are ministrant to the intellect of the soul. *Intellect, however, is the satellite of Deity*. For God is the most excellent, and the leader and ruler of all things. And for the sake of these, it is necessary that other goods should be present. For the general, indeed, is the leader of the army; the pilot, of the ship; God, of the world; and intellect, of soul. But prudence is the leader of the felicity pertaining to life. For prudence is nothing else than the science of the felicity which respects human life, or the science of the goods which naturally pertain to man.

And the felicity, indeed, and life of God are most excellent; but the felicity of man consists of science, and virtue, and in the third place of prosperity⁶ corporalized. But I mean by science, the wisdom 158 pertaining to things divine and demoniacal; and by prudence, the wisdom pertaining to human concerns, and the affairs of life. For it is requisite to call the virtues which employ reasonings and demonstrations, sciences. But it is fit to denominate virtue ethical, and the best habit of the irrational part of the soul, according to which we are said to possess certain qualities pertaining to manners; *viz.* by which we are called liberal, just, and temperate. But it is requisite to call prosperity, the preter-rational presence of goods, [or a supply of goods without the assistance of reason,] and which is not effected on account of it. Since therefore virtue and science are in our power, but prosperity is not; and since also felicity consists in the contemplation and performance of things [truly] beautiful; but contemplations and actions, when they are not prosperous, are attended with ministrant offices and necessity, but when they proceed in the right path, produce delight and felicity; and these things are effected in prosperity;—this being the case, it is evident that *felicity is nothing else than the use of virtue in prosperity*. Hence the good man is disposed with respect to prosperity, in the same manner as he who has an excellent and robust body. For such a one is able to endure heat and cold, to raise a great burden, and to sustain easily many other molestations.

Since therefore felicity is the use of virtue in prosperity, we must speak concerning virtue and prosperity, and in the first place concerning prosperity. For of goods, some indeed do not admit of excess, and this is the case with virtue. For there is not any virtue which is excessive, nor any worthy man who is beyond measure good. For virtue has the fit and becoming for a rule, and is the habit of the decorous in practical concerns. But prosperity receives excess and diminution. And when it is excessive indeed, it generates certain vices, and removes a man from his natural habit; so that he frequently through this opposes the constitution of virtue. And this is not only the case with prosperity, but many other causes likewise may effect the same thing. For it is by no means proper to wonder, that some of those who play on the pipe should be arrogant men, who, bidding farewell to truth, ensnare by a certain false imagination those who are unskilled in music; and to disbelieve that a thing of this kind does not take place in virtue. For the more venerable a thing is, so much the more numerous are those that pretend to the possession of it. For

159

there are many things which distort the habit and form of virtue; some of which are insidious arts and affectation; others are kindred physical passions, which sometimes produce an indecorum[7] contrary to the true disposition [of virtue]. This also is effected through manners in which men have been nurtured for a long time; and it not unfrequently happens that it is produced through youth or old age, and through prosperity or adversity; and by other very numerous ways. Hence, we ought never to wonder, if sometimes a distorted judgment is formed of all things, the true disposition being changed.[8] Thus we see that the most excellent carpenter frequently errs in the works which are the subjects of his art; and this is also the case with the general, the pilot, the painter, and in short, with all artists. And yet at the same time we do not deprive them of the habit which they possess. For as we do not rank among bad men him who at certain times acts intemperately, or unjustly, or timidly; so neither do we place him in the class of good men, who does something right in things pertaining to temperance, or justice, or fortitude. But it must be said that the conduct of bad men in things of this kind is casually right, and that good men [sometimes] err. A true judgment however [in these instances] is to be formed, not by looking to a certain occasion, or to a certain extent of time, but to the whole of life. But as indigence and excess are injurious to the body, yet excess and what are called superfluities, are naturally adapted to produce greater diseases [than those caused by indigence]; thus also prosperity or adversity injure the soul, when they unseasonably happen; yet that which is called by all men prosperity, is naturally adapted to produce greater diseases [than adversity], since it intoxicates like wine the reasoning power of good men.

160

Hence it is more difficult to bear prosperity in a becoming manner than adversity. For all men when they continue in adversity, are seen for the most part to be moderate and orderly in their manners; but in prosperity they are brave, magnificent, and magnanimous [when they bear it in a becoming manner]. For adversity has the power of contracting and depressing the soul; but prosperity, on the contrary, elevates and expands it. Hence all those that are unfortunate, are in their manners cautious and prudent; but those that are fortunate are insolent and confident. But the boundary of prosperity, is that which a good man would deliberately choose to co-operate with him in his own proper actions; just as the [proper] magnitude of a ship, and the [proper] magnitude of a rudder, are such as will enable a good pilot to sail over a great extent of sea, and to accomplish a great voyage. An excess of prosperity, however, is not naturally adapted to be vanquished by, but to vanquish the soul. For as a [very] splendid light causes an obscuration of sight in the eyes; thus also excessive prosperity darkens the intellect of the soul. And thus much may suffice concerning prosperity.

FROM

THEAGES,

IN HIS TREATISE

ON THE VIRTUES.

————————

The order of the soul subsists in such a way, that one part of it is the reasoning power, another is anger, and another is desire. And the reasoning power, indeed, has dominion over knowledge; anger over impetus; and desire intrepidly rules over the appetitions of the soul. When therefore these three parts pass into one, and exhibit one appropriate composition, then virtue and concord are produced in the soul. But when they are divulsed from each other by sedition, then vice and discord are produced in the soul. It is necessary, however, that virtue should have these three things, *viz.* reason, power, and deliberate choice. The virtue, therefore, of the reasoning power of the soul is prudence; for it is a habit of judging and contemplating. But the virtue of the irascible part, is fortitude; for it is a habit of resisting, and enduring things of a dreadful nature. And the virtue of the epithymetic or appetitive part is temperance; for it is a moderation and detention of the pleasures which arise through the body. But the virtue of the whole soul is justice. For men indeed become bad, either through vice, or through incontinence, or through a natural ferocity. But they injure each other, either through gain, or through pleasure, or through ambition. Vice, therefore, more appropriately belongs to the reasoning part of the soul. For prudence indeed is similar to art;

162 but vice to pernicious art. For it invents contrivances for the purpose of acting unjustly. But incontinence rather pertains to the appetitive part of the soul. For continence consists in subduing, and incontinence in not subduing pleasures. And ferocity pertains to the irascible part of the soul. For when some one, through acting ill from desire, is gratified not as a man should be, but as a wild beast, then a thing of this kind is denominated ferocity. The effects also of these dispositions are consequent to the things for the sake of which they are performed. For avarice is consequent to vice; but vice is consequent to the reasoning part of the soul. And ambition, indeed, follows from the irascible part; and this becoming excessive, generates ferocity. Again, pleasure pertains to the appetitive part; but this being sought after more vehemently, generates incontinence. Hence, since the acting unjustly is produced from so many causes, it is evident that acting justly is effected through an equal number of causes. For virtue, indeed, is naturally beneficent and profitable; but vice is productive of evil, and is noxious.

Since, however, of the parts of the soul, one is the leader, but the other follows, and the virtues and the vices subsist about these, and in these; it is evident that with respect to the virtues also, some are leaders, others are followers, and others are composed from these. And the leaders, indeed, are such as prudence; but the followers are such as fortitude and temperance; and the composites from these, are such as justice. The passions, however, are the matter of virtue; for the virtues subsist about, and in these. But of the passions, one is voluntary, but another is involuntary. And the voluntary, indeed, is pleasure; but the involuntary is pain. Men also, who have the political virtues, give intension and remission to these, co-harmonizing the other parts of the soul, to that part which possesses reason. But the

163 boundary of this co-adaptation, is for intellect not to be prevented from accomplishing its proper work, either by indigence, or excess. For that which is less excellent, is co-arranged for the sake of that which is more excellent. Thus in the world, every part that is always passive, subsists for the sake of that which is always moved. And in the conjunction of animals, the female subsists for the sake of the male. For the latter sows, generating a soul; but the former alone imparts matter to that which is generated. In the soul however, the irrational subsists for the sake of the rational part. For anger and desire are co-arranged in subserviency to the first part of the soul; the former as a certain satellite, and guardian of the body; but the latter as a dispensator and provident curator of necessary wants. But intellect being established in the highest summit of the body, and having a prospect in that which is on all sides splendid and transparent,[9] investigates the wisdom of [real] beings. And this is the work of it according to nature, *viz.* having investigated, and obtained the possession [of truth] to follow those beings who are more excellent and more honorable than itself. For *the knowledge of things divine and most honorable, is the principle, cause, and rule of human blessedness.*

FROM

METOPUS,

IN HIS TREATISE

CONCERNING VIRTUE.

The virtue of man is the perfection of the nature of man. For every being becomes perfect, and arrives at the summit of excellence according to the proper nature of its virtue. Thus the virtue of a horse, is that which leads the nature of a horse to its summit. And the same reasoning is applicable to the several parts of a thing. Thus the virtue of the eyes is acuteness of vision: and this in the nature of the eyes is the summit. The virtue of the ears also, is acuteness of hearing: and this is the summit of the nature of the ears. Thus too, the virtue of the feet is swiftness: and this is the summit of the nature of the feet. It is necessary however, that every virtue should have these three things, reason, power, and deliberate choice; reason indeed, by which it judges and contemplates; power, by which it prohibits and vanquishes; and deliberate choice, by which it loves and delights in [what is proper]. To judge, therefore, and contemplate, pertain to the dianoetic part of the soul; but to prohibit and vanquish are the peculiarity of the irrational[10] part of the soul; and to love and delight in what is proper, pertain to both the rational and irrational parts. For deliberate choice consists of dianoia [or the discursive energy of reason] and appetite. Dianoia therefore, belongs to the rational, but appetite to the irrational part of the soul. The multitude however, of all the virtues, may be perceived from the parts of the soul; and in a similar manner the generation and nature of virtue. For of the parts of the soul, there are two that rank as the first, *viz.* the rational and the irrational parts. And the rational part indeed, is that by which we judge and contemplate; but the irrational part is that by which we are impelled and desire. These however, are either concordant or discordant with each other. But the contest and dissonance between them, are produced through excess and defect. It is evident therefore, that when the rational vanquishes the irrational part of the soul, endurance and continence are produced; and that when the former leads, and the latter follows, and both accord with each other, then virtue is generated. Hence, endurance and continence are generated accompanied with pain; but endurance resists pain, and continence pleasure. Incontinence however, and effeminacy, neither resist nor vanquish [pleasure]. And on this account it happens that men fly from good through pain, but reject it through pleasure. Praise likewise, and blame, and every thing beautiful in human conduct are produced in these parts of the soul. And in short, the nature of virtue derives its subsistence after this manner.

The species however, and the parts of it, may be surveyed as follows: Since there are two parts of the soul, the rational and the irrational; the latter is divided into the irascible and appetitive. And the rational part indeed, is that by which we judge and contemplate; but the irrational part is that by which we are impelled and desire. And of this, that which is as it were adapted to defend us, and revenge incidental molestations, is denominated the irascible part; but that which is as it were orectic of, and desires to preserve the proper constitution of the body, is the appetitive part. It is evident therefore, that the multitude of the virtues, their differences, and their peculiarities, follow conformably to these parts of the soul.

CLINIAS.

Every virtue is perfected, as was shown by us in the beginning, from reason, deliberate choice, and power. Each of these, however, is not by itself a part of virtue, but the cause of it. Such therefore, as have the intellective and gnostic part of virtue,[11] are denominated skilful and intelligent; but such as have the ethical and pre-elective part of it, are denominated useful and equitable.[12] Since however, man is naturally adapted to act unjustly from exciting causes; and these are three, the love of pleasure in corporeal enjoyments; avarice, in the accumulation of wealth; and ambition, in surpassing those that are equal and similar to him;—this being the case, it is necessary to know, that it is possible to oppose to these such things as procure fear, shame, and desire in men; *viz.* fear through the laws, shame through the Gods, and desire through the energies of reason. Hence, it is necessary that youth should be taught from the first to honor the Gods and the laws. For from these, it will be manifest, that every human work, and every kind of human life, by the participation of sanctity and piety, will sail prosperously [over the sea of generation].

FROM

THEAGES,

IN HIS TREATISE

ON THE VIRTUES.

———————

The principles of all virtue are three; knowledge, power, and deliberate choice. And knowledge indeed, is that by which we contemplate and form a judgment of things; power is as it were a certain strength of the nature[13] from which we derive our subsistence, and is that which gives stability to our actions; and deliberate choice is as it were certain hands of the soul by which we are impelled to, and lay hold on the objects of our choice. The order of the soul also subsists as follows: One part of it is the reasoning power, another part is anger, and another is desire. And the reasoning power indeed, is that which has dominion over knowledge; anger is that which rules over the ardent impulses of the soul; and desire is that which willingly rules over appetite. When therefore, these three pass into one, so as to exhibit one co-adaptation, then virtue and concord are produced in the soul; but when they are seditious, and divulsed from each other, then vice and discord are generated in the soul. And when the reasoning power prevails over the irrational parts of the soul, then endurance and continence are produced; endurance indeed, in the retention of pains; but continence in the abstinence from pleasures. But when the irrational parts of the soul prevail over the reasoning power, then effeminacy and incontinence are produced; effeminacy indeed, in flying from pain; but incontinence, in the being vanquished by pleasures. When however, the better part of the soul governs, but the less excellent part is governed; and the former leads, but the latter follows, and both consent, and are concordant with each other, then virtue and every good are generated in the whole soul. When likewise the appetitive follows the reasoning part of the soul, then temperance is produced; but when this is the case with the irascible part, fortitude is produced; and when it takes place in all the parts of the soul, then justice is the result. For justice is that which separates all the vices and all the virtues of the soul from each other. And justice is a certain established order of the apt conjunction of the parts of the soul, and perfect and supreme virtue. For every good is contained in this; but the other goods of the soul cannot subsist without this. Hence justice possesses great strength both among Gods and men. For this virtue contains the bond by which the whole and the universe are held together, and also by which Gods and men are connected. Justice therefore, is said to be Themis among the celestial, but Dice among the terrestrial Gods; and Law among men. These assertions however, are indications and symbols, that justice is the supreme virtue. Hence virtue, when it consists in contemplating and judging, is called prudence; when in sustaining things of a dreadful nature, it is denominated fortitude; when in restraining pleasure, temperance; and when in abstaining from gain, and from injuring our neighbours, justice.

170   Moreover, the arrangement of virtue according to right reason, and the transgression of it contrary to right reason, produce [in the former case] a tendency to the decorous as the final mark, and [in the latter] the frustration of it. The decorous however, is that which ought to be. But this does not require either addition or ablation; since it is that which it is requisite to be. But of the indecorous there are two species; one of which is excess, and the other defect. And excess indeed, is more, but deficiency is less, than is decorous. Virtue also, is a certain habit of the decorous. Hence it is directly, both a summit and a medium. For thus, things that are decorous are both media and summits. They are media indeed, because they fall between excess and deficiency; but they are summits, because they do not require either addition or ablation. For they are the very things

themselves which they ought to be.

Since however, the virtue of manners is conversant with the passions, but of the passions pleasure and pain are supreme, it is evident that virtue does not consist in extirpating the passions of the soul, pleasure and pain, but in co-harmonizing them. For neither does health, which is a certain apt mixture of the powers of the body, consist in expelling the cold and the hot, the moist and the dry; but in these being [appropriately] mingled together. For it is as it were, a certain symmetry of these. Thus too, in music, concord does not consist in expelling the sharp and the flat; but when these are co-harmonized, then concord is produced, and dissonance is exterminated. In a similar manner, the hot and the cold, the moist and the dry, being harmoniously mingled together, health is produced, and disease destroyed. But when anger and desire are co-harmonized, the vices and the [other] passions are extirpated, and the virtues and manners are ingenerated. Deliberate choice however, in beautiful conduct, is the greatest peculiarity of the virtue of manners. For it is possible to use reason and power without virtue; but it is not possible to use deliberate choice without it. For deliberate choice indicates the dignity of manners. Hence also, the reasoning power subduing *by force* anger and desire, produces continence and endurance. And again, when the reasoning power is violently dethroned by the irrational parts, then incontinence and effeminacy are produced. Such dispositions however, of the soul as these, are half-perfect virtues, and half-perfect vices. For the reasoning power of the soul is [according to its natural subsistence] in a healthy, but the irrational parts are in a diseased condition. And so far indeed, as anger and desire are governed and led by the rational part of the soul, continence and endurance become virtues; but so far as this is effected by violence, and not voluntarily, they become vices. For it is necessary that virtue should perform such things as are fit, not with pain, but with pleasure. Again, so far as anger and desire govern the reasoning power, effeminacy and incontinence are produced, which are certain vices. But so far as they gratify the passions with pain, knowing that they are erroneous, in consequence of the eye of the soul being sane, —so far as this is the case, they are not vices. Hence, it is evident that virtue must necessarily perform what is fit voluntarily; that which is

171

involuntary indeed, not being without pain and fear; and that which is voluntary, not subsisting without pleasure and delight.

By division also it will at the same time be found that this is the case. For knowledge and the perception of things, are the province of the rational part of the soul; but power pertains to the irrational part. For not to be able to resist pain, or to vanquish pleasure, is the peculiarity of the irrational part of the soul. But deliberate choice subsists in both these, *viz.* in the rational, and also in the irrational part. For it consists of dianoia and appetite; of which, dianoia indeed, pertains to the rational, but appetite to the irrational part. Hence every virtue consists in a co-adaptation of the parts of the soul; and both will and deliberate choice, entirely subsist in virtue.

Universally therefore, virtue is a certain co-adaptation of the irrational parts of the soul to the rational part. Virtue however, is produced through pleasure and pain receiving the boundary of that which is fit. For true virtue is nothing else than the habit of that which is fit. But the fit, or the decorous, is that which ought to be; and the unfit, or indecorous, is that which ought not to be. Of the indecorous however, there are two species, *viz.* excess and defect. And excess indeed, is more than is fit; but defect is less than is fit. But since the fit is that which ought to be, it is both a summit and a middle. It is a summit indeed, because it neither requires ablation, nor addition; but it is a middle, because it subsists between excess and defect. The fit, however, and the unfit, are to each other as the equal and the unequal, that which is arranged, and that which is without arrangement; and both the two former and the two latter are finite and infinite.[14] On this account, the parts of the unequal are referred to the middle, but not to each other. For the angle is called obtuse which is greater than a right angle; but that is called acute, which is less than a right angle. The right line also [in a circle] is greater, which surpasses that which is drawn from the center. And the day is longer indeed, which exceeds that of the equinox. Diseases, likewise, of the body are generated, through the body becoming more hot or more cold [than is proper]. For that which is more hot [than is fit] exceeds moderation; and that which is more cold [than is fit] is below mediocrity. The soul also, and such things as pertain to it, have this disposition and analogy. For audacity indeed, is an excess of the

172

173

decorous in the endurance of things of a dreadful nature; but timidity is a deficiency of the decorous. And prodigality is an excess of what is fit in the expenditure of money; but illiberality is a deficiency in this. And rage indeed, is an excess of the decorous in the impulse of the irascible part of the soul; but insensibility is a deficiency of this. The same reasoning likewise applies to the opposition of the other dispositions of the soul. It is necessary however, that virtue, since it is a habit of the decorous, and a medium of the passions, should neither be [wholly] impassive, nor immoderately passive. For impassivity indeed, causes the soul to be unimpelled, and to be without an enthusiastic tendency to the beautiful in conduct; but immoderate passivity causes it to be full of perturbation, and inconsiderate. It is necessary therefore, that passion should so present itself to the view, in virtue, as shadow and outline in a picture. For the animated and the delicate, and that which imitates the truth, in conjunction with goodness of colors, are especially effected in a picture through these [*i.e.* through shadow and outline]. But the passions of the soul are animated by the natural incitation and enthusiasm of virtue. For virtue is generated from the passions, and when generated, again subsists together with them; just as that which is well harmonized consists of the sharp and the flat, that which is well mingled consists of the hot and the cold, and that which is in equilibrium derives its equality of weight from the heavy and the light. It is not therefore necessary to take away the passions of the soul; for neither would this be profitable; but it is requisite that they should be co-harmonized with the rational part, in conjunction with fitness and mediocrity.

FROM

THE TREATISE OF

ARCHYTAS

ON ETHICAL ERUDITION.

———————

I say that virtue will be found sufficient to the avoidance of infelicity, and vice to the non-attainment of felicity, if we judiciously consider the habits [by which these are produced]. For it is necessary that the bad man should always be miserable; whether he is in affluence, for he employs it badly; or whether he is in penury; just as the blind man, whether he has light, and the most splendid visible object before him, or whether he is in the dark [is always necessarily without sight]. But the good man is not always happy; for felicity does not consist in the possession, but in the use of virtue. For neither does he who has sight always see; for he will not see, if he is without light. Life, however, is divided into two paths; one of which is more arduous, and in which the patient Ulysses walked; but the other is more free from molestation, and is that in which Nestor proceeded. I say therefore that virtue desires the latter, but is able to proceed in the former of these paths. The nature however of felicity proclaims it to be a desirable and stable life, because it gives perfection to the decision of the soul. Hence the virtuous man who does not obtain such a life as this, is not indeed happy, nor yet entirely miserable. No one therefore will dare to say that the good man should be exempt from disease, and pain, and sorrow. For as we leave certain painful things to the body, so 175

141

likewise we must permit them to be present with the soul. The sorrows, however, of fools are most irrational; but those of wise men proceed only as far as reason, which gives limitation to things, permits. Moreover, the boast of apathy dissolves the generosity of virtue, when it opposes itself to things of an indifferent nature, and not to evils such as death, and pain, and poverty. For things which are not evils are easily vanquished. We should therefore exercise ourselves in the mediocrity of the passions, as we shall then equally avoid insensibility, and too much passivity, and shall not speak higher of our nature than we ought.

FROM

ARCHYTAS,

IN HIS TREATISE ON

THE GOOD AND HAPPY MAN.

I say then that the good man is one who uses in a beautiful manner great things and opportunities. He likewise is able to bear well both prosperity and adversity. In beautiful and honorable circumstances also, he becomes worthy of the condition in which he is placed; and when his fortune is changed, receives it in a proper manner. In short, on all occasions, he contends well from contingencies that may arise. Nor does he only thus prepare himself [for whatever may happen], but likewise those who confide in and contend together with him.

FROM

CRITO,

IN HIS TREATISE ON

PRUDENCE AND PROSPERITY.

Prudence and prosperity subsist, with reference to each other, as follows: Prudence indeed is effable and possesses reason; for it is something orderly and definite. But prosperity is ineffable and irrational; for it is something disorderly and indefinite. And prudence, indeed, is prior, but prosperity is posterior in beginning and in power. For the former is naturally adapted to govern and define; but the latter to be governed and defined. Moreover, both prudence and prosperity receive co-adaptation, since they concur in one and the same thing. For it is always necessary that the thing which bounds and co-arranges, should have a nature which is effable and participates of reason; but that the thing which is bounded and co-arranged, should be naturally ineffable and irrational. For the reason of the nature of the infinite and of that which bounds, thus subsists in all things. For infinites are always naturally disposed to be bounded and co-arranged by things which possess reason and prudence, since the former have the order of matter and essence with relation to the latter. But finites are co-arranged and bounded from themselves, since they have the order of cause, and of that which is energetic.

The co-adaptation, however, of these natures in different things, produces a great and various difference of co-adapted substances. For

in the comprehension of the whole of things, the co-adaptation of
both the natures, *i.e.* of the nature which is always moved, and of that
which is always passive, is the world. For it is not possible for the
whole and the universe to be otherwise saved, than by that which is
generated being co-adapted to that which is divine, and that which is
always passive to that which is always moved.[15] In man, likewise, the
co-adaptation of the irrational to the rational part of the soul, is
virtue. For it is not possible in these, when there is sedition in both
the parts, that virtue should have a subsistence. In a city also, the co-
adaptation of the governors to the governed, produces strength and
concord. For to govern is the peculiarity of the better nature; but to be
governed, is easier to the subordinate [than to the more excellent]
nature. And strength and concord are common to both. There is,
however, the same mode of adaptation in the universe and in a family:
for allurements[16] and erudition concur with reason in one and the
same thing; and likewise pains and pleasures, prosperity and adversity.
For the life of man requires intension and remission, sorrow and
gladness, prosperity and adversity. For some things are able to collect
and retain the intellect to industry and wisdom; but others impart
relaxation and delight, and thus render the intellect vigorous and
prompt to action. If however one of these prevails in life, then the life
of man becomes of one part, and verges to one part, tending either to
sorrow and difficulty, or to remission and levity. But the co-
adaptation of all these ought to subsist with reference to prudence. For
this separates and distinguishes[17] bound and infinity in actions. Hence
prudence is the leader and mother of the other virtues. For all of them
are co-harmonized and co-arranged with reference to the reason and
law of this virtue. And now my discussion of this subject is
terminated. For the irrational and the effable are in all things. And
the latter defines and bounds; but the former is defined and bounded.
That, however, which consists of both these, is the apt composition of
the whole and the universe.

The following beautiful fragment of CRITO on Prudence, is from the Physical Eclogues of Stobæus, p. 198, and is omitted by Gale in his Collection of Pythagoric Ethical Fragments in Opusc. Mythol. Etc.

God fashioned man in such a way as to render it manifest, that he is not through the want of power, or of deliberate choice, incapable of being impelled to what is beautiful in conduct. For he implanted in him a principle of such a kind as to comprehend at one and the same time the possible and the pre-eligible; so that man might be the cause of power, and the possession of good, but God of impulse and incitation according to right reason. On this account also, he made him tend to heaven, gave him an intellective power, and implanted in him a sight called intellect, which is capable of beholding God. For it is not possible without God to discover that which is best and most beautiful, nor without intellect to see God, since every mortal nature is established in conjunction with a kindred privation of intellect. This however is not imparted to it by God, but by the essence of generation, and by that impulse of the soul which is without deliberate choice.

FROM

ARCHYTAS,

IN HIS TREATISE ON

THE GOOD AND HAPPY MAN.

———————

The prudent [*i.e.* the wise] man will especially become so as follows: In the first place, being naturally sagacious, possessing a good memory, and being a lover of labor, he should exercise his dianoetic power immediately from his youth in reasonings and disciplines, and in accurate theories, and adhere to genuine philosophy. But after this he should acquire knowledge and experience in what pertains to the Gods, the laws, and human lives. For there are two things from which the disposition of prudence is produced; one of which consists in obtaining a mathematical and gnostic habit; but the other, in a man perceiving by himself many theorems and things, and understanding other things through a certain different mode. For neither is he sufficient to the possession of prudence, who immediately from his youth has exercised his dianoetic power in reasonings and disciplines; nor he who being destitute of these, has heard and has been conversant with a multitude of things. But the latter will have his dianoetic power blind, through judging of particulars; and the former through always surveying universals. For as in computations the amount of the whole is obtained by the addition of the parts, thus also in things, reason is able to delineate the theory of universals; but experience has the power of forming a judgment of particulars.

FROM

ALCINOUS

HANDBOOK

THE TRUTH AND SOPHIA

The purpose of the good man will specially become as follows. In the first place, being actually experience, possessing a good memory and being a lover of labor he should reserve for similar power immediately in his search in theorems; and adhere to if in some theorems, and adhere to general philosophy. For after this shall acquire knowledge and experience in what pertains to the theoretic lives. Innate basis for the theoretic lives, from which the disposition of prudence is produced, one of which consists in obtaining a mathematical and gnostic habit, but the other in a man's perceiving by himself the theorems and things, and understanding other things through a certain different mode. For neither it is sufficient to the possession of prudence and immediate truth, from his youth has exerted his dianoetic power in reasonings and disciplines; nor he who being destitute of these, has found and has been conversant with a multitude of things; but the latter will have his dianoetic power blind, through judging of particulars; and the former thinking always surveying universals, nor as in comprehension the amount of the whole is obtained by the adding of the parts; thus also in things, reason is able to delineate the theory of universals, but experience has the power of forming a judgment of particulars.

ARCHYTAS,

IN HIS TREATISE

ON DISCIPLINES.

———————

It is necessary that you should become scientific, either by learning from another person, or by discovering yourself the things of which you have a scientific knowledge. If, therefore, you learn from another person, that which you learn is foreign; but what you discover yourself is through yourself, and is your own. Moreover, if you investigate, discovery will be easy, and soon obtained; but if you do not know how to investigate, discovery will be to you impossible. And [right] reasoning indeed, when discovered, causes sedition to cease, and increases concord. For through this the inexhaustible desire of possessing is suppressed, and equality prevails; since by this we obtain what is just in contracts. Hence, on account of this, the poor receive from those who are able to give; and the rich give to those that are in want, both of them believing that through this they shall obtain the equal. This however will be a rule and an impediment to those that act unjustly, *viz.* that men who possess scientific knowledge will appease their anger, prior to the comm-ission of an injury, being persuaded that the perpetrators of it will not be concealed when it is committed; but that those who do not possess scientific knowledge, becoming manifest in the commission of an injury, will be restrained from acting unjustly.

FROM

POLUS,

IN HIS TREATISE

ON JUSTICE.

It appears to me that the justice which subsists among men, may be called the mother and the nurse of the other virtues. For without this a man can neither be temperate, nor brave, nor prudent. For it is the harmony and peace, in conjunction with elegance, of the whole soul. The strength however of this virtue will become more manifest, if we direct our attention to the other habits. For they have a partial utility, and which is referred to one thing; but this is referred to whole systems, and to a multitude. In the world therefore, it conducts the whole government of things, and is providence, harmony, and Dice, by the decree of a certain genus of Gods. But in a city it is justly called peace, and equitable legislation. And in a house, it is the concord between the husband and wife; the benevolence of the servant towards the master; and the anxious care of the master for the welfare of the servant. In the body likewise, which is the first and dearest thing to all animals, [so far as they are animals,] it is the health and entireness of all the parts. But in the soul, it is the wisdom, which among men subsists from science and justice. If therefore, this virtue thus disciplines and saves both the whole and the parts [of every thing] rendering things concordant and familiar with each other, how is it possible it should not be called by the decision of all men, the mother and the nurse of all things?

183 The following fragments also, from the Treatise of Archytas on Wisdom, are preserved by Iamblichus, in the 3rd Chapter of his Protreptics, or Exhortations to Philosophy.

"Archytas therefore, in the beginning of his Treatise on Wisdom, exhorts to the possession of it as follows:

1. "Wisdom as much excels in all human affairs as the sight does the [other] corporeal senses, intellect the soul, and the sun the stars. For the sight is the most far-darting, and the most multiform of all the senses; intellect is the supreme part of the soul, judging by reason and dianoia what is fit, and existing as the sight and power of the most honorable things; and the sun is the eye and soul of things which have a natural subsistence. For through it all things become visible, are generated, and rise into existence.[18] Deriving also their roots, and being generated from thence, they are nourished, increased and excited by it in conjunction with sense.

2. "Man was generated by far the wisest of all [terrestrial] animals. For he is able to contemplate the things which exist, and to obtain from all things science and wisdom. To which also it may be added, that divinity has engraved and exhibited in him the system of universal reason, in which all the forms of things in existence are distributed, and the significations of nouns and verbs. For a place is assigned for the sounds of the voice, *viz.* the pharynx, the mouth, and the nostrils. But as man was generated the instrument of the sounds, through which nouns and verbs are signified, so likewise of the conceptions which are beheld in the things that have an existence. And this appears to me to be the work of wisdom, for the accomplishment of which man was generated and constituted, and received organs and powers from divinity.

184 3. "Man was generated and constituted, for the purpose of contemplating the reason of the whole of nature, and in order that, being himself the work of wisdom, he might survey the wisdom of the things which exist.—For if the reason of man is contemplative of the reason of the whole of nature, and the wisdom also of man perceives and contemplates the wisdom of the things in existence,—this being acknowledged, it is at the same time demonstrated, that man is a part of universal reason, and of the whole of the intellectual nature.

4. "Wisdom is not conversant with a certain definite existing thing, but is simply conversant with all the things that exist. And it is requisite, that it should not first investigate the principles of itself, but the common principles of all beings. For wisdom so subsists with reference to all beings, that it is the province of it to know and contemplate the universal accidents of all things. And on this account wisdom discovers the principles of all beings.

5. "Whoever, therefore, is able to analyze all the genera which are contained under one and the same principle, and again to compose and con-numerate them, he appears to me to be the wisest of men, and to possess the most perfect veracity. Farther still, he will also have discovered a beautiful place of survey, from which it will be possible to behold divinity, and all things that are in co-ordination with, and successive to him, subsisting separately, or distinct from each other.[19] Having likewise entered this most ample road, being impelled in a right direction by intellect, and having arrived at the end of his course, he will have conjoined beginnings with ends, and will know that God is the principle, middle, and end, of all things which are accomplished according to justice and right reason."[20]

PYTHAGORIC ETHICAL SENTENCES

FROM

STOBÆUS,

Which are omitted in the Opuscula Mythologica, etc. of Gale.

Do not even *think* of doing what ought not to be done.

Choose rather to be strong in soul than in body.

Be persuaded that things of a laborious nature contribute more than pleasures to virtue.

Every passion of the soul is most hostile to its salvation.

It is difficult to walk at one and the same time in many paths of life.[21]

Pythagoras said, it is requisite to choose the most excellent life; for custom will make it pleasant. Wealth is an infirm anchor, glory is still more infirm; and in a similar manner the body, dominion, and honor. For all these are imbecile and powerless. What then are powerful anchors? Prudence, magnanimity, fortitude. These no tempest can shake. This is the law of God, that virtue is the only thing that is strong; and that every thing else is a trifle.

All the parts of human life, in the same manner as those of a statue, ought to be beautiful.

A statue indeed standing on its basis, but a worthy man on the subject of his deliberate choice, ought to be immovable.

Frankincense ought to be given to the Gods, but praise to good *187* men.

It is requisite to defend those who are unjustly accused of having acted injuriously, but to praise those who excel in a certain good.

Neither will the horse be judged to be generous, that is sumptuously adorned, but the horse whose nature is illustrious; nor is the man worthy who possesses great wealth, but he whose soul is generous.

When the wise man opens his mouth, the beauties of his soul present themselves to the view, like the statues in a temple.[22]

Remind yourself that all men assert that wisdom is the greatest good, but that there are few who strenuously endeavour to obtain this greatest good.[23] Pythagoras.

Be sober, and remember to be disposed to believe; for these are the nerves of wisdom. Epicharmus.

It is better to live lying on the grass, confiding in divinity and yourself, than to lie on a golden bed with perturbation.

You will not be in want of any thing, which it is in the power of Fortune to give and take away.[24]

Despise all those things, which when liberated from the body you will not want; and exercising yourself in those things of which when liberated from the body you will be in want, invoke the Gods to become your helpers.[25]

Neither is it possible to conceal fire in a garment, nor a base deviation from rectitude in time.

188   Wind indeed increases fire, but custom love.[26]

Those alone are dear to divinity, who are hostile to injustice.[27]

Those things which the body necessarily requires, are easily to be procured by all men, without labor and molestation; but those things to the attainment of which labor and molestation are requisite, are objects of desire, not to the body, but to depraved opinion. Aristoxenus Pythag. Stob. p. 132.

Of desire also, he [*i.e.* Pythagoras] said as follows: This passion is various, laborious, and very multiform. Of desires however, some are acquired and adventitious, but others are connascent. But he defined desire itself to be a certain tendency and impulse of the soul, and an appetite of a plenitude or presence of sense, or of an emptiness and absence of it, and of non-perception. He also said, that there are three most known species of erroneous and depraved desire, *viz.* the indecorous, the incommensurate, and the unseasonable. For desire is either immediately indecorous, troublesome, and illiberal; or it is not absolutely so, but is more vehement and lasting than is fit. Or in the third place, it is impelled when it is not proper, and to objects to which it ought not to tend. Ex Aristoxeni Pythag. Sententiis. Stob. p. 132.

Endeavour not to conceal your errors by words, but to remedy them by reproofs. Pythagoras. Stob. p. 146.

It is not so difficult to err, as not to reprove him who errs. Pythagoras. Stob. p. 147.

As a bodily disease cannot be healed, if it is concealed, or praised; thus also, neither can a remedy be applied to a diseased soul, which is badly guarded and protected. Pythagoras. Stob. p. 147·

The grace of freedom of speech, like beauty in season, is productive of greater delight. *189*

It is not proper either to have a blunt sword, or to use freedom of speech ineffectually.

Neither is the sun to be taken from the world, nor freedom of speech from erudition.

As it is possible for one who is clothed with a sordid robe, to have a good habit of body; thus also he whose life is poor may possess freedom of speech.[28]

Be rather delighted with those that reprove, than with those that flatter you; but avoid flatterers, as worse than enemies. Pythagoras. Stob. p. 149.

The life of the avaricious resembles a funeral banquet. For though it has all things [requisite to a feast,] yet no one present rejoices. Stob. p. 155.[29]

Acquire continence as the greatest strength and wealth. Pythagoras. Stob. p. 156.

"Not frequently man from man," is one of the exhortations of Pythagoras; by which he obscurely signifies, that it is not proper to be frequently engaged in venereal connexions. Stob. p. 156.

It is impossible that he can be free who is a slave to his passions. Pythagoras. Stob. p. 165.

Pythagoras said, that intoxication is the meditation of insanity. Stob. p. 165.

Pythagoras being asked, how a lover of wine might be cured of intoxication, answered, if he frequently surveys what his actions were when he was intoxicated. Stob. p. 165.

190   Pythagoras said, that it was either requisite to be silent, or to say something better than silence. Stob. p. 215.

Let it be more eligible to you to throw a stone in vain, than to utter an idle word. Pythagoras. Stob. p. 215.

Do not say a few things in many words, but much in a few words. Pythagoras. Stob. p. 216.

Genius is to men either a good or an evil dæmon. Epicharmus. Stob. p. 220.

Pythagoras being asked, how a man ought to conduct himself towards his country, when it had acted iniquitously with respect to him, replied, as to a mother. Stob. p. 227.

Travelling teaches a man frugality, and the way in which he may be sufficient to himself. For bread made of milk and flour, and a bed of grass, are the sweetest remedies of hunger and labor.

To the wise man every land is eligible as a place of residence; for the whole world is the country of the worthy soul.[30] Stob. p. 231.

Pythagoras said, that luxury entered into cities in the first place, afterwards satiety, then lascivious insolence, and after all these destruction. Stob. p. 247.

Pythagoras said, that of cities that was the best, which contained worthy men. Stob. p. 247.

Do those things which you judge to be beautiful, though in doing them you should be without renown. For the rabble is a bad judge of a good thing. [Despise therefore the reprehension of those whose praise you despise.] Demophilus. Stob. p. 310.[31]

Those that do not punish bad men, wish that good men may be injured. Pythagoras. Stab. p. 321.

191   It is not possible for a horse to be governed without a bridle, or riches without prudence. Pythagoras. Stob. p. 513.

It is the same thing to think greatly of yourself in prosperity, as to contend in the race in a slippery road. Stob. p. 563.

There is not any gate of wealth so secure, which the opportunity of Fortune may not open. Stob. p. 563.[32]

Expel by reasoning the unrestrained grief of a torpid soul. Stob. p. 572.

It is the province of a wise man to bear poverty with equanimity. Stob. p. 572.[33]

Spare your life, lest you consume it with sorrow and care. Pythagoras. Stob. p. 616.

Nor will I be silent as to this particular, that it appeared both to Plato and Pythagoras, that old age was not to be considered with reference to an egress from the present life, but to the beginning of a blessed life. From Phavorinus on Old Age. Stob. p. 585.

The two following extracts are from Clemens Alexandrinus in Stromat. lib. 3. p. 413.

The ancient theologists and priests testify that the soul is conjoined to the body through a certain punishment, and that it is buried in this body as in a sepulchre. Philolaus.

Whatever we see when awake, is death; and when asleep, a dream. Pythagoras.

PYTHAGORIC SENTENCES,

FROM THE

PROTREPTICS OF IAMBLICHUS.[34]

As we live through soul, it must be said that by the virtue of this we live well; just as because we see through the eyes, we see well through the virtue of these.

It must not be thought that gold can be injured by rust, or virtue by baseness.

We should betake ourselves to virtue as to an inviolable temple, in order that we may not be exposed to any ignoble insolence of soul with respect to our communion with, and continuance in life.

We should confide in Virtue as in a chaste wife; but trust to Fortune as to an inconstant mistress.

It is better that virtue should be received accompanied with poverty, than wealth with violence; and frugality with health, than veracity with disease.

An abundance of nutriment is noxious to the body; but the body is preserved when the soul is disposed in a becoming manner.

It is equally dangerous to give a sword to a madman, and power to a depraved man.

As it is better for a part of the body which contains purulent matter to be burnt, than to continue in the state in which it is, thus also it is better for a depraved man to die than to live.

The theorems of philosophy are to be enjoyed as much as possible, as if they were ambrosia and nectar. For the pleasure arising from them is genuine, incorruptible, and divine. They are also capable of producing magnanimity; and though they cannot make us eternal beings, yet they enable us to obtain a scientific knowledge of eternal natures.

If vigor of sensation is considered by us to be an eligible thing, we should much more strenuously endeavour to obtain prudence; for it is as it were the sensitive vigor of the practical intellect which we contain. And as through the former we are not deceived in sensible perceptions, so through the latter we avoid false reasoning in practical affairs.

We shall venerate Divinity in a proper manner, if we render the intellect that is in us pure from all vice, as from a certain stain.

A temple, indeed, should be adorned with gifts, but the soul with disciplines.

As the lesser mysteries are to be delivered before the greater, thus also discipline must precede philosophy.

The fruits of the earth, indeed, are annually imparted, but the fruits of philosophy at every part of the year.

As land is especially to be attended to by him who wishes to obtain from it the most excellent fruit, thus also the greatest attention should be paid to the soul, in order that it may produce fruit worthy of its nature.

Notes

Introduction

1. Οἶδα μέν οὖν καί Πλάτωνα τὸν μέγαν, καί μετά τουτόν ἀνδρα τοις χρόνοις μέν, οὐ τῇ μήν φύσει, καταδεεστέρον, τὸν Χαλκιδέα φημι τὸν Ἰαμβλιχον, κ. λ. Julian. Orat. IV.

Thus too the celebrated Bullialdus, in his Notes on Theo of Smyrna, speaks of Iamblichus as a man of a most acute genius.

2. [See: Thomas Taylor, *The Philosophical and Mathematical Commentaries of Proclus on the First Book of Euclid's Elements, and his Life by Marinus. With a preliminary Dissertation on the Platonic Doctrine of Ideas. To which are added A History of the Restoration of the Platonic Theology by the later Platonists*, 2 vols. (1792)]

3. There is a Greek and Latin edition of this admirable work by Gale, under the title of Iamblichus De Mysteriis.

[See also Taylor's translation of the same work, completed 3 years after the present work, titled: *Iamblichus on the Mysteries of the Egyptians, Chaldeans, and Assyrians* (1821)]

4. Ἀλλά καί τὸ της λέξεως κομμάτικον, καί ἀφοριστικόν, καί τό τῶν ἔννοιων πραγματικόν, καί γλαφυρόν, καί ἔνθουν, κ. λ. See the Testimonies prefixed by Gale to his edition of the above-mentioned work.

5. This Sopater succeeded Plotinus in his philosophical school.

6. The exact time of Iamblichus' death is unknown. It is however certain that it was during the reign of Constantine; and according to the accurate Fabricius, prior to the year of Christ 333. Vid. Biblioth. Græc. Tom. IV. p. 283.

7. This Sextus is probably the same that Seneca so greatly extols, and from whom he derives many of those admirable sentences with which his works abound. Vid. Senecæ Epistolas, 59, 64, 98, et lib. 2 de Irâ, c. 36, et lib. 3. c. 36.

8. All these were published in one vol. 12mo. by Mr. Bridgman, under the title of *Translations from the Greek*, in the year 1804, and well deserve to be perused by the liberal reader. [see the Appendix in the present work]

Life of Pythagoras

1. *i.e.* Having black leaves.

2. *i.e.* It must not be admitted, that Apollo was actually connected with Pythaïs; for this would be absurd in the extreme; but the assertion of Epimenides, Eudoxus, and Xenocrates must be considered as one of those mythological narrations in which heroes are said to have Gods for their fathers, or Goddesses for their mothers, and the true meaning of it is as

follows: According to the ancient theology, between those perpetual attendants of a divine nature called *essential* heroes, who are impassive and pure, and the bulk of human souls who descend to earth with passivity and impurity, it is necessary there should be an order of human souls who descend with impassivity and purity. For as there is no vacuum either in incorporeal or corporeal natures, it is necessary that the last link of a superior order, should coalesce with the summit of one proximately inferior. These souls were called by the ancients, *terrestrial* heroes, on account of their high degree of proximity and alliance to such as are essentially heroes. Hercules, Theseus, Pythagoras, Plato, etc. were souls of this kind, who descended into mortality both to benefit other souls, and in compliance with that necessity by which all natures inferior to the perpetual attendants of the Gods are at times obliged to descend.

But as, according to the arcana of ancient theology, every God beginning from on high produces his proper series as far as to the last of things, and this series comprehends many essences different from each other, such as Dæmoniacal, Heroical, Nymphical, and the like; the lowest powers of these orders, have a great communion and physical sympathy with the human race, and contribute to the perfection of all their natural operations, and particularly to their procreations.

"Hence," says Proclus in MSS. Schol. in Crat., "it often appears, that *heroes* are generated from the mixture of these powers with mankind; for those that possess a certain prerogative above human nature, are properly denominated *heroes*."

He adds:

"Not only a dæmoniacal genus of this kind sympathizes physically with men, but other kinds sympathize with other natures, as Nymphs with trees, others with fountains, and others with stags or serpents."

Olympiodorus, in his Life of Plato, observes of that philosopher, that:

"an Apolloniacal spectre is said to have had connexion with Perictione his mother, and that appearing in the night to his father Aristo, it commanded him not to sleep with Perictione during the time of her pregnancy; which mandate Aristo obeyed."

The like account of the divine origin of Plato, is also given by Apuleius, Plutarch, and Hesychius.

3. *i.e.* The priests of Jupiter.

4. From what has been said in the note, p. 3, respecting the divine origin of Pythagoras, it follows that he was a *terrestrial hero* belonging to the series of Apollo. Thus too the Esculapius who once lived on the earth, and was the inventor of medicine, proceeded, according to the ancient mythology, from

the God Esculapius, who subsists in Apollo, just as the hero Bacchus proceeded from the Bacchus who subsists in Jupiter. Hence the Emperor Julian (apud Cyril.) says of Esculapius:

"I had almost forgotten the greatest of the gifts of Jupiter and the Sun, but I have very properly reserved it to the last. For it is not peculiar to us only, but is common also, I think, to our kindred the Greeks. For Jupiter, in intelligibles, generated from himself Esculapius; but he was unfolded into light on the earth, through the prolific light of the sun. He therefore, proceeding from heaven to the earth, appeared uniformly in a human shape about Epidaurus. But thence becoming multiplied in his progressions, he extended his saving right hand to all the earth. He came to Pergamus, to Ionia, to Tarentum, and afterwards to Rome. Thence he went to the island Co, afterwards to Ægas, and at length to wherever there is land and sea. Nor did we individually, but collectively, experience his beneficence. And at one and the same time, he corrected souls that were wandering in error, and bodies that were infirm."

5. Those Gods, according to the Orphic theology, that contain in themselves the first principle of stability, sameness, and being, and who also were the suppliers of conversion to all things, are of a male characteristic; but those that are the causes of all-various progressions, separations, and measures of life, are of a feminine peculiarity.

6. This inventor of names was called by the Egyptians Theuth, as we are informed by Plato in the Philebus and Phædrus; in the latter of which dialogues, Socrates says:

"I have heard, that about Naucratis in Egypt, there was one of the ancient Gods of the Egyptians, to whom a bird was sacred, which they call Ibis; but the name of the dæmon himself was Theuth. According to tradition, this God first discovered number and the art of reckoning, geometry and astronomy, the games of chess and hazard, and likewise letters."

On this passage I observe as follows, in Vol. 3 of my translation of Plato: The genus of disciplines belonging to Mercury, contains gymnastic, music, arithmetic, geometry, astronomy, and the art of speaking and writing, This God, as he is the source of invention, is called the son of Maia; because *investigation*, which is implied by *Maia*, produces *invention:* and as unfolding the will of Jupiter, who is an intellectual God, he is the cause of mathesis or discipline. He first subsists in Jupiter, the artificer of the world; next among the supermundane Gods; in the third place, among the liberated Gods; fourthly, in the planet Mercury; fifthly, in the Mercurial order of dæmons; sixthly, in human souls, who are the attendants of this God; and in the seventh degree, his properties subsist in certain animals, such as the ibis, the ape, and sagacious dogs. The narration of Socrates in this place, is both allegorical and anagogic or reductory. Naucratis is a region of Egypt eminently subject to the influence of Mercury, though the whole of Egypt is allotted to this divinity. Likewise, in this city a man once flourished full of the Mercurial power, because his soul formerly existed in the heavens of the Mercurial order. But he was first called Theuth, that is, Mercury, and a God, because his soul subsisted according to the perfect similitude of this divinity. But afterwards a dæmon, because from the God Mercury, through a Mercurial dæmon, gifts of this kind are transmitted to a Mercurial soul.

7. Iamblichus derived this very beautiful passage from Heraclides Ponticus, as is evident from Cicero, Tusc. Quæst. lib. v. 3. who relates the same thing of Pythagoras, from the aforesaid author.

8. *i.e.* With intelligibles properly so called.

9. Iliad, lib. 17. The translation by Pope.

10. "The Pythagoreans," says Simplicius, in his Commentary on the 2nd book of Aristotle's treatise *On the Heavens*, "said, that an harmonic sound was produced from the motion of the celestial bodies, and they scientifically collected this from the analogy of their intervals; since not only the ratios of the sun and moon, of Venus and Mercury, but also of the other stars, were discovered by them."

Simplicius adds:

"Perhaps the objection of Aristotle to this assertion of the Pythagoreans, may be solved according to the philosophy of those men, as follows: All things are not commensurate with each other, nor is every thing sensible to every thing, even in the sublunary region. This is evident from dogs who scent animals at a great distance, and which are not smelt by men. How much more, therefore, in things which are separated by so great an interval as those which are incorruptible from the corruptible, and celestial from terrestrial natures, is it true to say, that the sound of divine bodies is not audible by terrestrial ears? But if any one like Pythagoras, who is reported to have heard this harmony, should have his terrestrial body exempt from him, and his luminous and celestial vehicle* and the senses which it contains purified, either through a good allotment, or through probity of life, or through a perfection arising from sacred operations, such a one will perceive things invisible to others, and will hear things inaudible by others. With respect to divine and immaterial bodies, however, if any sound is produced by them, it is neither percussive nor destructive, but it excites the powers and energies of sublunary sounds, and perfects the sense which is co-ordinate with them. It has also a certain analogy to the sound which concurs with the motion of terrestrial bodies. But the sound which is with us in consequence of the sonorific nature of the air, is a certain energy of the motion of their impassive sound. If, then, air is not passive there, it is evident that neither will the sound which is there be passive. Pythagoras, however, seems to have said that he heard the celestial harmony, as understanding the harmonic proportions in numbers, of the heavenly bodies, and that which is audible in them. Some one, however, may very properly doubt why the stars are seen by our visive sense, but the sound of them is not heard by our ears? To this we reply that neither do we see the stars themselves; for we do not see their magnitudes, or their figures, or their surpassing beauty. Neither do we see the motion through which the sound is produced; but we see as it were such an illumination of them, as that of the light of the sun about the earth, the sun himself not being seen by us. Perhaps too, neither will it be wonderful, that the visive sense, as being more immaterial, subsisting rather according to energy than according to passion, and very much transcending the other senses, should be thought worthy to receive the splendor and illumination of the celestial bodies, but that the other senses should not be adapted for this purpose. Of these, however, and such like particulars, if any one can assign more probable causes, let him be considered as a friend, and not as an enemy."

---

* The soul has three vehicles, one etherial, another aerial, and the third this terrestrial body. The first, which is luminous and celestial, is connate with the essence of the soul, and in which alone it resides in a state of bliss in the stars. In the second, it suffers the punishment of its sins after death. And from the third it becomes an inhabitant of earth.

11. *i.e.* Of the discursive energy of reason, or that part of the soul that reasons scientifically, deriving the principles of its reasoning from intellect.

12. Kuster, one of the editors of this Life of Pythagoras, not perceiving that these auditions are both questions and answers, has made them to be questions only, and in consequence of this was completely at a loss to conceive the meaning of ὅπερ ἐστὶν ἡ ἁρμονία, ἐν ᾗ αἱ Σειρῆνες. Hence, he thinks it should be, τι ἐστὶν ἡ ἁρμονία ἡ ἧδον αἱ Σειρῆνες; but is not satisfied with this reading after all. Something I have no doubt is wanting; but the sense of the passage is, I conceive, that which is given in the above translation.

13. "Pythagoras," says Proclus in MSS. Schol. in Cratylum, "being asked what was the wisest of things, said it was number; and being asked what was the next in wisdom, said, he who gave names to things. But by number, he obscurely signified the intelligible order, which comprehends the multitude of intellectual forms: for there that which is the first, and properly number, subsists after the superessential one.*

This likewise supplies the measures of essence to all beings, in which also true wisdom, and knowledge which is of itself, and which is converted to and perfects itself, subsist. And as there the intelligible, intellect, and intelligence, are the same, so there also number and wisdom are the same. But by the founder of names, he obscurely signified the soul, which indeed subsists from intellect, and is not things themselves like the first intellect, but possesses the images and essential transitive reasons of them as statues of beings. Being, therefore, is imparted to all things from intellect, which knows itself and is replete with wisdom; but that they are denominated is from soul, which imitates intellect. Pythagoras therefore said, that it was not the business of any casual person to fabricate names, but of one looking to intellect and the nature of things."

---

* *i.e.* Number according to cause, which subsists at the extremity of the intelligible order. For number according to hyparxis or essence, subsists at the summit of the order which is intelligible and at the same time intellectual. See the 3rd book of my translation of Proclus on the Theology of Plato.

14. The words περὶ πυθαγόρειων are omitted in the original, but from the Protrept. of Iamblichus evidently ought to be inserted.

15. The same thing is said by the Pythagoreans to have befallen the person who first divulged the theory of incommensurable quantities. See the first scholium on the 10th book of Euclid's Elements, in Commandine's edition, fol. 1572.

16. Iamblichus, in this list of Pythagoreans, must not be supposed to enumerate those only who were contemporary with Pythagoras: since, if he did, he contradicts what he says of Philolaus in Chap. 31, *viz.* that "he was many ages posterior to Pythagoras"; but those in general who came from the school of Pythagoras, and were his most celebrated disciples.

17. From this passage it is evident that Iamblichus had many sources of information, which are unknown to modern critics; and this circumstance alone ought to check their pedagogical impertinence.

18. For αυτα here I read, conformably to the version of Obrechtus, αλλα.

19. For δῆγμους here, I read ὀδυρμους; as I do not see what morsus has to do with this place. Obrechtus has in his version "pectorisque morsus"; but I have no doubt *lamentations* is the proper word, which aptly associates with despondency.

20. "Well-instituted polities," says Proclus in MS. Comment. in Alcibiad. Prior., "are averse to the art of playing on wind-instruments; and

therefore neither does Plato admit it. The cause of this is the variety of this instrument, the pipe, which shows that the art which uses it should be avoided. For instruments called Panarmonia, and those consisting of many strings, are imitations of pipes. For every hole of the pipe emits, as they say, three sounds at least; but if the cavity above the holes be opened, then each hole will emit more than three sounds."

21. Odyss. lib. 4.

22. Iamblichus derived what he has said in this chapter about music, from Nicomachus.

23. The first part of this sentence in the original is ξένου τινὸς ἐκβεβληκότος ἐν ᾿Ασκληπιείῳ Ζώνην χρυσίον ἐχουσαν, and in translating it I have followed the version of Obrechtus, because it appeared to me to convey the meaning of Iamblichus, though the translation is certainly forced, and not such as the natural construction of the words will admit. The translation of Arcerius is, "Cum hospes quidam in æde Æsculapii fœminam zonam auream habentem ejecisset"; and this is perfectly conformable to the natural construction of the words, but then it is void of sense.

24. This history is copiously narrated in chap. 33.

25. See chap. 33.

26. These lines are as the numbers 4, 3, 2. For 4 to 3 is sesquitertian, 3 to 2 is sesquialter, and 2 is an arithmetical medium between 4 and 3.

27. For an explanation of this assertion of Plato in the Republic, see my Theoretic Arithmetic [1816].

28. "The Pythagoreans," says Syrianus in Aristot. Metaphys. Lib. 13., "received from the theology of Orpheus, the principles of intelligible and intellectual numbers, they assigned them an abundant progression, and extended their dominion as far as to sensibles themselves. Hence that proverb was peculiar to the Pythagoreans, that *all things are assimilated to number.* Pythagoras, therefore, in THE SACRED DISCOURSE, clearly says, that 'number is the ruler of forms and ideas, and is the cause of Gods and dæmons.' He also supposes, that 'to the most ancient and artificially ruling deity, number is the canon, the artificial reason, the intellect also, and the most undeviating balance of the composition and generation of all things.'"

Αὐτός μέν Πυθᾰγόρας, ἐν τῷ ἱερῳ λογῳ, διαρρήδην μορφῶν καί ἰδέων κράντορα τόν ἀριθμόν ἔλεγεν ἐιναι, καί θέων καί διαμόνων ἄιτιον· καί τῷ πρέσβυτατῳ καί κρατιστεύοντι τέχνιτῃ θέῳ κανονα, καί λογον τεχνικόν, νουν τε καί σταθμάν ἀκλῖνέστατᾰν τόν ἀριθμόν ὑπεικε συστάσιος καί γενέσεως τῶν πάντων.

Syrianus adds:

"But Philolaus declared that number is the governing and self-begotten bond of the eternal permanency of mundane natures."

Φιλόλαυς δε, τῆς τῶς κοσμικῶν ἀιωνιας διαμόνης τῆς κρατιστεύουσαν καί αὐτογενή συοχην ἐιναι ἀπεφηνατο τόν ἀριθμόν.

"And Hippasus, and all those who were destined to a quinquennial silence, called number the judicial instrument of the maker of the universe, and the first paradigm of mundane fabrication."

ὁι δε πέρα Ἱππασον ἀκουσματικόι ἐιπον κρῐτῐκόν κοσμουργόυ θέου ὄργᾰνον, καί παράδειγμα πρωτόν κοσμοποιΐας.

"But how is it possible they could have spoken thus sublimely of number, unless they had considered it as possessing an essence separate from sensibles, and a transcendency fabricative, and at the same time paradigmatic?"

29. *i.e.* To spheres; Iamblichus indicating by this, that Pythagoras as well as Orpheus considered a spherical figure as the most appropriate image of divinity. For the universe is spherical; and, as Iamblichus afterwards observes, the Gods have a nature and *morphe* similar to the universe; *morphe*, as we learn from Simplicius, pertaining to the color, figure, and magnitude of superficies. Kiessling, having no conception of this meaning, and supposing the whole passage to be corrupt, has made nonsense of it by his alterations. For according to his version, Pythagoras, after the manner of Orpheus, worshipped the Gods not bound to a human form, but *to divine numbers*. For instead of ἱδρυμασι he reads ἀριθμοις. But divine numbers both according to Orpheus and Pythagoras are the Gods themselves.

30. *i.e.* Futurity is long; Pythagoras signifying by this, that those who do not take an oath religiously, will be punished in some future period, if they are not at present.

31. *i.e.* From the time in which the Gods are fabulously said to have reigned in Egypt.

32. I wonder that the learned Obrechtus should translate ἡβηδὸν, *cum omni juventute sua*. Had his translation, which is on the whole very excellent, been reviewed by English or Scotch critics, they would have immediately said from this circumstance, that he did not understand Greek.

33. Iamblichus here alludes to a right-angled triangle, and the Pythagoric theorem of 47. 1 of Euclid. For the square described on the longest side is equal to the two squares described on the two other sides. The longest side therefore is said by geometricians to be equal in power to the powers of the other sides. This however Kiessling not understanding, says that:

"power is the space contained between the concurring lines of figures, and is the area of the triangle."

"Δύναμις idem est, quod ἐμβαδον, spatium, quod intra concurrentes lineas figurarum continetur, area trigoni."

But Kiessling, though a good verbalist, is a bad geometrician, and no philosopher.

34. In the original, δέκατον, *the tenth month;* but as it very seldom happens that a woman is in a state of pregnancy more than nine months, it appears to me that for δέκατον we should read ἑκτον the sixth month, as in the above translation.

35. Obrechtus by translating περὶ δὲ δόξης in this place, "De fama et gloria," has evidently mistaken the meaning of Iamblichus.

36. The wise and magnanimous Pythagoreans, Platonists, Peripatetics and Stoics, among the ancients, looked to virtue as its own reward, and performed what is right, because it is right to do so. And though they firmly believed in the immortality of the soul, their conduct was not at all influenced by the hope of future reward. This great truth indeed, that virtue brings with it its own recompense, is almost at present obsolete; and it is no unusual thing to hear a man, when afflicted, exclaiming with Methodistical cant,

> "The many troubles that I meet,
> In getting to a Mercy-seat!"

37. These energies are called beneficent, because they are of a purifying character. Hence Plato in the Timæus says, that a deluge is the consequence of the Gods *purifying* the earth by water.

38. Iamblichus a little before informs us, that Pythagoras suspected that Phalaris intended to put him to death, but at the same time knew that he was not destined to die by Phalaris. This being the case therefore, Pythagoras has no claim to fortitude in this instance, in being free from the fear of death. But he has great claim to it, when it is considered that he was in the power of a tyrant who might have caused him to suffer tortures worse than death.

39. *i.e. Humble* (τᾰπεινῆς οὐσης). With the Pythagoreans, therefore, humility was no virtue, though in modern times it is considered to be the greatest of the virtues. With Aristotle likewise it is no virtue: for in his Nicomachean Ethics he says, that "all humble men are flatterers, and all flatterers are humble."

40. See the Cave of Plato, in the 7th book of his Republic.

41. The original is, Μητρόδωρός τε ὁ Θύρσου τοῦ πατρὸς Ἐπιχάρμου, which Obrechtus erroneously translates, "Metrodorus Epicharmi filius Thyrsi nepos."

42. This observation applies also to those of the present day, who, from a profound ignorance of human nature, attempt to enlighten by education the lowest class of mankind. For this, as I have elsewhere observed, is an attempt to break the golden chain of beings, to disorganise society, and to render the vulgar dissatisfied with the servile situations in which God and nature

intended them to be placed. See p. 73 of the introduction to my translation of Select Works of Plotinus.

43. This also is asserted, as I have before observed, in the Scholia on the 10th book of Commandine's edition of Euclid's Elements, p. 122.

44. Obrechtus has omitted to translate the words ἤδη πρεσβύτην ὄντα, "being now an elderly man."

45. In the original, ἄκρατος, which Obrechtus very erroneously translates *impotens*.

46. *i.e.* To the Pythagoreans.

47. The whole of this paragraph, the greater part of which is a repetition of what has been said elsewhere, does not certainly belong to this place.

48. In the original, καὶ τὴν γην ἀνάδαστον ἐποίησαν, which Obrechtus erroneously translates, "et agrorum divisionem introduxerunt."

49. The words within the brackets are from a Latin Manuscript, which was in the possession of Fabricius.

Ethical Fragments

1. In the original οὐδέν γάρ αὐτάρκες, ο τουτῶν τῶν μορίων ποιεῖ τὸ ὅλον. This Canter erroneously translates, "Quandoquidem horum nulla pars totum queat constituere." And Gale has not noticed the error.

2. Gale says in his notes, that after ὀφθαλμῶν he adds φύσιος, but he should evidently have added ἀρετα, as in the above translation.

3. In the original σύν τα ὀξυδορκία, which Canter very defectively translates, *videndi facultate*.

4. For ου μετρίαν here, I read ἀσυμμετρίαν.

5. *i.e.* So far as he is considered as energizing in conjunction with the body; but so far as he has an energy independent of the body, *viz.* so far as he is a rational soul, the body is not to be considered as a part of his essence. And the energy of the rational soul by itself alone, without any assistance from the corporeal organs, constitutes the true man, into the definition of which body does not enter.

6. Canter, in his version of these Pythagoric fragments, uniformly translates εὐτύχια *felicitas*, contrary to the obvious meaning of the word, as is evident in this, and many other passages. It is also directly contrary to what Aristotle says in cap. 13. lib. 7. of his Nicomachean Ethics:

δια δε το προσδεισθαι της τυχης, δοκει τισι ταυτον ειναι η ευτυχια τη ευδαιμονια, ουκ ουσα· επει και αυτη υπερβαλλουσα, εμποδιος εστι.

i.e. "Because felicity requires fortune, it appears to some persons that prosperity is the same with felicity. This however is not the case; since

prosperity, when it is excessive, is an impediment to felicity."
But Canter did not, I believe, pretend to have any knowledge of philosophy: and Gale, who did, has not corrected him in this and many other places in which he has erred through the want of this knowledge. Gale however, though verbally learned, was but a garrulous smatterer in philosophy, as is evident from his notes on Iamblichus de Mysteriis.

7. For ἐπιπρέπειαν here, I read ἀπρέπειαν.

8. In the original: ὥστε οὐδέποκα δεῖ θαύμαινεν, εἰ παντ' ἀντεστραμμένως ἐνιόκα κρίνεται, τὰς ἀληθινας διαθέσιος μεταπίπτοισας, which Canter erroneously translates as follows: "Quocirca mirandum non est, si cuncta nonnunquam, verâ affectione mutatâ, aliter eveniunt." Nor is the error noticed by Gale.

9. *i.e.* In the etherial vehicle of the soul, which when the soul energizes intellectually is spherical, and is moved circularly. This vehicle also is αὐγοειδής, or luciform, throughout diaphanous, and of a star-like nature. Hence Marcus Antoninus beautifully observes:

σφαῖρα ψυχῆς αὐτοειδής, (lege αὐγοειδής) ὅταν μήτε ἐκτείνηται ἐπι τι, μήτε ἔσω συντρέχῃ μήτε συνιζάνῃ, ἀλλά φῶτι λαμπήται, ᾧ τὴν ἀλήθειαν ὁρᾷ τὴν πάντων, καὶ τὴν ἐν αὐτῃ. Lib. II.

i.e. The sphere of the soul is then luciform, when the soul is neither extended to anything [external] nor inwardly concurs with it, nor is depressed by it, but is illuminated with a light by which she sees the truth of all things, and the truth that is in herself."

10. M. Meibomius observes, that Canter did not see that λογιστικω should be written in this place for ἄλογω. Canter however was right in retaining ἀλογω. For the dianoetic is the same with the logistic part of the soul; and it is evident that a part of the soul different from the dianoetic is here intended to be signified. Besides, as Aristotle shows in his Nicomachean Ethics, when the irrational becomes obedient to the rational part of the soul, the former then prohibits and vanquishes base appetites in conjunction with the latter.

11. *viz.* Such as have the theoretic virtues.

12. *i.e.* Such as have the ethical and political virtues.

13. The original is, ἁ δὲ δύναμις, οἷον ἀλκά τις τω σκάνεος ᾇ ὑφιστάμεθα, καὶ ἐμμένομες τοῖς πράγμασιν. This sentence in its present state is certainly unintelligible. For σκάνεος therefore, I read φύσεως, and then the sense will be as in the above translation. The version of Canter is certainly absurd; for it is "Facultas tanquam robur et causæ, quo ferimus, et in rebus permanemus." And Gale, as usual, takes no notice of the absurdity.

14. *viz.* The equal and that which is arranged, belong to the order of bound, and the unequal and that which is without arrangement, to the order of

infinity. And bound and infinity are the two great principles of things after the ineffable cause of all. See the third book of my translation of Proclus, *On the Theology of Plato*.

15. *viz*. The salvation of the universe arises from the co-adaptation of the sublunary region to the heavens.

16. In the Greek ἐπῳδὰς; on which Gale observes, "Forte ἀμᾶθίας nisi aliud subsit mysterium." But it appears to me that there is no occasion to substitute any other word for ἐπῳδὰς. For in the education of youth, it is certainly requisite to unite allurement with erudition. And the substitution of ἀμᾶθίας, *ignorance*, is monstrous.

17. In the original αὐτὰ γὰρ ἁ διενεργῦσα, instead of which Gale proposes to read αὐτὰ γὰρ ἁδε ἐνεργοισα, which still leaves the sentence involved in obscurity. But if for διενεργῦσα we read διοριζοῦσα as in the above translation, the meaning is clear.

18. For νοῆται in this place, I read φυεται.

19. Neither of the Latin translators North and Arcerius have understood this passage, and therefore have erroneously translated it. For the original is:

καί πάντα τὰ ἐν τᾳ συστοιχείᾳ καὶ τάξει τα ἐκείνου κατακεχωρισμένα.

This North translates:

"Atque omnia in rerum serie et ordine ab illo separata."

But Arcerius:

"Atque omnia quæ sunt in naturæ cognatione ordineque ab illo separata."

By the things however co-ordinate with, and successive to God, Archytas means the other Gods, who, though subordinate to the supreme, yet in consequence of partaking of the same nature, are said to be co-ordinate with him. Gale, likewise, did not perceive the error of the Latin translators.

20. Plato says this of God in his Laws.

21. The above sentences are from Stobæi Sententiæ, p. 3. (the edition that of 1609,) and are ascribed to Pythagoras.

22. The above seven sentences are to be found in p. 4. of Stobæus, and as it appears to me are erroneously ascribed to Socrates. For I conceive them to have been written either by Democrates or Demophilus.

23. Stob. p. 48.

24. Hence the dogma of the Stoics derived its origin, that the wise man is independent of Fortune.

25. Stob. p. 65. These three sentences are ascribed to Pythagoras.

26. Stob. p. 80. These two sentences are ascribed to Socrates, but I have no doubt originally formed a part of the sentences of Demophilus.

27. Stob. p. 104. This sentence is ascribed to Democritus in Stobæus, but has doubtless either Democrates or Demophilus for its author.

28. Stob. p. 147. The above four sentences, are in Stobæus ascribed to Socrates; but I refer them either to Democrates or Demophilus.

29. This sentence in Stobæus is ascribed to Socrates, as is also the one which immediately precedes it, *viz.* "The wealth of the avaricious man, like the sun descending under the earth, delights no living thing." But as this sentence is to be found among the Similitudes of Demophilus, there can be no doubt of the other belonging to the same work.

30. This and the preceding sentence, are in Stobæus ascribed to Democritus, but I attribute them to Democrates or Demophilus.

31. This sentence in Stobæus is ascribed to Pythagoras, but, excepting the part within the brackets, is to be found among the sentences of Demophilus.

32. This sentence in Stobæus, is ascribed to Democritus, and that immediately preceding it, to Socrates; but I ascribe both of them to Democrates, or Demophilus.

33. This and the preceding sentences, together with two other sentences that accompany them, are in Stobæus ascribed to Democritus; but as the other two are to be found in the Collection of Democrates, there can be no doubt that all of them are from the same author.

34. Several of these sentences as published by Arcerius, are in a very defective state; but which, as the learned reader will perceive, I have endeavoured to amend in my translation of them.

Additional Notes.

P. 28. Better worth saving than ten thousand corporeal eyes.

Iamblichus here alludes to what Plato says in the seventh book of his Republic, respecting the mathematical disciplines. For he there says that:

> "the soul through these disciplines has an organ purified and enlightened, which is blinded and buried by studies of another kind, an organ better worth saving than ten thousand eyes, since truth becomes visible through this alone."

P. 33. That in which the Sirens subsist.

> "The divine Plato," says Proclus in his MS. Scholia on the Cratylus, "knew that there are three kinds of Sirens: the celestial, which is under the government of Jupiter; that which produces generation, and is under the government of Neptune; and that which is cathartic, and is under the government of Pluto. It is common to all these to incline all things through an harmonic motion to their ruling Gods. Hence, when the soul is in the heavens, the Sirens are desirous of uniting it to the divine life which flourishes there. But it is proper that souls living in generation should sail beyond them, like the Homeric Ulysses, that they may not be allured by generation, of which the sea is an image. And when souls are in Hades, the Sirens are desirous of uniting them through intellectual conceptions to Pluto. So that

204 Plato knew that in the kingdom of Hades there are Gods, dæmons, and souls, who dance as it were round Pluto, allured by the Sirens that dwell there."

See more concerning the Sirens in my translation of Proclus on the Theology of Plato, Book the 6th.

P. 34. *That it is requisite to put the shoe on the right foot first.*

This audition is taken from what forms the 12th Symbol in the Protreptics of Iamblichus, and is as follows:

"When stretching forth your feet to have your sandals put on, first extend your right foot; but when about to use a foot bath, first extend your left foot."

See the Appendix for Iamblichus' explanation of this symbol.

P. 34. *That it is not proper to walk in the public ways.*

This is the 5th Symbol in the Protreptics of Iamblichus, but is there differently expressed, for it is:

"Declining from the public ways, walk in unfrequented paths."

See the Appendix for Iamblichus' explanation of this symbol.

205 P. 34. *Do not assist a man in laying a burden down.*

This in the Protreptics is the 11th Symbol. See the Appendix for Iamblichus' explanation.

P. 34. *Do not draw near to a woman for the sake of begetting children, if she has gold.*

In the Protreptics of Iamblichus (Symbol 35) this is expressed as follows:

"Draw not near to that which has gold, in order to produce children."

See the Appendix for Iamblichus' explanation of this symbol.

P. 34. *Speak not about Pythagoric concerns without light.*   *206*

This is the 13th Symbol in the Protreptics. See the Appendix for Iamblichus' explanation.

P. 34. *Wear not the image of God in a ring.*

This in the Protreptics is the 24th Symbol; but instead of *wear*, it is there *inscribe*. See the Appendix for Iamblichus' explanation.

P. 34. *Nor is it proper to sacrifice a white cock; for this also is a*   *207*
suppliant, and is sacred to the moon.

In the Protreptics, the 18th Symbol is partly the same with, and partly different from this. For it is:

"Nourish a cock; but sacrifice it not; for it is sacred to the sun and the moon."

See the Appendix for Iamblichus' explanation of this symbol.

P. 36. *It is proper to sacrifice, and to enter temples, unshod.*

This in the Protreptics is the 3rd Symbol; but is thus enunciated by Iamblichus:

"Sacrifice and adore unshod."

See the Appendix for Iamblichus' explanation of this symbol.

P. 43. *Enter not into a temple negligently, nor, in short, adore*   *208*
carelessly, not even though you should stand at the very doors
themselves.

This in the Protreptics is the 2nd Symbol. See the Appendix for Iamblichus' explanation.

P. 45. *These, therefore, he ordered not to eat the heart.*

This is the 30th Symbol in the Protreptics. See the Appendix for Iamblichus' explanation.

209   P. 45. *Nor the brain.*

This is the 31st Symbol in the Protreptics. See the Appendix for Iamblichus' explanation.

210   P. 45. *To abstain from mallows, etc.*

The 38th Symbol in the Protreptics is:

"Transplant mallows in your garden, but eat them not."

See the Appendix for Iamblichus' explanation of this symbol.

P. 45. *Thus too he ordered them to abstain from the fish Melanurus.*[1]

The 6th Symbol in the Protreptics is:

"Abstain from melanurus; for it belongs to the terrestrial Gods."

See the Appendix for Iamblichus' explanation of this symbol.

211   P. 45. *And also not to receive the fish Erythynus.*

This in the Protreptics is the 33rd Symbol. See the Appendix for Iamblichus' explanation.

P. 45. *He likewise exhorted them to abstain from beans.*

In the Protreptics this is the 37th Symbol; and Iamblichus has not developed for us the more mystical signification of this symbol. For he only says that: "it admonishes us to beware of every thing which is corruptive of our converse with the Gods and divine prophecy."

But Aristotle appears to have assigned the true mystical reason why the Pythagoreans abstained from beans. For he says (apud Laert.) that:

"Pythagoras considered beans as a symbol of generation [*i.e.* of the whole of a visible and corporeal nature,] which subsists according to a right line, and is without inflection; because a bean alone of almost all spermatic plants, is perforated through the whole of it, and is not obstructed by any intervening joints."

Hence he adds: "it resembles the gates of Hades."

For these are perpetually open without any impediment to souls descending into generation. The exhortation, therefore, to abstain from beans, is equivalent to admonishing us to beware of a continued and perpetual descent into the realms of generation. Hence the true meaning of the following celebrated lines in Virgil:

> —————— facilis descensus Averno.
> Noctes atque dies patet atri janua Ditis:
> Sed revocare gradum, superasque evadere ad auras,
> Hoc opus, hic labor est.

i.e.

> The gates of Hell are open night and day,
> Smooth the descent, and easy is the way;
> But to return, and view the cheerful skies,
> In this, the mighty task and labor lies.
>
> DRYDEN.

P. 55. Such as infallible predictions of earthquakes, rapid expulsions of pestilence, etc. etc.

Since Pythagoras, as Iamblichus informs us, p. 7, was initiated in all the mysteries of Byblus and Tyre, in the sacred operations of the Syrians, and in the mysteries of the Phœnicians, and also (p. 9) that he spent two and twenty years in the adyta of temples in Egypt, associated with the Magi in Babylon, and was instructed by them in their venerable knowledge;—it is not at all wonderful that he was skilled in magic or theurgy, and was therefore able to perform things which surpass *merely human power*, and which appear to be perfectly incredible to the vulgar. For "magic," as we learn from Psellus in his MS. treatise on dæmons, "formed the last part of the sacerdotal science." He farther likewise informs us, that:

> "magic investigates the nature, power, and quality of every thing sublunary; *viz.* of the elements and their parts, of animals, all-various plants, and their fruits, of stones, and herbs: and in short, it explores the essence and power of every thing. From hence, therefore, it produces its effects. And it forms statues which procure health, makes all-various figures, and things which become the instruments of disease. It asserts too, that eagles and

dragons contribute to health; but that cats, dogs, and crows, are symbols of vigilance, to which therefore they contribute. But for the fashioning of certain parts, wax and clay are used. Often, too, celestial fire is made to appear through magic; and then statues laugh, and lamps are spontaneously enkindled."

See the original in the Notes to my Pausanias, p. 325. And that theurgy was employed by the ancients in their mysteries, I have fully proved in my treatise On the Eleusinian and Bacchic Mysteries.[2]

Conformably to this, Plato also in the First Alcibiades says, that the magic of Zoroaster consisted in the worship of the Gods, on which passage, I shall present the reader with what I have said, in the first volume of my Plato, p. 63, as it will enable him to see that the theurgy of the ancients is founded in a theory equally scientific and sublime.

"The following account of magic by Proclus, originally formed, as it appears to me, a part of the Commentary written by him on the present passage. For the MS. Commentary of Proclus, which is extant on this dialogue, does not extend to more than a third part of it; and this Dissertation on Magic, which is only extant in Latin, was published by Ficinus the translator, immediately after his Excerpta from this Commentary. So that it seems highly probable, that the manuscript from which Ficinus translated his Excerpta, was much more perfect, than that which has been preserved to us, in consequence of containing this account of the magic of the ancients.

"In the same manner as lovers gradually advance from that beauty which is apparent in sensible forms, to that which is divine; so the ancient priests, when they considered that there is a certain alliance and sympathy in natural things to each other, and of things manifest to occult powers, and discovered that all things subsist in all, they fabricated a sacred science from this mutual sympathy and similarity. Thus they recognized things supreme in such as are subordinate, and the subordinate in the supreme: in the celestial regions, terrene properties subsisting in a causal and celestial manner; and in earth celestial properties, but according to a terrene condition. For how shall we account for those plants called heliotropes, that is, attendants on the sun, moving in correspondence with the revolution of its orb, but selenitropes, or attendants on the moon, turning in exact conformity to her motion? It is because all things pray, and hymn the leaders of their respective orders; but some intellectually, and others rationally; some in a natural, and others after a sensible manner. Hence the sun-flower, as far as it is able, moves in a circular dance towards the sun; so that if any one could hear the pulsation made by its circuit in the air, he would perceive something composed by a sound of this kind, in honor of its king, such as a plant is capable of framing. Hence, too, we may behold the sun and moon in the earth, but according to a terrene quality; but in the celestial regions, all plants, and stones, and animals, possessing an intellectual life according to a celestial nature. Now the ancients, having contemplated this mutual sympathy of things, applied for occult purposes, both celestial and terrene natures, by means of which, through a certain similitude, they deduced divine virtues into this inferior abode. For, indeed, similitude itself is a sufficient cause of binding things together in union and consent. Thus, if a piece of paper is heated, and afterwards placed near a lamp, though it does not touch the fire, the paper will be suddenly inflamed, and the flame will descend from the superior to the inferior parts. This heated paper we may compare to a certain relation of inferiors to superiors; and its approximation to the lamp, to the opportune use of things according to time, place, and matter. But the procession of fire into the paper, aptly represents the presence of divine light, to that nature which is capable of its reception. Lastly, the inflammation of the paper may be compared to the deification of mortals, and to the illumination of material natures, which are afterwards carried upwards like the enkindled paper, from a certain participation of divine seed.

"Again, the lotus, before the rising of the sun, folds its leaves into itself, but gradually expands them on its rising: unfolding them in proportion to the sun's ascent to the zenith; but as gradually contracting them, as that luminary descends to the west. Hence this plant, by the expansion and contraction of its leaves, appears no less to honor the sun, than men by the gesture of their eye-lids, and the motion of their lips. But this imitation and certain participation of supernal light, is not only visible in plants, which possess nothing more than a vestige of life, but likewise in particular stones. Thus the sun-stone, by its golden rays, imitates those of the sun; but the stone called the eye of heaven, or of the sun, has a figure similar to the pupil of an eye, and a ray shines from the middle of the pupil. Thus too the lunar stone, which has a figure similar to the moon when horned, by a certain change of itself, follows the lunar motion. Lastly, the stone called helioselenus, *i.e.* of the sun and moon, imitates, after a manner, the congress of those luminaries, which it images by its color. So that all things are full of divine natures; terrestrial natures receiving the plenitude of such as are celestial, but celestial of supercelestial essences;[3] while every order of things proceeds gradually in a beautiful descent from the highest to the lowest. For whatever particulars are collected into one above the order of things, are afterwards dilated in descending, various souls being distributed under their various ruling divinities.

216

"In the next place, there are many solar animals, such as lions and cocks, which participate, according to their nature, of a certain solar divinity; whence it is wonderful how much inferiors yield to superiors in the same order, though they do not yield in magnitude and power. Hence it is said, that a cock is very much feared, and as it were reverenced, by a lion; the reason of which we cannot assign from matter or sense, but from the contemplation alone of a supernal order. For thus we shall find that the presence of the solar virtue accords more with a cock than with a lion. This will be evident from considering that the cock, as it were, with certain hymns, applauds and calls to the rising sun, when he bends his course to us from the antipodes; and that solar angels sometimes appear in forms of this kind, who though they are without shape, yet present themselves to us who are connected with shape, in some sensible form. Sometimes too there are dæmons with a leonine front, who, when a cock is placed before them, unless they are of a solar order, suddenly disappear; and this, because those natures which have an inferior rank in the same order, always reverence their superiors; just as many, on beholding the images of divine men, are accustomed, from the very view, to be fearful of perpetrating any thing base.

"In fine, some things turn round correspondent to the revolutions of the sun, as the plants which we have mentioned, and others after a manner imitate the solar rays, as the palm and the date; some the fiery nature of the sun, as the laurel; and others a different property. For, indeed, we may perceive that the properties which are collected in the sun, are every where distributed to subsequent natures constituted in a solar order; that is, to angels, dæmons, souls, animals, plants, and stones. Hence the authors of the ancient priesthood discovered from things apparent, the worship of superior powers, while they mingled some things and purified others. They mingled many things indeed together, because they saw that some simple substances possessed a divine property (though not taken singly) sufficient to call down that particular power, of which they were participants. Hence, by the mingling of many things together, they attracted upon us a supernal influx; and by the composition of one thing from many, they produced an assimilation to that one which is above many; and composed statues from the mixture of various substances conspiring in sympathy and consent. Besides this, they collected composite odours, by a divine art, into one, comprehending a multitude of powers, and symbolizing with the unity of a divine essence; considering that division debilitates each of these, but that mingling them together, restores them to the idea of their exemplar. 217

"But sometimes one herb, or one stone, is sufficient to a divine operation. Thus, a thistle is sufficient to procure the sudden appearance of some superior power; but a laurel, raccinum, (or a thorny kind of sprig) the land and sea onion, the coral, the diamond, and the jasper, operate as a safeguard. The heart of a mole is subservient to divination, but sulphur and marine water to purification. Hence, the ancient priests, by the mutual relation and sympathy of things to each other, collected their virtues into one, but expelled them by repugnancy and antipathy; purifying when it was requisite with sulphur and bitumen, and sprinkling with marine water. For sulphur purifies, from the sharpness of its odour; but marine water, on account of its fiery portion. Besides this, in the worship of the Gods, they offered animals, and other substances congruous to their nature; and received, in the first place, the powers of dæmons, as proximate to natural substances and operations; and by these natural substances they convoked into their presence those powers to which they approached. Afterwards, they proceeded from dæmons to the powers and energies of the Gods; partly, indeed, from dæmoniacal instruction, but partly by their own industry, interpreting convenient symbols, and ascending to a proper 218 intelligence of the Gods. And lastly, laying aside natural substances and their operations, they received themselves into the communion and fellowship of the Gods."

It will doubtless be objected by most of the present period, who believe in nothing beyond the information of their senses, that plants, animals, and stones, no longer possess those wonderful sympathetic powers, which are mentioned by Proclus in the above extract. In answer to any such objector, whose *little* soul, (in the language of the Emperor Julian) is indeed acute, but sees nothing with a vision healthy and sound, it must be said, that this is not at all wonderful at a period, when, as the author of the Asclepian dialogue justly observes:

> "there is a lamentable departure of divinity from man, when nothing worthy of heaven, or celestial concerns, is heard or believed, and when every divine voice is by a *necessary* silence dumb."[4]

But to the philosophic reader, it must be observed, that as in the realms of generation, or in other words, the sublunary region, wholes, *viz.* the spheres of the different elements, remain perpetually according to nature; but their parts are sometimes according, and some times contrary to nature; this must also be true of the parts of the earth. When those circulations therefore take place, during which the parts of the earth subsist according to nature, and which are justly called, by Plato, fertile periods, the powers of plants, animals, and stones, magically sympathize with superior natures, in consequence of a more abundant participation of them, through a greater degree of aptitude to receive, and alliance to the participated powers. But during those circulations, in which the parts of the earth subsist contrary to nature, as at present, and which Plato calls barren periods, the powers of plants, animals, and stones, no longer possess a magic sympathy, and consequently are no longer capable of producing magical operations.

219

P. 60. *The eternal essence of number is the most providential principle of the universe, etc.*

The following account of the manner in which the Pythagoreans philosophized about numbers, is extracted from my Theoretic Arithmetic, and the information contained in it is principally derived from the great Syrianus.

"The Pythagoreans, turning from the vulgar paths, and delivering their philosophy in secret to those alone who were worthy to receive it, exhibited it to others through mathematical names. Hence, they called forms, numbers, as things which are the first separated from impartible union; for the natures which are above forms, are also above separation.[5] The all-perfect multitude of forms, therefore, they obscurely signified through the duad; but they indicated the first formal principles by the monad and duad, as not being numbers; and also by the first triad and tetrad, as being the first numbers, the one being odd, and the other even, from which by addition the decad is generated; for the sum of 1, 2, 3, and 4, is ten. But after numbers, in secondary and multifarious lives, introducing geometrical prior to physical magnitudes; these also they referred to numbers, as to formal causes and the principles of these; referring the point indeed, as being impartible, to the monad; but a line, as the first interval, to the duad; and again, a superficies, as having a more abundant interval, to the triad; and a solid to the tetrad. They also called, as is evident from the testimony of Aristotle, the first length the duad; for it is not simply length, but the *first* length, in order that by this they might signify *cause.* In a similar manner also, they denominated the *first* breadth, the triad; and the *first* depth the tetrad. They also referred to formal principles all psychical knowledge. And intellectual knowledge indeed, as being contracted according to impartible union, they referred to the monad; but scientific knowledge, as being evolved, and as proceeding from cause to the thing caused, yet through the inerratic, and always through the same things, they referred to the duad; and opinion to the triad, because the power of it is not always directed to the same thing, but at one time inclines to the true, and at another to the false. And they referred sense to the tetrad, because it has an apprehension of bodies; for in the duad, indeed, there is one interval from one monad to the other; but in the triad there are two intervals from any one monad to the rest; and in the tetrad there are three. They referred, therefore, to principles every thing knowable, *viz.* beings, and the gnostic powers of these. But they divided beings

220

not according to breadth, but according to depth; into intelligibles, objects of science, objects of opinion, and sensibles. In a similar manner, also, they divided knowledge into intellect, science, opinion, and sense. The extremity, therefore, of the intelligible triad, or animal itself, as it is called by Plato in the Timæus, is assumed from the division of the objects of knowledge, manifesting the intelligible order, in which forms themselves, *viz.* the first forms and the principles of these, are contained, *viz.* the idea of the one itself, of the first length, which is the duad itself, and also the ideas of the first breadth and the first depth; (for in common the term *first* is adapted to all of them), *viz.* to the triad itself, and the tetrad itself.

221

"Again, the Pythagoreans and Plato did not denominate idea from one thing, and ideal number from another. But since the assertion is eminently true, that all things are similar to number, it is evident that number, and especially every ideal number, was denominated on account of its paradigmatic peculiarity. If any one, however, wishes to apprehend this from the appellation itself, it is easy to infer that idea was so called, from rendering as it were its participants similar to itself, and imparting to them *form, order, beauty,* and *unity;* and this in consequence of always preserving the same form, expanding its own power to the infinity of particulars, and investing with the same species its eternal participants. *Number* also, since it imparts proportion and elegant arrangement to all things, was allotted this appellation. For the ancients, says Syrianus,[6] call to *adapt* or *compose* ἄρσαι *arsai,* whence is derived ἀριθμός *arithmos number.* Hence ἀνάρσιον *anarsion* among the Greeks signifies *incomposite.* Hence too, those Grecian sayings, *you will adapt the balance, they placed number together with them,* and also *number and friendship.* From all which number was called by the Greeks *arithmos,* as that which measures and orderly arranges all things, and unites them in amicable league.

"Farther still, some of the Pythagoreans discoursed about inseparable numbers alone, *i.e.* numbers which are inseparable from mundane natures, but others about such as have a subsistence separate from the universe, in which as paradigms they saw those numbers are contained, which are perfected by nature. But others, making a distinction between the two, unfolded their doctrine in a more clear and perfect manner. If it be requisite, however, to speak concerning the difference of these monads, and their privation of difference, we must say that the monads which subsist in quantity, are by no means to be extended to essential numbers; but when we call essential numbers monads, we must assert that all of them mutually differ from each other by *difference* itself, and that they possess a privation of difference from *sameness*. It is evident also, that those which are in the same order, are contained through mutual comparison, in *sameness* rather than in difference, but that those which are in different orders are conversant with much diversity, through the dominion of *difference*.

"Again, the Pythagoreans asserted that nature produces sensibles by numbers; but then these numbers were not mathematical but physical; and as they spoke symbolically, it is not improbable that they demonstrated every property of sensibles by mathematical names. However, says Syrianus, to ascribe to them a knowledge of sensible numbers alone, is not only ridiculous, but highly impious. For they received indeed, from the theology of Orpheus, the principles of intelligible and intellectual numbers, they assigned them an abundant progression, and extended their dominion as far as to sensibles themselves."

Again, their conceptions about mathematical and physical number, were as follow:

"As in every thing, according to the doctrine of Aristotle, one thing corresponds to matter, and another to form, in any number, as for instance the pentad, its five monads, and in short its quantity, and the number which is the subject of participation, are derived from the duad itself; but its form, *i.e.* the pentad itself, is from the monad: for every form is a monad, and unites its subject quantity. The pentad itself, therefore, which is a monad, proceeds from the principal monad, forms its subject quantity, which is itself formless, and connects it to its own form. For there are two principles of mathematical numbers in our souls: the monad, which comprehends in itself all the forms of numbers, and corresponds to the monad in intellectual natures; and the duad, which is a certain generative principle of infinite power, and which on this account, as being the image of the never-failing and intelligible duad, is called indefinite. While this proceeds to all things, it is not deserted in its course by the

222

223

monad, but that which proceeds from the monad continually distinguishes and forms boundless quantity, gives a specific distinction to all its orderly progressions, and incessantly adorns them with forms. And as in mundane natures, there is neither any thing formless, nor any vacuum among the species of things, so likewise in math-ematical number, neither is any quantity left innumerable; for thus the forming power of the monad would be vanquished by the indefinite duad, nor does any medium intervene between the consequent numbers, and the well-disposed energy of the monad.

"Neither, therefore, does the pentad consist of substance and accident, as a white man; nor of genus and difference, as man of animal and biped; nor of five monads mutually touching each other, like a bundle of wood; nor of things mingled, like a drink made from wine and honey; nor of things sustaining position, as stones by their position complete the house; nor lastly, as things numerable, for these are nothing else than particulars. But it does not follow that numbers themselves, because they consist of indivisible monads, have nothing else besides monads, (for the multitude of points in continued quantity is an indivisible multitude, yet it is not on this account that there is a completion of something else from the points themselves); but this takes place because there is something in them which corresponds to matter, and something which corresponds to form. Lastly, when we unite the triad with the tetrad, we say that we make seven. The assertion, however, is not true: for monads conjoined with monads, produce indeed the subject of the number 7, but nothing more. Who then imparts the heptadic form to these monads? Who is it also that gives the form of a bed to a certain number of pieces of wood? Shall we not say that the soul of the carpenter, from the art which he possesses, fashions the wood, so as to receive the form of a bed, and that the numerative soul, from possessing in herself a monad which has the relation of a principle, gives form and subsistence to all numbers? But in this only consists the difference, that the carpenter's art is not naturally inherent in us, and requires manual operation, because it is conversant with sensible matter; but the numerative art is naturally present with us, and is therefore possessed by all men, and has an intellectual matter which it instantaneously invests with form. And this is that which deceives the multitude, who think that the heptad is nothing besides seven monads. For the imagination of the vulgar, unless it first sees a thing unadorned, afterwards the supervening energy of the adorner, and lastly, above all the thing itself, perfect and formed, cannot be persuaded that it has two natures, one formless, the other formal, and still further, that which beyond these imparts form; but asserts that the subject is one, and without generation. Hence, perhaps, the ancient theologists and Plato ascribed temporal generations to things without generation, and to things which are perpetually adorned, and regularly disposed, privation of order and ornament, the erroneous and the boundless, that they might lead men to the knowledge of a formal and effective cause. It is, therefore, by no means wonderful, that though seven sensible monads are never without the heptad, these should be distinguished by science, and that the former should have the relation of a subject, and be analogous to matter, but the latter should correspond to species and form.

"Again, as when water is changed into air, the water does not become air, or the subject of air, but that which was the subject of water becomes the subject of air, so when one number unites itself with another, as for instance the triad with the duad, the species or forms of the two numbers are not mingled, except in their immaterial reasons (or productive principles), in which at the same time that they are separate, they are not impeded from being united, but the quantities of the two numbers which are placed together, become the subject of the pentad. The triad, therefore, is one, and also the tetrad, even in mathematical numbers: for though in the ennead or number nine, you may conceive a first, second, and third triad, yet you see one thing thrice assumed; and in short, in the ennead there is nothing but the form of the ennead in the quantity of nine monads. But if you mentally separate its subject, (for form is impartible) you will immediately invest it with forms corresponding to its division; for our soul cannot endure to see that which is formless, unadorned, especially as she possesses the power of investing it with ornament.

"Since also separate numbers possess a demiurgic or fabricative power, which mathematical numbers imitate, the sensible world likewise contains images of those numbers by which it is adorned; so that all things are in all, but in an appropriate manner in each. The sensible world, therefore, subsists from immaterial and energetic reasons, and from more ancient causes. But those who do not admit that nature herself is full of productive powers, lest they should be obliged to double things themselves, these wonder how from things void of magnitude and gravity, magnitude and gravity are composed; though they are never composed from things of this kind which are void of gravity and magnitude, as from parts. But magnitude is generated from essentially impartible elements; since form and matter are the elements of bodies; and still much more is it generated from those truer causes which are considered in demiurgic reasons and forms. Is it not therefore necessary that all dimensions, and all moving masses, must from these receive their generation? For either bodies are unbegotten, like incorporeal natures; or of things with interval, things without interval are the causes; of partibles impartibles; and of sensibles and contraries, things insensible and void of contact: and we must assent to those who assert that things possessing magnitude are thus generated from impartibles. Hence the Pythagorean Eurytus, and his followers, beholding the images of things themselves in numbers, rightly attributed certain numbers to certain things, according to their peculiarity. In consequence of this, he said that a particular number is the boundary of this plant, and again, another number of this animal; just as of a triangle 6 is the boundary, of a square 9, and of a cube 8. As the musician, too, harmonizes his lyre through mathematical numbers, so nature through her own natural numbers, orderly arranges, and modulates her productions.

"Indeed, that numbers are participated by the heavens, and that there is a solar number, and also a lunar number, is manifest according to the adage, even to the blind. For the restitutions of the heavenly bodies to their pristine state (ἀποκαταστάσεις) would not always be effected through the same things, and in the same manner, unless one and the same number had dominion in each. Yet all these contribute to the procession of the celestial spheres, and are contained by their perfect number. But there is also a certain natural number belonging to every animal. For things of the same species would not be distinguished by organs after the same manner, nor would they arrive at puberty and old age about the same time, or generate, nor

226

would the fœtus be nourished or increase, according to regular periods, unless they were detained by the same measure of nature. According to the best of the Pythagoreans also, Plato himself, number is the cause of better and worse generations. Hence though the Pythagoreans sometimes speak of the squares and cubes of natural numbers, they do not make them to be monadic, such as the number 9, and the number 27; but they signify through these names, from similitude, the progression of natural numbers into, and dominion about, generations. In like manner, though they call them equal or double, they exhibit the dominion and symphony of ideas in these numbers. Hence different things do not use the same number, so far as they are different, nor do the same things use a different number, so far as they are the same.

"In short, physical numbers are material forms divided about the subject which receives them. But material powers are the sources of connexion and modification to bodies. For form is one thing, and the power proceeding from it another. For form itself is indeed impartible and essential; but being extended, and becoming bulky, it emits from itself, as if it were a blast, material powers which are certain qualities. Thus, for instance, in fire, the form and essence of it is impartible, and is truly the image of the cause of fire; for in partible natures, the impartible has a subsistence. But from form which is impartible in fire, and which subsists in it as number, an extension of it accompanied with interval takes place about matter, from which the powers of fire are emitted, such as heat, or refrigeration, or moisture, or something else of the like kind. And these qualities are indeed essential, but are by no means the essence of fire. For essences do not proceed from qualities, nor are essence and power the same thing. But the essential every where precedes power. And from this being one the multitude of powers proceeds, and the distributed from that which is undistributed; just as many energies are the progeny of one power."

228   P. 60. *For Pythagoras always proclaimed, that nothing*
admirable pertaining to the Gods, or divine dogmas, should be
disbelieved.

This in the Protreptics forms the fourth symbol. See the Appendix
for Iamblichus' explanation.

229   P. 50. *After this manner therefore it is said that music was*
discovered by Pythagoras.

The following particulars relative to music are added for the
purpose of elucidating what is said about it in this chapter.

"Take two brazen chords, such as are used in harps; for those chords
which are made from the intestines of sheep are for the most part
either false or obnoxious to the change of the air.

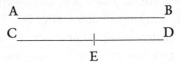

"Let these chords be perfectly equal, and equally stretched, so as to be
in unison, *i.e.* so that there may be only one sound, though there are
two strings. But it is requisite that they should be placed upon some
oblong and polished rule. The ancients called this rule an harmonic
rule, or also a monochord, by which instrument all consonances and
dissonances, and likewise musical intervals, were tried. Let now one of
230 these chords be bisected in E. Afterwards under the point E place what
is vulgarly called the *tactus*, but which was denominated by the
ancients, from its figure, a hemisphere. The tactus, therefore, being
placed under E, press there the chord, so that one half of it only, as for
instance ED, may be wholly struck and resound. Having therefore
struck each of the chords at the same time, *viz.* the whole of AB, and
the half ED, so that they may resound at one and the same time, you
will hear the sweetest of all consonances, composed from the sound of
the whole chord AB, and the sound of the half ED. This consonance
the ancients called diapason, *i.e. through all* [the chords], because in the
musical instruments of the ancients, the two extreme chords, *i.e.* the
most grave, and the most acute of all the chords, contained this
consonance; so that, from the gravest chord having made a transition

through all the chords to the supreme and most acute of all, they would hear this sweetest consonance. It was, likewise, said to be in a duple ratio of the proportion of one sound to the other. For the sound of the chord AB is doubly greater or more grave than the sound of the half ED. For as sounding bodies are to each other, so are their sounds. But the chord AB is the double of ED. This, however, is now commonly called the octave, because from the first sound, and that the gravest, which is called *ut*, as far as to that sound which corresponds to it in the consonance diapason, there are these eight sounds, *ut, re, mi, fa, sol, re, mi, fa*. And of these the first *ut*, and the last *fa*, which is the eighth, produce the consonance diapason, or the double, or the octave.

"Again, let the same chord CD be divided into three equal parts in the points F, G.

FD, therefore, will be two-thirds as well of the whole CD as of the whole AB. Let the tactus now be placed in F, and let AB and FD be struck at the same time, and a consonance very sweet and perfect will indeed be heard, yet not so sweet as the diapason. This the ancients called diapente (*i.e.* through five chords), because the first and the fifth chord produce this consonance. But according to proportion it is called sesquialter, because the chord AB is sesquialter to FD, and consequently the sounds of these chords also are in the same ratio. But sesquialter ratio is when the greater quantity AB contains the less FD once, and the half of it besides. It is, indeed, commonly called the fifth, because it is composed from the first sound *ut*, and the fifth, *sol*. {231}

Again, let the same chord be cut into four equal parts in the points H, E, I,

so that the chord HD, may be three-fourths of the whole CD. The tactus, therefore, being placed in H, let AB and HD be struck at one and the same time, and a consonance will be heard, indeed, yet more imperfect than the preceding two. This was called by the ancients diatessaron, *i.e.* through four chords or sounds, for a similar reason to that by which the former were denominated. With reference, however, to the ratio of the chords and sounds, it is called sesquitertian, because the greater AB contains the less once, and a third part of it besides. But it is now commonly called a fourth, because it is found between the first sound *ut*, and the fourth *fa*. If now the point F be added in the preceding figure, and at one and the same time two chords HD and FD are compared in arithmetical ratios, we shall find that the greater HD will have to the less FD a sesquioctave[7] ratio, and the sound of the greater HD to the less FD will have the same ratio, *i.e.* in modern terms, that between *fa* and *sol* there is a sesquioctave ratio. But if these two sounds are heard together, they will be discordant to the ear. Again, the distance between these sounds *fa*, *sol*, or between the chords HD and FD, or between the two harmonic intervals HD and FD, the ratio of which was sesquioctave, was called by the ancients a tone. Afterwards they divided the whole of CD into nine equal parts, the first of which is divided in K, so that the whole CD may have to the remainder KD, which contains eight of those parts, a sesquioctave ratio. This, in like manner, will be the interval of a tone, the first sound of which, *i.e.* of the whole CD, is now called *ut*, but the second sound of the rest of the chord KD is called *re*. Afterwards they in a similar manner divided the remainder KD into nine parts, the first part of which is marked in the point L. And for the same reason between the chord KD and the chord LD, and their sounds, there will be a sesquioctave ratio. The sound of the chord LD is now called *mi*; but the interval which remains between the chord LD and the chord HD has not a sesquioctave ratio, but less than it almost by half, and therefore an interval of this kind was called a semitone, and also diesis or a division. But that interval which remains between the points F and E they divided after the same manner as the space between C and H was divided, and they again found the same sounds. Let those divisions be marked by the points M and N; and here, also, between N and E, or between *mi* and *fa*, there is in like manner another semitone. These eight sounds, therefore, are *ut, re, mi, fa, sol, re, mi, fa*, which compose the whole diapason. For as we have before observed, between *ut* and the last *fa* is the consonance diapason, or between the chord CD or AB, and the chord ED. But from the intervals which are 233 between the sounds there are two semitones, *viz.* one between *mi* and *fa*, denoted by the letters L, N, and the other between the last *mi* and *fa*, denoted by the letters N, E. The remaining five intervals are entire tones. It must, also, be observed, that from *ut* to the first *sol* is the consonance diapente, which contains three tonic intervals, and one semitone; nevertheless in all there are five sounds, *ut, re, mi, fa, sol.*

Again, from sol to the last *fa* there are four sounds, *sol, re, mi, fa,* which are perfectly similar to the first four, *ut, re, mi, fa.* Nevertheless these are more grave, but those are more acute. And as from *ut* to the first *fa* is the diatessaron, so likewise from *sol* to the last *fa* is another diatessaron; from which, in the last place, it must be observed, it follows that the two consonances diatessaron and diapente constitute the whole diapason; or that the diapason is divided into one diatessaron, and one diapente. For from *ut* to *sol* is the diapente, but from *sol* to the last *fa* is the diatessaron. This will also be the case if we should say that from *ut* to the first *fa* is the diatessaron, as is evident from the division of the chord; but from the first *fa* to the last *fa* is the diapente, as is evident from the four intervals of the chord, three of which are tones, and the remaining interval is a semitone, which also in the other diapente were contained between *ut* and *sol.*

Now again, let the tactus be placed in I; but I is the fourth part of the whole CD. Let, also, AB and ID be struck at one and the same time, and the sweetest consonance, called bisdiapason, will be produced; which is so denominated, because it is composed from two diapasons, of which the first is between AB or CD, and ED, but the second is between ED and ID; for the ratio of these is double as well as of those. The ratio, also, of the bisdiapason is quadruple, as is evident from the division; and is commonly called a fifteenth, because from 234 the first *ut* to this sound, which is also denominated *fa*, there would be fifteen sounds, if the interval EI were divided after the same manner as the first CE is divided.

Farther still, let GD be a third part of the whole CD, and let the tactus be placed in G. Then at one and the same time let AB and GD be struck, and a sweet consonance will be heard, which is called diapasondiapente, because it is composed from one diapason contained by the interval CE, or the two chords CD, ED, and one diapente, contained by the interval EG, or the chords ED, GD. For the chord ED is sesquialter to the chord GD; which ratio constitutes the nature of the diapente. The proportion, also, of this consonance is triple. For the chord AB or CD is triple of GD; and it is commonly called the twelfth, because between *ut* and *sol*, denoted by the letter G, there would be twelve sounds, if the interval EG received its divisions. From all which it is manifest by the experience of the ear, that there are altogether five consonances, three simple, the diapason, the diapente, and the diatessaron; but two composite, the bisdiapason, and the diapasondiapente.

In the last place, it is necessary to observe that those ancient Greeks differently denominated these sounds, *ut*, *re*, etc. For the first, *i.e.* the gravest sound or chord, which is now called *ut*, they denominated hypate, and the others in the following order:

Ut,	Hypate,	*i.e.* Principalis.
Re,	Parhypate,	— Postprincipalis.
Mi,	Lychanos,	— Index.
Fa,	Mese,	— Media.
Sol,	Paramese,	— Postmedia.
Re,	Trite,	— Tertia.
Mi,	Paranete,	— Antepenultima.
Fa,	Nete,	— Ultima, vel suprema

P. 61. *I swear by him who the tetractys found.*

The tetrad was called by the Pythagoreans every number, because it comprehends in itself all the numbers as far as to the decad, and the decad itself; for the sum of 1, 2, 3, and 4, is 10. Hence both the decad and the tetrad were said by them to be every number; the decad indeed in energy, but the tetrad in capacity. The sum likewise of these four numbers was said by them to constitute the tetractys, in which all harmonic ratios are included. For 4 to 1, which is a quadruple ratio, forms the symphony bisdiapason; the ratio of 3 to 2, which is sesquialter, forms the symphony diapente; 4 to 3, which is sesquitertian, the symphony diatessaron; and 2 to 1, which is a duple ratio, forms the diapason.

In consequence, however, of the great veneration paid to the tetractys by the Pythagoreans, it will be proper to give it a more ample discussion, and for this purpose to show from Theo of Smyrna,[8] how many tetractys there are:

"The tetractys," says he, "was not only principally honored by the Pythagoreans, because all symphonies are found to exist within it, but also because it appears to contain the nature of all things."

Hence the following was their oath:

"Not by him who delivered to our soul the tetractys, which contains the fountain and root of everlasting nature."

But by him who delivered the tetractys they mean Pythagoras; for the doctrine concerning it appears to have been his invention. The above-mentioned tetractys, therefore, is seen in the composition of the first numbers 1. 2. 3. 4. But the second tetractys arises from the increase by multiplication of even and odd numbers beginning from the monad.

Of these, the monad is assumed as the first, because, as we have before observed, it is the principle of all even, odd, and evenly-odd numbers, and the nature of it is simple. But the three successive numbers receive their composition according to the even and the odd; because every number is not alone even, nor alone odd. Hence the even and the odd receive two tetractys, according to multi-plication; the even indeed, in a duple ration; for 2 is the first of even numbers, and increases from the monad by duplication. But the odd number is increased in a triple ratio; for 3 is the first of odd numbers, and is itself increased from the monad by triplication. Hence the monad is common to both these, being itself even and odd. The second number, however, in even and double numbers is 2; but in odd and triple numbers 3. The third among even numbers is 4; but among odd numbers is 9. And the fourth among even numbers is 8; but among odd numbers is 27.

$$\left\{ \begin{array}{cccc} 1. & 2. & 4. & 8. \\ 1. & 3. & 9. & 27. \end{array} \right\}$$

In these numbers the more perfect ratios of symphonies are found; and in these also a tone is comprehended. The monad, however, contains the productive principle of a point. But the second numbers 2 and 3 contain the principle of a side, since they are incomposite, and first, are measured by the monad, and naturally measure a right line. The third terms are 4 and 9, which are in power a square superficies, since they are equally equal. And the fourth terms 8 and 27 being equally equal, are in power a cube. Hence from these numbers, and this tetractys, the increase takes place from a point to a solid. For a side follows after a point, a superficies after a side, and a solid after a superficies. In these numbers also, Plato in the Timæus constitutes the soul. But the last of these seven numbers, *i.e.* 27, is equal to all the numbers that precede it; for 1+2+3+4+8+9=27. There are, therefore, two tetractys of numbers, one of which subsists by addition, but the other by multiplication, and they comprehend musical, geometrical, and arithmetical ratios, from which also the harmony of the universe consists.

But the third tetractys is that which according to the same analogy or proportion comprehends the nature of all magnitude. For what the monad was in the former tetractys, that a point is in this. What the numbers 2 and 3, which are in power a side, were in the former tetractys, that the extended species of a line, the circular and the right, are in this; the right line indeed subsisting in conformity to the even number, since it is terminated[9] by two points; but the circular in conformity to the odd number, because it is comprehended by one line which has no end. But what in the former tetractys the square numbers 4 and 9 were, that the two-fold species of planes, the rectilinear and the circular, are in this. And what the cube numbers 8 and 27 were in the former, the one being an even, but the other an odd number, that the two solids, one of which has a hollow superficies, as the sphere and the cylinder, but the other a plane superficies, as the cube and pyramid, are in this tetractys. Hence, this is the third tetractys, which gives completion to every magnitude, from a point, a line, a superficies, and a solid.

The fourth tetractys is of the simple bodies fire, air, water, and earth, which have an analogy according to numbers. For what the monad was in the first tetractys, that fire is in this. But the duad is air, the triad is water, and the tetrad is earth. For such is the nature of the elements according to tenuity and density of parts. Hence fire has to air the ratio of 1 to 2; but to water, the ratio of 1 to 3; and to earth, the ratio of 1 to 4. In other respects also they are analogous to each other.   *238*

The fifth tetractys is of the figures of the simple bodies. For the pyramid, indeed, is the figure of fire; the octaedron, of air; the icosaedron, of water; and the cube, of earth.

The sixth tetractys is of things rising into existence through the vegetative life. And the seed, indeed, is analogous to the monad and a point. But if it increases in length it is analogous to the duad and a line; if in breadth, to the triad and a superficies; but if in thickness, to the tetrad and a solid.

The seventh tetractys is of communities; of which the principle indeed, and as it were monad, is man; the duad is a house; the triad a street; and the tetrad a city. For a nation consists of these. And these indeed are the material and sensible tetractys.

The eighth tetractys consists of the powers which form a judgment of things material and sensible, and which are of a certain intelligible nature. And these are, intellect, science, opinion, and sense. And intellect, indeed, corresponds in its essence to the monad; but science to the duad; for science is the science of a certain thing. Opinion subsists between science and ignorance; but sense is as the tetrad. For the touch which is common to all the senses being fourfold, all the senses energize according to contact.

The ninth tetractys is that from which the animal is composed, the soul and the body. For the parts of the soul, indeed, are the rational, the irascible, and the epithymetic, or that which desires external good; and the fourth is the body in which the soul subsists.

The tenth tetractys is of the seasons of the year, through which all things rise into existence, *viz.* the spring, the summer, the autumn, and the winter.

And the eleventh is of the ages of man, *viz.* of the infant, the lad, the man, and the old man.

Hence there are eleven tetractys. The first is that which subsists   *239* according to the composition of numbers. The second, according to the multiplication of numbers. The third subsists according to magnitude. The fourth is of the simple bodies. The fifth is of figures.

The sixth is of things rising into existence through the vegetative life. The seventh is of communities. The eighth is the judicial power. The ninth is of the parts of the animal. The tenth is of the seasons of the year. And the eleventh is of the ages of man. All of them however are proportional to each other. For what the monad is in the first and second tetractys, that a point is in the third; fire in the fourth; a pyramid in the fifth; seed in the sixth; man in the seventh; intellect in the eighth; and so of the rest. Thus, for instance, the first tetractys is 1. 2. 3. 4. The second is the monad, a side, a square, and a cube. The third is a point, a line, a superficies, and a solid. The fourth is fire, air, water, earth. The fifth the pyramid, the octaedron, the icosaedron, and the cube. The sixth, seed, length, breadth and depth. The seventh, man, a house, a street, a city. The eighth, intellect, science, opinion, sense. The ninth, the rational, the irascible, and the epithymetic parts, and the body. The tenth, the spring, summer, autumn, winter. The eleventh, the infant, the lad, the man, and the old man.

The world also, which is composed from these tetractys, is perfect, being elegantly arranged in geometrical, harmonical, and arithmetical proportion; comprehending every power, all the nature of number, every magnitude, and every simple and composite body. But it is perfect, because all things are the parts of it, but it is not itself the part of any thing. Hence, the Pythagoreans are said to have first used the beforementioned oath, and also the assertion that "all things are assimilated to number."

240   *P. 62. This number is the first that partakes of every number, and when divided in every possible way, receives the power of the numbers subtracted, and of those that remain.*

Because 6 consists of 1, 2 and 3, the two first of which are the principles of all number, and also because 2 and 3 are the first even and odd, which are the sources of all the species of numbers; the number 6 may be said to partake of every number. In what Iamblichus afterwards adds, I suppose he alludes to 6 being a perfect number and therefore equal to all its parts.

P. 75. *Not to step above the beam of the balance.*

This is the 14th Symbol in the Protreptics of Iamblichus. See the Appendix for Iamblichus' explanation.

The following extract also from my Theoretic Arithmetic, (p. 194), will in a still greater degree elucidate this symbol. The information contained in it is derived from the anonymous author of a very valuable work entitled Θεολογούμενα 'Αριθμητικῆς *Theologumena Arithmeticæ*, and which has lately been reprinted at Leipsic.

"The Pythagoreans called the pentad providence and justice, *241* because it equalizes things unequal, justice being a medium between excess and defect, just as 5 is the middle of all the numbers that are equally distant from it on boths sides as far as to the decad, some of which it surpasses, and by others is surpassed, as may be seen in the following arrangement:

$$1. \quad 4. \quad 7.$$
$$2. \quad 5. \quad 8.$$
$$3. \quad 6. \quad 9.$$

For here, as in the middle of the beam of a balance, 5 does not depart from the line of the equilibrium, while one scale is raised, and the other is depressed.

In the following arrangement also, *viz.* 1, 2, 3, 4, 5, 6, 7, 8, 9, it will be found that the sum of the numbers which are posterior, is triple the sum of those that are prior to 5; for 6+7+8+9=30; but 1+2+3+4=10. If therefore the numbers on each side of 5 represent the beam of a balance; 5 being the tongue of it, when a weight depresses the beam, an obtuse angle is produced by the depressed part of the tongue, and an acute angle by the elevated part of the beam. Hence it is worse to do than to suffer an injury: and the authors of the injury verge downward as it were to the infernal regions; but the injured tend upward as it were to the Gods, imploring the divine assistance. Hence the meaning of the Pythagoric symbol is obvious, "Pass not above the beam of the balance." Since however injustice pertains to inequality, in order to correct this, equalization is requisite, that the beam of the balance may remain on both sides without obliquity. But equalization is effected by addition and subtraction. Thus if 4 is added to 5, and 4 is also taken from 5, the number 9 will be produced on one side, and 1 on the other, each of which is equally distant from 5. Thus too, if 3 is added to 5, and is also subtracted from it, on the one side 8 will be produced, and on the other 2. If 2 is added to 5, and likewise taken from it, 7 and 3 will be produced. And by adding 1 to 5, and subtracting 1 from it, 6 and 4 will be the result; in all which instances, the numbers produced are equidistant from 5, and the sum of each couple is equal to 10."

P. 89. *Such as dig not fire with a sword.*

This is the 9th Symbol in the Protreptics. See the Appendix for Iamblichus' explanation.

P. 112. *But this follows from the whole being naturally prior to the part, and not the part to the whole.*

For whole co-subverts, but is not co-subverted by part: since if whole is taken away, part also is taken away; but the contrary does not follow.

P. 133. *Such therefore as have the intellective and gnostic part of virtue, are denominated skilful and intelligent: but such as have the ethical and pre-elective part of it, are denominated useful and equitable.*

The following account of the virtues is extracted from the Notes to my Translation of the Phædo of Plato: The first of the virtues are the physical, which are common to brutes, being mingled with the temperaments, and for the most part contrary to each other; or rather pertaining to the animal. Or it may be said that they are illuminations from reason, when not impeded by a certain bad temperament: or that they are the result of energies in a former life. Of these Plato speaks in the Politicus and the Laws. The ethical virtues, which are above these, are ingenerated by custom and a certain right opinion, and are the virtues of children when well educated. These virtues also are to be found in some brute animals. They likewise transcend the temperaments, and on this account are not contrary to each other. These virtues Plato delivers in the Laws. They pertain however at the same time both to reason and the irrational nature. In the third rank above these are the political virtues, which pertain to reason alone; for they are scientific. But they are the virtues of reason adorning the irrational part as its instrument; through prudence adorning the gnostic, through fortitude the irascible, and through temperance the epithymetic power, (or the power which is the source of desire;) but adorning all the parts of the irrational nature through justice. And of these virtues Plato speaks much in the Republic. These virtues too follow each other. Above these are the cathartic virtues, which pertain to reason alone, withdrawing from other things to itself, throwing aside the instruments of sense as vain, repressing also the energies through *244* these instruments, and liberating the soul from the bonds of generation. Plato particularly unfolds these virtues in the Phædo. Prior to these however are the theoretic virtues, which pertain to the soul, introducing itself to natures superior to itself, not only gnostically, as some one may be induced to think from the name, but also orectically: for it hastens to become, as it were, intellect instead of soul; and intellect possesses both desire and knowledge. These virtues are the converse of the political: for as the latter energize about things subordinate according to reason, so the former about things more excellent according to intellect. These virtues Plato delivers in the Theætetus.

According to Plotinus, there is also another gradation of the virtues besides these, *viz.* the paradigmatic. For, as our eye, when it is first illuminated by the solar light, is different from that which illuminates, as being illuminated, but afterwards is in a certain respect united and conjoined with it, and becomes, as it were, solar-form; so also our soul at first indeed is illuminated by intellect, and energizes according to the theoretic virtues, but afterwards becomes, as it were, that which is illuminated, and energizes uniformly according to the paradigmatic virtues. And it is the business indeed of philosophy to make us intellect; but of theurgy to unite us to intelligibles, so that we may energize paradigmatically. And as when possessing the physical virtues, we know mundane bodies (for the subjects to virtues of this kind are bodies); so from possessing the ethical virtues, we know the fate of the universe, because fate is conversant with irrational lives. For the rational soul is not under fate; and the ethical virtues are irrational, because they pertain to the irrational part. According to the political virtues we know mundane affairs, and according to the cathartic supermundane; but as possessing the theoretic we know intellectual, and from the paradigmatic intelligible natures. Temperance also pertains to the ethical virtues; justice to the political, on account of compacts; fortitude to the cathartic, through not verging to matter; and prudence to the theoretic. Observe too, that Plato in the Phædo calls the physical virtues servile, because they may subsist in servile souls; but he calls the ethical σκιογράφιαι *adumbrations*, because their possessors only know that the energies of such virtues are right, but do not know *why* they are so. It is well observed too here, by Olympiodorus, that Plato calls the cathartic and theoretic virtues, those which are in reality true virtues. He also separates them in another way, *viz.* that the political are not telestic, *i.e.* do not pertain to mystic ceremonies, but that the cathartic and theoretic are telestic. Hence, Olympiodorus adds, the cathartic virtues are denominated from the purification which is used in the mysteries; but the theoretic from perceiving things divine. On this account he accords with the Orphic verses, that:

> The soul that uninitiated dies,
> Plung'd in the blackest mire in Hades lies.

For initiation is the divinely-inspired energy of the virtues. Olympiodorus also further observes, that by the thyrsus-bearers, Plato means those that energize according to the political virtues, but by the Bacchuses those that exercise the cathartic virtues. For we are bound in matter as Titans, through the great partibility of our nature; but we rise from the dark mire as Bacchuses. Hence we become more prophetic at the time of death: and Bacchus is the inspective guardian of death, because he is likewise of every thing pertaining to the Bacchic sacred rites.

All the virtues likewise exhibit their proper characters, these being every where common, but subsisting appropriately in each. For the characteristic property of fortitude is the not declining to things subordinate; of temperance, a conversion from an inferior nature; of justice, a proper energy, and which is adapted to being; and of prudence, the election and selection of things good and evil.

Olympiodorus farther observes, that all the virtues are in the Gods. For many Gods, says he, are adorned with their appellations; and all goodness originates from the Gods. Likewise, prior to things which sometimes participate the virtues, as is our case, it is necessary there should be natures which always participate them. In what order, therefore, do the virtues appear? Shall we say in the psychical? For virtue is the perfection of the soul; and election and pre-election are the energies and projections of the soul. Hence the Chaldæan oracles conjoin fontal virtue with fontal soul, or in other words, with soul subsisting according to cause. But may it not also be said, that the virtues naturally wish to give an orderly arrangement to that which is disordered? If this be admitted, they will originate from the demiurgic order. How then will they be cathartic there? May we not say, Olympiodorus adds, that through the cathartic virtues considered according to their causal subsistence in Jupiter the demiurgus, he is enabled to abide in his accustomed mode, as Plato says in the Timæus? And farther still, according to ancient theologists, he ascends to the tower of Saturn, who is a *pure* intellect.

As this distribution of the virtues, however, is at present no less novel than important, the following discussion of them from the Ἀφορμαὶ πρὸς τὰ νόητα, or AUXILIARIES TO INTELLIGIBLES, of Porphyry, is added for the sake of the genuinely philosophic reader:

"There is one kind of virtues pertaining to the political character, and another to the man who tends to contemplation, and on this account is called theoretic, and is now a beholder. And there are also other virtues pertaining to intellect, so far as it is intellect, and separate from soul. The virtues indeed of the political character, and which consist in the moderation of the passions, are characterised by following and being obedient to the reasoning about that which is becoming in actions. Hence, looking to an innoxious converse with neighbours, they are denominated, from the aggregation of fellowship, political. And prudence indeed subsists about the reasoning part; fortitude about the irascible part; temperance, in the consent and symphony of the epithymetic with the reasoning part; and justice in each of these performing its proper employment with respect to governing and being governed. But the virtues of him who

247

proceeds to the contemplative life, consist in a departure from terrestrial concerns. Hence also, they are called purifications, being surveyed in the refraining from corporeal actions, and avoiding sympathies with the body. For these are the virtues of the soul elevating itself to true being. The political virtues, therefore, adorn the mortal man, and are the forerunners of purifications. For it is necessary that he who is adorned by these, should abstain from doing any thing precedaneously in conjunction with body. Hence in purifications, not to opine with body, but to energize alone, gives subsistence to prudence; which derives its perfection through energizing intellectually with purity. But not to be similarly passive with the body, constitutes temperance. Not to fear a departure from body as into something void, and nonentity, gives subsistence to fortitude. But when reason and intellect are the leaders, and there is no resistance [from the irrational part,] justice is produced. The disposition therefore, according to the political virtues, is surveyed in the moderation of the passions; having for its end to live as man conformable to nature. But the disposition according to the theoretic virtues, is beheld in apathy;[10] the end of which is a similitude to God.

248   "Since, however, of purification one kind consists in purifying, but another pertains to those that are purified, the cathartic virtues are surveyed according to both these significations of purification; for they purify the soul, and are present with purification. For the end of purification is to become pure. But since purification, and the being purified, are an ablation of every thing foreign, the good resulting from them will be different from that which purifies; so that if that which is purified was good prior to the impurity with which it is defiled, purification is sufficient. That, however, which remains after purification, is good, and not purification. The nature of the soul also was not good, but is that which is able to partake of good, and is boniform. For if this were not the case, it would not have become situated in evil. The good, therefore, of the soul consists in being united to its generator; but its evil, in an association with things subordinate to itself. Its evil also is twofold; the one

arising from an association with terrestrial natures; but the other from doing this with an excess of the passions. Hence all the political virtues, which liberate the soul from one evil, may be denominated virtues, and are honorable. But the cathartic are more honorable, and liberate it from evil, so far as it is soul. It is necessary, therefore, that the soul when purified should associate with its generator. Hence the virtue of it after its conversion consists in a scientific knowledge of [true] being; but this will not be the case unless conversion precedes.

"There is therefore another genus of virtues after the cathartic and political, and which are the virtues of the soul energizing intellectually. And here, indeed, wisdom and prudence consist in the contemplation of those things which intellect possesses. But justice consists in performing what is appropriate in a conformity to, and energizing according to intellect. Temperance is an inward conversion of the soul to intellect. And fortitude is apathy; according to a similitude of that to which the soul looks, and which is naturally impassive. These virtues, also, in the same manner as the others, alternately follow each other.

249

"The fourth species of the virtues is that of the paradigms subsisting in intellect; which are more excellent than the psychical virtues, and exist as the paradigms of these; the virtues of the soul being the similitudes of them. And intellect indeed is that in which all things subsist at once as paradigms. Here, therefore, prudence is science; but intellect that knows [all things] is wisdom. Temperance is that which is converted to itself. The proper work of intellect, is the performance of its appropriate duty, [and this is justice"]. But fortitude is sameness, and the abiding with purity in itself, through an abundance of power. There are therefore four genera of virtues; of which, indeed, some pertain to intellect, concur with the essence of it, and are paradigmatic. Others pertain to soul now looking to intellect, and being filled from it. Others belong to the soul of man, purifying itself, and becoming purified from the body, and the irrational passions. And others are the virtues of the soul of man, adorning the man, through giving measure and bound to the irrational nature, and producing moderation in the passions.

And he, indeed, who has the greater virtues has also necessarily the less; but the contrary is not true, that he who has the less has also the greater virtues. Nor will he who possesses the greater, energize precedaneously according to the less, but only so far as the necessities of the mortal nature require. The scope also of the virtues, is, as we have said, generically different in the different virtues. For the scope of the political virtues, is to give measure to the passions in their practical energies according to nature. But the scope of the cathartic virtues, is entirely to obliterate the remembrance of the passions. And the scope of the rest subsists *250* analogously to what has been before said. Hence, he who energizes according to the practical virtues, is a *worthy* man: but he who energizes according to the cathartic virtues, is a *dæmoniacal man*, or is also *a good dæmon*. He who energizes according to the intellectual virtues alone, is *a God*. But he who energizes according to the paradigmatic virtues, *is the father of the Gods*. We, therefore, ought especially to pay attention to the cathartic virtues, since we may obtain these in the present life. But through these, the ascent is to the more honorable virtues. Hence it is requisite to survey to what degree purification may be extended. For it is a separation from body, and from the passive motion of the irrational part. But how this may be effected, and to what extent, must now be said.

"In the first place, indeed, it is necessary that he who intends to acquire this purification, should, as the foundation and basis of it, know himself to be a soul bound in a foreign thing, and in a different essence. In the second place, as that which is raised from this foundation, he should collect himself from the body, and as it were from different places, so as to be disposed in a manner perfectly impassive with respect to the body. For he who energizes uninterruptedly according to sense, though he may not do this with an adhering affection, and the enjoyment resulting from pleasure, yet at the same time his attention is dissipated about the body, in consequence of becoming through sense[12] in contact with it. But we are addicted to the pleasures or pains of sensibles, in conjunction with a promptitude, and converging sympathy; from which disposition it is requisite to be purified.

This, however, will be effected by admitting necessary pleasures, and the sensations of them, merely as remedies, or as a liberation from pain, in order that [*the rational part*] *may not be impeded* [*in its energies.*] Pain also must be taken away. But if this is not possible, it must be mildly diminished. And it will be diminished, if the soul is not copassive with it. Anger, likewise, must as much as possible be taken away; and must by no means be premeditated. But if it cannot be entirely removed, deliberate choice must not be mingled with it, but the unpremeditated motion must be the impulse of the irrational part. *That however which is unpremeditated is imbecile and small.* All fear, likewise, must be expelled. For he who acquires this purification, will fear nothing. Here, however, if it should take place, it will be unpremeditated. Anger therefore and fear must be used for the purpose of admonition. But the desire of every thing base must be exterminated. Such a one also, so far as he is a cathartic philosopher, will not desire meats and drinks. Neither must there be the unpremeditated in natural venereal connexions; *but if this should take place, it must only be as far as to that precipitate imagination which energizes in sleep.* In short, the intellectual soul itself of the purified man, must be liberated from all these [corporeal propensities]. He must likewise endeavour that what is moved to the irrational nature of corporeal passions, may be moved without sympathy, and without animadversion; so that the motions themselves may be immediately dissolved, through their vicinity to the reasoning power. This, however, will not take place while the purification is proceeding to its perfection; but will happen to those in whom reason rules without opposition. Hence in these, the inferior part will so venerate reason, that it will be indignant, if it is at all moved, in consequence of not being quiet when its master is present, and will reprove itself for its imbecility. These, however, are yet only moderations of the passions, but at length terminate in apathy. For when co-passivity is entirely exterminated, then apathy is present with him who is purified from it. For passion becomes moved, when reason imparts excitation, through verging [to the irrational nature]."

251

P. 163. *The theorems of philosophy are to be enjoyed, as much as possible, as if they were ambrosia and nectar, etc. etc.*

This Sentence in the original of Arcerius is as follows:

τῶν κατὰ φιλοσοφίαν θεωρημάτων ἀπολαυστεον, ἐφ’ ὅσον οἱόν, καθάπερ ἀμβροσίας καὶ νέκταρος· ἀκήρατόν τε γὰρ τὸ ἀπ’ αὐτῶν ἡδὺ καὶ τὸ θεῖον τὸ μεγαλόψυχον δύναταί τε ποιεῖν, καὶ εἰ μὴ ἀϊδίους, ἀϊδίων γε ἐπιστήμονας.

In the edition of the Protreptics by Kiessling, which I did not see, till the greater part of this work was printed, σοφίαν is substituted for φιλοσοφίαν, but in my opinion very erroneously; and this German editor, from not perceiving the necessity of reading ἀκήρατόν τε γὰρ τὸ ἀπ’ αὐτῶν ἡδὺ καὶ θεῖον, τὸ μεγαλόψυχον, κ. λ. instead of retaining the reading of Arcerius, has made nonsense of this part of the Sentence. For his version of it is:

"Nam et sincera est eorum dulcedo, et divinam naturam, animum magnum efficere possunt."

THE END.

Notes

1. According to Ælian and Suidas also, *melanurus* is a fish; but as the word signifies that which has a black termination, it is very appropriately used as a symbol of a material nature.

2. See the second edition of this work in Nos. 15 and 16 of the Pamphleteer [1816].

3. *i.e.* Natures which are not connected with body.

4. See an extract of some length, and of the greatest importance, from this dialogue, in my translation of Select Works of Plotinus, p. 553, etc.

5. Forms subsist at the extremity of the intelligible triad, which triad consists of *being*, *life*, and *intellect*. But being and life, with all they contain, subsist here involved in impartible union. See my Proclus on the Theology of Plato.

6. In Aristot. Metaphys. Lib. 13.

7. Because ¾ is to ⅔ as 9 to 8.

8. In Mathemat. p. 147.

9. Instead of περιττόυται, it is necessary to read περατόυται; the necessity of which emendation, I wonder the learned Bullialdus did not observe.

10. This philosophic apathy is not, as is stupidly supposed by most of the present day, insensibility, but a perfect subjugation of the passions to reason.

11. The words καὶ δικαιοσύνη are omitted in the original. But it is evident from Plotinus, that they ought to be inserted.

12. Instead of κατ' αὐτὴν here, it is necessary to read κατ' αἴσθησιν.

Appendix

Appendix

The Pythagoric Sentences of Demophilus

Translated by Thomas Taylor
(Originally published in *Sallust on the Gods and the World*, 1793)

1. Request not of the divinity such things as when obtained you cannot preserve; for no gift of divinity can ever be taken away; and on this account he does not confer that which you are unable to retain.

2. Be vigilant in your intellectual part; for sleep about this has an affinity with real death.

3. Divinity sends evil to men, not as being influenced by anger, but for the sake of purification;[1] for anger is foreign from divinity, since it arises from circumstances taking place contrary to the will: but nothing contrary to the will can happen to a god.

4. When you deliberate whether or not you shall injure another, you will previously suffer the evil yourself which you intended to commit: but neither must you expect any good from the evil; for the manners of everyone are correspondent to his life and actions: for every soul is a repository; that which is good, of things good, and that which is evil, of things depraved.

5. After long consultation, engage either in speaking or acting; for you have not the ability to recall either your discourses or deeds.

6. Divinity does not principally esteem the tongue, but the deeds of the wise; for a wise man, even when he is silent, honours divinity.

7. A loquacious and ignorant man, both in prayer and sacrifice, contaminates a divine nature: the wise man therefore is alone a priest, is alone the friend of divinity, and only knows how to pray.

8. The wise man being sent hither naked, should naked invoke him

by whom he was sent; for he alone is heard by divinity who is not burdened by foreign concerns.

9. It is impossible to receive from divinity any gift greater than virtue.[2]

10. Gifts and victims confer no honour on the divinity, nor is he adorned with offerings suspended in temples; but a soul divinely inspired, solidly conjoins us with divinity; for it is necessary that like should approach to like.

11. It is more painful to be subservient to passions than to tyrants themselves.

12. It is better to converse more with yourself than with others.

13. If you are always careful to remember, that in whatever place either your soul or body accomplishes any deed, divinity is present as an inspector of your conduct; in all your discourses and actions you will venerate the presence of an inspector from whom nothing can be concealed, and will at the same time possess divinity as an intimate associate.

14. Believe that you are furious and insane, in proportion as you are ignorant of yourself.

15. It is necessary to search for those wives and children which will remain after a liberation from the present life.

16. The self-sufficient and needy philosopher lives a life truly similar to divinity, and considers the non-possession of external and unnecessary goods as the greatest wealth; for the acquisition of riches sometimes inflames desire; but not to act in any respect unjustly is sufficient to the enjoyment of a blessed life.

17. True goods are never produced by indolent habits.

18. Esteem that to be eminently good, which, when communicated to another, will be increased to yourself.[3]

19. Esteem those to be eminently your friends, who assist your soul rather than your body.

20. Consider both the praise and reproach of every foolish person as ridiculous, and the whole life of an ignorant man as a disgrace.

21. Endeavour that your familiars may reverence rather than fear you; for love attends upon reverence, but hatred upon fear.

22. The sacrifices of fools are the aliment of the fire; but the offerings which they suspend in temples are the supplies of the sacrilege.

23. Understand that no dissimulation can be long concealed.

24. The unjust man suffers greater evil while his soul is tormented with a consciousness of guilt, than when his body is scourged with whips.

25. It is by no means safe to discourse concerning divinity with men of false opinions; for the danger is equally great in speaking to such as these, things either fallacious or true.

26. By everywhere using reason as your guide, you will avoid the commission of crimes.

27. By being troublesome to others, you will not easily escape molestation yourself.

28. Consider that as great erudition, through which you are able to bear the want of erudition in the ignorant.

29. He who is depraved does not listen to the divine law; and on this account lives without law.

30. A just man, who is a stranger, is not only superior to a citizen, but is even more excellent than a relation.

31. As many passions of the soul, so many fierce and savage despots.

32. No one is free who has not obtained the empire of himself.

33. Labour, together with continence, precedes the acquisition of every good.

34. Be persuaded that those things are not your riches which you do not possess in the penetralia of cogitation.

35. Do that which you judge to be beautiful and honest, though you should acquire no glory from the performance; for the vulgar is a depraved judge of beautiful deeds.

36. Make trial of a man rather from his deeds than his discourses; for many live badly and speak well.

37. Perform great things, at the same time promising nothing great.

38. Since the roots of our natures are established in divinity, from which also we are produced, we should tenaciously adhere to our root; for streams also of water, and other offspring of the earth, when their roots are cut off become rotten and dry.

39. The strength of the soul is temperance; for this is the light of a soul destitute of passions: but it is much better to die than to darken the soul through the intemperance of the body.

40. You cannot easily denominate that man happy who depends either on his friends or children, or on any fleeting and fallen nature; for all these are unstable and uncertain; but to depend on oneself and on divinity is alone stable and firm.

41. He is a wise man, and beloved by divinity, who studies how to labour for the good of his soul, as much as others labour for the sake of the body.

42. Yield all things to their kindred and ruling nature except liberty.

43. Learn how to produce eternal children, not such as may supply the wants of the body in old age, but such as may nourish the soul with perpetual food.

44. It is impossible that the same person can be a *lover of pleasure, a lover of body, a lover of riches*, and *a lover of divinity*: for a lover of pleasure is also a lover of body; but a lover of body is entirely a lover of riches; but a lover of riches is necessarily unjust; and the unjust is necessarily profane towards divinity, and lawless with respect to men. Hence, though he should sacrifice hecatombs, he is only by this means the more impious, unholy, atheistical, and sacrilegious with respect to his intention: and on this account it is necessary to avoid every lover of pleasure as an atheist and polluted person.

45. The divinity has not a place in the earth more allied to his nature than a pure and holy soul.

THE END OF THE PYTHAGORIC SENTENCES OF DEMOPHILUS

The Similitudes of Demophilus

OR

The Remedy of Life,

From the PYTHAGOREANS.

Translated by William Bridgman (1804)

1. Flattery is like painted armour, because it affords delight, but is of no use.

2. Learning is similar to a golden crown; for it is both honourable, and advantageous.

3. Flighty men, like empty vessels, are easily laid hold of by the ears.[4]

4. Life, like a musical instrument, being harmonized by remission and intention, becomes more agreeable.

5. Reason, like a good potter, introduces a beautiful form to the soul.

6. The intellect of wise men, like gold, possesses the greatest weight.

7. Boasting, like gilt armour, is not the same within, as without.

8. Reason has the same power as an ointment; for it benefits us when we are disordered, but delights us when well.

9. Of a bad man, as of a bad dog, the silence is more to be dreaded than the voice.

10. It is neither becoming to prefer a mistress to a wife; nor flattery to a friend.

11. Garrulous men, like magpies,[5] by their continued loquacity destroy the pleasures of conversation.

12. The furies pursue the sins of bad men who are impious, and those also of the stupid and daring, when they grow old.

13. It is necessary that a well educated man should depart from life elegantly, as from a banquet.

14. A port is a place of rest to a ship, but friendship, to life.

15. The reproof of a father is a pleasant medicine; for it is more advantageous than severe chastisements.

16. It is necessary that a worthy man, like a good wrestler, should oppose his weight to fortune, when acting the part of an antagonist.

17. The possession of self-sufficiency,[6] like a short and pleasant road, has much grace and but little labour.

18. Restive horses are led by the bridle, but irritable minds, by reasoning.

19. Jests, like salt, should be used sparingly.

20. Both a well adapted shoe, and a well harmonized life, are accompanied with but little pain.

21. Garments reaching to the feet impede the body;[7] and immoderate riches, the soul.

22. To those who run in the stadium, the reward of victory is in the end of the race; but to those who delight to labour in wisdom, the reward is in old age.

23. It is necessary that he who hastens to behold virtue as his country, should pass by pleasures, as he would the Sirens.

24. As those who sail in fair weather are wont to have things prepared against a storm, so also those who are wise in prosperity, should prepare things necessary for their assistance against adversity.

25. Garments that are made clean and bright become soiled again by use; but the soul being once purified from ignorance, remains splendid for ever.

26. Fugitive slaves, although they are not pursued, are, affrighted; but the unwise suffer perturbation, though they have not yet acted badly.

27. The wealth of the avaricious, like the sun when it has descended under the earth, delights no living thing.

28. The fruits of the earth spring up once a year; but the fruits of friendship at all times.

29. It is the business of a musician to harmonize every instrument; but of a well educated man to adapt himself harmoniously to every fortune.

30. Neither the blows of a sick man, nor the threats of a stupid one, are to be feared.

31. It is necessary to provide an inward garment for the protection of the breast, and intellect as a protection against pain.

32. The diet of the sick, and the soul of the unwise, are full of fastidiousness.

33. Untaught boys confound letters, but uneducated men, things.

34. The intellect derived from philosophy is similar to a charioteer; for it is present with our desires, and always conducts them to the beautiful.

35. Time, indeed, will render the herb absinthium sweeter than honey, but circumstances may sometimes make an enemy preferable to a friend.

36. A good pilot sometimes suffers shipwreck, and a worthy man is sometimes unfortunate.

37. Thunder especially frightens children; but threats, the unwise.

38. Figure adorns a statue; but actions adorn a man.

39. It is the same thing to drink a deadly medicine from a golden cup, and to receive counsel from an injudicious friend.

40. Swallows signify fair weather; but the discourses of philosophy, exemption from pain.

41. Orphan children have not so much need of guardians as stupid men.

42. Fortune is like a depraved rewarder of contests; for she frequently crowns him who accomplishes nothing.

43. There is need of a pilot and a wind for a prosperous navigation; but of reasoning and fortune, to effect a happy life.

44. A timid man bears armour against himself; and a fool employs riches for the same purpose.

45. It is the same thing to moor a boat by an infirm anchor, and to place hope in a depraved mind.

46. Clouds frequently obscure the sun; but the passions, the reasoning power.

47. Neither does a golden bed benefit a sick man; nor splendid fortune, a stupid man.

48. Pure water dissolves inflammation; but mild discourse dissolves anger.

49. Austere wine is not adapted for copious drinking nor rustic manners for conversation.

50. The anger of an ape, and the threats of a flatterer, are to be alike regarded.

51. Of life, the first part is childhood, on which account all men are attentive to it, as to the first part of a drama.

52. It is necessary that we should be cautious in our writings, but splendid in our actions.

53. As in plants, so also in youth, the first blossoms indicate the fruit of virtue.

54. In banquets, he who is not intoxicated with wine is the more pleasant; but in prosperity,[8] he who does not conduct himself illegally.

55. It is the same thing to nourish a serpent, and to benefit a depraved man; for gratitude is produced from neither.

56. It is rare to suffer shipwreck in fair weather; and equally so not to suffer shipwreck from want of counsel.

57. Wind inflates empty bladders; but false opinions puff up stupid men.

58. It is necessary that he who exercises himself should avoid fatigue, and he who is prosperous, envy.

59. "Measure is most excellent," says one of the wise[9] men; to which also we being in like manner persuaded, O most friendly and pious Asclepiades, here finish the curations of life.

THE END OF THE SIMILITUDES OF DEMOPHILUS.

The Golden Sentences of Democrates

Translated by William Bridgman (1804)

1. If any one will give his mind to these sentences, he will obtain many things worthy of a man, and be free from many things that are base.

2. The perfection of the soul will correct the depravity of the body;[10] but the strength of the body without reasoning, does not render the soul better.

3. He who loves the goods of the soul will love things more divine; but he who loves the goods of its transient habitation will love things human.

4. It is beautiful to impede an unjust man; but, if this be not possible, it is beautiful not to act in conjunction with him.

5. It is necessary to be good, rather than to appear so.

6. The felicity of a man does not consist either in body or in riches, but in upright conduct and justice.

7. Sin should be abstained from, not through fear, but for the sake of the becoming.

8. It is a great thing to be wise where we ought in calamitous circumstances.

9. Repentance after base actions is the salvation of life.

10. It is necessary to be a speaker of the truth, and not to be loquacious.

11. He who does an injury is more unhappy than he who receives one.

12. It is the province of a magnanimous man to bear with mildness the errors of others.

13. It is comely not to oppose the law, nor a prince, nor one wiser than yourself.

14. A good man pays no attention to the reproofs of the depraved.

15. It is hard to be governed by those who are worse than ourselves.

16. He who is perfectly vanquished by riches, can never be just.

17. Reason is frequently more persuasive than gold itself.

18. He who admonishes a man that *fancies* he has intellect, labours in vain.

19. Many who have not learnt to argue rationally, still live according to reason.

20. Many who commit the basest actions often exercise the best discourse.

21. Fools frequently become wise under the pressure of misfortunes.

22. It is necessary to emulate the works and actions, and not the words of virtue.

23. Those who are naturally well disposed know things beautiful, and are themselves emulous of them.

24. Vigour and strength of body are the nobility of cattle; but rectitude of manners is the nobility of man.

25. Neither art nor wisdom can be acquired without preparatory learning.

26. It is better to reprove your own errors, than those of others.

27. Those whose manners are well ordered, will also be orderly in their lives.

28. It is good not only to refrain from doing an injury, but even from the very wish.

29. It is proper to speak well of good works; for to do of such as are base is the property of a fraudulent man and an impostor.

30. Many that have great learning have no intellect.

31. It is necessary to endeavour to obtain an abundance of intellect, and not pursue an abundance of erudition.

32. It is better that counsel should precede actions, than that repentance should follow them.

33. Put not confidence in all men, but in those that are worthy; for to do the former is the province of a stupid man, but the latter of a

wise man.

34. A worthy and an unworthy man are to be judged not from their actions only, but also from their will.

35. To desire immoderately is the province of a boy, and not of a man.

36. Unseasonable pleasures bring forth pains.

37. Vehement desires about any one thing render the soul blind with respect to other things.

38. The love is just which, unattended with injury, aspires after things becoming.

39. Admit nothing as pleasant which is not advantageous.

40. It is better to be governed by, than to govern, the stupid.

41. Not argument but calamity is the preceptor to children.

42. Glory and wealth without wisdom are not secure possessions.

43. It is not indeed useless to procure wealth but to procure it from injustice is the most pernicious of all things.

44. It is a dreadful thing to imitate the bad, and to be unwilling to imitate the good.

45. It is a shameful thing for a man to be employed about the affairs of others, but to be ignorant of his own.

46. To be always intending to act renders action imperfect.

47. Fraudulent men, and such as are only seemingly good, do all things in words and nothing in deeds.

48. He is a blessed man who has both property and intellect, for he will use them well in such things as are proper.

49. The ignorance of what is excellent is the cause of error.

50. Prior to the performance of base things, a man should reverence himself.

51. A man given to contradiction, and very attentive to trifles, is naturally unadapted to learn what is proper.

52. Continually to speak without being willing to hear, is arrogance.

53. It is necessary to guard against a depraved man, lest he should take advantage of opportunity.

54. An envious man is the cause of molestation to himself, as to an enemy.

55. Not only he is an enemy who acts unjustly, but even he who

deliberates about so acting.

56. The enmity of relations is far more bitter than that of strangers.

57. Conduct yourself to all men without suspicion; and be accommodating and cautious in your behaviour.

58. It is proper to receive favours, at the same time determining that the retribution shall surpass the gift.

59. When about to bestow a favour, previously consider him who is to receive it, lest being a fraudulent character he should return evil for good.

60. Small favours seasonably bestowed, become things of the greatest consequence to those that receive them.

61. Honours, with wise men, are capable of effecting the greatest things, if at the same time they understand that they are honoured.

62. The beneficent man is one who does not look to retribution; but who deliberately intends to do well.

63. Many that appear to be friends are not, and others, who do not appear to be friends, are so.

64. The friendship of one wise man is better than that of every fool.

65. He is unworthy to live, who has not one worthy friend.

66. Many turn from their friends, if, from affluence, they fall into adversity.

67. The equal is beautiful in every thing; but excess and defect to me do not appear to be so.

68. He who loves no one does not appear to me to be loved by any one.

69. He is an agreeable old man who is facetious, and abounds in interesting anecdote.

70. The beauty of the body is merely animal unless supported by intellect.

71. To find a friend in prosperity, is very easy; but in adversity, it is the most difficult of all things.

72. Not all relations are friends, but those who accord with what is mutually advantageous.

73. Since we are men, it is becoming not to deride, but bewail, the calamities of men.

74. Good scarcely presents itself, even to those who investigate it; but evil is obvious without investigation.

75. Men who delight to blame others are not naturally adapted to friendship.

76. A woman should not be given to loquacity; for it is a dreadful thing.

77. To be governed by a woman is the extremity of insolence and unmanliness.[11]

78. It is the property of a divine intellect to be always intently thinking about the beautiful.

79. He who believes that Divinity beholds all things, will not sin either secretly or openly.

80. Those who praise the unwise do them a great injury.

81. It is better to be praised by another than by oneself.

82. If you cannot reconcile to yourself the praises you receive, think that you are flattered.

83. The world is a scene; life a transition. You came, you saw, you departed.

84. The world is a mutation: life a vain opinion.

THE END OF THE GOLDEN SENTENCES.

The Pythagoric Symbols,
with the Explanations of Iamblichus

Translated by William Bridgman (1804),
with minor revisions by Thomas Taylor (1818)

All these Symbols are exhortatory in *common* to the whole of virtue; but *particularly* each to some particular virtue. Different Symbols also are differently adapted to parts of philosophy and discipline. Thus for instance the first Symbol directly exhorts to piety and divine science.

SYMBOL I

When going to the temple to adore Divinity neither say nor do any thing in the interim pertaining to the common affairs of life.

EXPLANATION

This Symbol preserves a divine nature such as it is in itself pure and undefiled: for the pure is wont to be conjoined with the pure. It also causes us to introduce nothing from human affairs into the worship of Divinity; for all such things are foreign from, and contrary to, religious worship. This Symbol also greatly contributes to scienc ; for in divine science it is necessary to introduce nothing of this kind; such as human conceptions, or those pertaining to the concerns of life. We are exhorted to nothing else, therefore, by these words than this; that we should not mingle sacred discourses and divine actions with the instability of human manners.

SYMBOL 2

Neither enter into a temple negligently nor in short adore carelessly, not even though you should stand at the very doors themselves.

EXPLANATION

With the preceding this Symbol also accords. For if the similar is friendly and allied to the similar, it is evident that since the Gods have a most principal essence among wholes, we ought to make the worship of them a principal object. But he who does this for the sake of any thing else, gives a secondary rank to that which takes the precedency of all things, and subverts the whole order of religious worship and knowledge. Besides, it is not proper to rank illustrious goods in the subordinate condition of human utility, nor to place our concerns in the order of an end, but things more excellent, whether they be works or conceptions, in the condition of an appendage.

SYMBOL 3

Sacrifice and adore unshod.

EXPLANATION

An exhortation to the same thing may also be obtained from this Symbol. For it signifies that we ought to worship the Gods, and acquire a knowledge of them in an orderly and modest manner, and in a way not surpassing our condition on the earth. It also signifies that in worshipping them, and acquiring this knowledge, we should be free from bonds, and properly liberated. But the Symbol exhorts that sacrifice and adoration should be performed not only in the body, but also in the energies of the soul; so that these energies may neither be detained by passions, nor by the imbecility of the body, nor by generation, with which we are externally surrounded. But every thing pertaining to us should be properly liberated, and prepared for the participation of the Gods.

SYMBOL 4

Disbelieve nothing wonderful concerning the gods, nor concerning divine dogmas.

EXPLANATION

This Symbol in like manner exhorts to the same virtue. For this dogma sufficiently venerates and unfolds the transcendency of the Gods, affording us a viaticum, and recalling to our memory that we ought not to estimate divine power from our judgment. But it is likely that some things should appear difficult and impossible to us, in consequence of our corporeal subsistence, and from our being conversant with generation and corruption; from our having a momentary existence; from being subject to a variety of diseases; from the smallness of our habitation; from our gravitating tendency to the middle; from our somnolency, indigence and repletion; from our want of counsel and our imbecility; from the impediments of our soul, and a variety of other circumstances, although our nature possesses many illustrious prerogatives. At the same time however we perfectly fall short of the Gods, and neither possess the same power with them, nor equal virtue. This Symbol therefore in a particular manner introduces the knowledge of the Gods, as beings who are able to effect all things. On this account it exhorts us to disbelieve nothing concerning the Gods. It also adds, nor about divine dogmas; *viz.* those belonging to the Pythagoric philosophy. For these being secured by disciplines and scientific theory, are alone true and free from falsehood, being corroborated by all-various demonstration, accompanied with necessity. The same Symbol, also, is capable of exhorting us to the science concerning the Gods: for it urges us to acquire a science of that kind, through which we shall be in no respect deficient in things asserted about the Gods. It is also able to exhort the same things concerning divine dogmas, and a disciplinative progression. For disciplines alone give eyes to, and produce light about, all things, in him who intends to consider and survey them. For from the participation of disciplines, one thing before all others is effected, *viz.* a belief in the nature, essence, and power of the Gods, and also in those Pythagoric dogmas, which appear to be prodigious to such as have not been introduced to, and are uninitiated in, disciplines. So that the precept *disbelieve not* is equivalent to *participate* and *acquire* those things through which you will not disbelieve; that is to say, acquire disciplines and scientific demonstrations.

SYMBOL 5

Declining from the public ways, walk unfrequented paths.

EXPLANATION

I think that this Symbol also contributes to the same thing as the preceding. For this exhorts us to abandon a popular and merely human life; but thinks fit that we should pursue a separate and divine life. It also signifies that it is necessary to look above common opinions; but very much to esteem such as are private and arcane; and that we should despise merely human delight; but ardently pursue that felicitous mode of conduct which adheres to the divine will. It likewise exhorts us to dismiss human manners as popular, and to exchange for these the religious cultivation of the gods, as transcending a popular life.

SYMBOL 6

Abstain from Melanurus;[12] for it belongs to the terrestrial gods.

EXPLANATION

This Symbol also is allied to the preceding. Other particulars therefore pertaining to it we shall speak of in our discourse about the Symbols.[13] So far then as it pertains to exhortation it admonishes us to embrace the celestial journey, to conjoin ourselves to the intellectual Gods, to become separated from a material nature, and to be led as it were in a circular progression to an immaterial and pure life. It further exhorts us to adopt the most excellent worship of the Gods, and especially that which pertains to the primary Gods.[14] Such, therefore, are the exhortations to the knowledge and worship of Divinity. The following Symbols exhort to wisdom.

SYMBOL 7

Govern your tongue before all other things, following the gods.

EXPLANATION

For it is the first work of wisdom to convert reason to itself and to accustom it not to proceed externally, but to be perfected in itself and in a conversion to itself. But the second work consists in following the gods. For nothing so perfects the intellect as when being converted into itself, it at the same time follows Divinity.

SYMBOL 8

The wind blowing, adore the sound.

EXPLANATION

This Symbol also is a token of divine wisdom. For it obscurely signifies that we ought to love the similitude of the divine essences and powers, and when their words accord with their energies, to honour and reverence them with the greatest earnestness.

SYMBOL 9

Cut not fire with a sword.

EXPLANATION

This Symbol exhorts to prudence. For it excites in us an appropriate conception with respect to the propriety of not opposing sharp words to a man full of fire and wrath, nor contending with him. For frequently by words you will agitate and disturb an ignorant man, and will yourself suffer things dreadful and unpleasant. Heraclitus also testifies to the truth of this Symbol, for he says, "it is difficult to fight with anger; for whatever is necessary to be done, benefits the soul." And this he says truly. For many by gratifying anger have changed the condition of their soul, and have made death preferable to life. But by governing the tongue and being quiet, friendship is produced from strife, the fire of anger being extinguished, and you yourself will not appear to be destitute of intellect.

SYMBOL 10

Remove from yourself every vinegar bottle.

EXPLANATION

The truth of the preceding is testified by the present Symbol. For it exhorts us to prudence and not anger; since that which is sharp in the soul and which we call anger is deprived of reasoning and prudence. For anger boils like a kettle heated by the fire, being attentive to nothing but its own emotions, and dividing the judgment into minute parts. It is proper therefore that the soul being established in quiet should turn from anger, which frequently attacks itself as if it touched sounding brass. Hence it is requisite to suppress this passion by the reasoning power.

SYMBOL 11

Assist a man in raising a burden; but do not assist him in laying it down.

EXPLANATION

This Symbol exhorts to fortitude, for whoever takes up burden signifies an action of labour and energy; but he who lays one down, of rest and remission. So that the Symbol has the following meaning. Do not become either to yourself or another the cause of an indolent and effeminate mode of conduct; for every useful thing is acquired by labour. But the Pythagoreans celebrate this Symbol as Herculean, thus denominating it from the labours of Hercules. For, during his association with men, he frequently returned from fire and every thing dreadful, indignantly rejecting indolence. For rectitude of conduct is produced from acting and operating, but not from sluggishness.

SYMBOL 12

When stretching forth your feet to have to have your sandals put on, first extend your right foot; but when about to use a foot-bath, first extend your left foot.

EXPLANATION

This Symbol exhorts to practical prudence, admonishing us to place worthy actions about us, as right-handed; but entirely to lay aside and throw away such as are base, as being left-handed.

SYMBOL 13

Speak not about Pythagoric concerns without light.

EXPLANATION

This Symbol exhorts to the possession of intellectual prudence. For this is similar to the light of the soul, to which being indefinite it gives bound, and leads, as it were, from darkness into light. It is proper, therefore, to place intellect as the leader of every thing beautiful in life, but especially in Pythagoric dogmas; for these cannot be known without light.

SYMBOL 14

Step not beyond the beam of the balance.

EXPLANATION

This Symbol exhorts us to the exercise of justice, to the honouring equality and moderation in an admirable degree, and to the knowledge of justice as the most perfect virtue, to which the other virtues give completion, and without which none of the rest are of any advantage. It also admonishes us that it is proper to know this virtue not in a careless manner, but through theorems[15] and scientific demonstration. But this knowledge is the business of no other art and science than the Pythagoric philosophy alone, which in a transcendent degree honours disciplines before every thing else.

SYMBOL 15

Having departed from your house, turn not back; for the furies will be your attendants.

EXPLANATION

This Symbol also exhorts to philosophy and a self-operating energy according to intellect. It clearly manifests too and predicts, that having applied yourself to philosophy, you should separate yourself from every thing corporeal and sensible, and truly meditate upon death, proceeding, without turning back, to things intelligible and which always subsist according to the same and after a similar manner, through appropriate disciplines: for journeying is a change of place; and death is the separation of the soul from the body. But we should philosophize truly and without sensible and corporeal energies, employing a pure intellect in the apprehension of the truth of things, which knowledge when acquired is wisdom. But having applied yourself to philosophy, turn not back nor suffer yourself to be drawn to former objects and to corporeal natures together with which you were nourished. For by so doing you will be attended by abundant repentance, in consequence of being impeded in sane apprehensions by the darkness in which corporeal natures are involved. But the Symbol denominates repentance, the furies.

SYMBOL 16

Being turned towards the sun, make not water.

EXPLANATION

The exhortation of this Symbol is as follows: Attempt to do nothing which is merely of an animal nature; but philosophize, looking to the heavens and the sun. Let the light of truth also be your leader, and remember that no abject conceptions must be admitted in philosophy; but ascend to the gods and wisdom through the survey of the celestial orbs. Having likewise applied yourself to philosophy and purified yourself by the light of truth which is in it; being also converted to a pursuit of this kind, to theology, to physiology, and astronomy, and to the knowledge of that cause which is above all these; no longer do any thing of a merely animal and brutal nature.

SYMBOL 17

Wipe not a seat with a torch.

EXPLANATION

This Symbol also exhorts the same thing. For since a torch is of a purifying nature in consequence of its rapid and abundant participation of fire, in the same manner as what is called sulphur, the Symbol not only exhorts not to defile it, since it is itself abstergent of defilements, nor to oppose its natural aptitude by defiling that which is an impediment to defilement; but rather that we should not mingle the peculiarities of wisdom with those of the merely animal nature.[16] For a torch through the bright light which it emits is compared to philosophy; but a seat through its lowly condition to the merely animal nature.

SYMBOL 18

Nourish a cock; but sacrifice it not; for it is sacred to the sun and the moon.

EXPLANATION

This Symbol advises us to nourish and strengthen the body and not neglect it, dissolving and destroying the mighty tokens of the union, connexion, sympathy, and consent of the world. So that it exhorts us to engage in the contemplation and philosophy of the universe. For though the truth concerning the universe is naturally occult, and sufficiently difficult of investigation, it must, however, at the same time, be inquired into and investigated by man, and especially through philosophy. For it is truly impossible to be discovered through any other pursuit. But philosophy receiving certain sparks, and as it were viatica, from nature, excites and expands them into magnitude, rendering them more conspicuous through the disciplines which it possesses. Hence, therefore, we should philosophize.

SYMBOL 19

Sit not upon a bushel.

EXPLANATION

This Symbol may be considered more Pythagorically, beginning from the same principles with those above. For since nutriment is to be measured by the corporeal and animal nature, and not by a bushel, do not pass your life in indolence nor without being initiated into philosophy; but dedicating yourself to this, rather provide for that part of you which is more divine, which is soul, and much more fur the intellect which soul contains; the nutriment of which is measured, not by a bushel, but by contemplation and discipline.

SYMBOL 20

Nourish not that which has crooked nails.

EXPLANATION

This Symbol also in a more Pythagoric manner advises us to communicate and impart, and prepare others to do so, accustoming them to give and receive without depravity and abundantly; not indeed receiving every thing insatiably and giving nothing. For the physical organization of animals with crooked nails is adapted to receive rapidly and with facility, but by no means to relinquish what they hold, or impart it to others, through the opposition of the nails in consequence of their being crooked; just as the fish called crangæ[17] are naturally adapted to draw any thing to themselves with celerity, but to relinquish it with difficulty, unless by turning from, we avoid them. But hands indeed were suspended from us by nature, that through them we might both give and receive, and the fingers also are naturally attached to the hands, straight and not crooked. In things of this kind, therefore, we must not imitate animals with crooked nails, since we are fashioned by our Maker in a different way, but should rather be communicative and impart to each other, being exhorted to a thing of this kind by the fabricators of names themselves, who denominated the right hand more honourable than the left, not only from receiving, but from being capable of imparting. We must act justly therefore, and through this philosophize. For justice is a certain retribution and remuneration equalizing the abounding and deficient by reciprocal gifts.[18]

SYMBOL 21

Cut not in the way.

EXPLANATION

This Symbol manifests that truth is one, but falsehood multifarious. But this is evident from hence, that what any particular thing *is* can be predicated only in one way, if it be properly predicated; but what it *is not*, may be predicated in infinite ways. Philosophy too appears to be a path or way. The Symbol therefore says, Choose that philosophy, and that path to philosophy in which there is no division, and in which you will not dogmatize things contradictory to each other, but such as are stable and the same with themselves, being established by scientific demonstration through disciplines and contemplation; which is the same thing as if it said, *Philosophize Pythagorically.* And this indeed is possible. But the philosophy which proceeds through things corporeal and sensible, and which is employed by the moderns even to satiety, which likewise considers Divinity, qualities, the soul, the virtues, and in short all the most principal causes of things to be body,—this philosophy easily eludes the grasp, and is easily subverted.[19] And this is evident from the various arguments of its advocates. On the other hand, the philosophy which proceeds through things incorporeal,[20] intelligible, immaterial, and perpetual,[21] and which always subsist according to the same, and in a similar manner, and never, as far as possible to them, admit either corruption or mutation, being similar to their subjects,—this philosophy is the artificer of firm, stable, and undeviating demonstration. The precept, therefore, admonishes us when we philosophize, and proceed in the way pointed out, to fly from the snares of, and avoid all connection with, things corporeal and multifarious, but to become familiar with the essence of incorporeal[22] natures, which at all times are similar to themselves, through the truth and stability which they naturally contain.

SYMBOL 22

Receive not a swallow into your house.

EXPLANATION

This Symbol admonishes as follows: Do not admit to your dogmas a man who is indolent, who does not labour incessantly, and who is not a firm adherent to the Pythagoric sect, and endued with intelligence; for these dogmas require continued and most strenuous attention, and an endurance of labour through the mutation and circumvolution of the various disciplines which they contain. But it uses the swallow as an image of indolence and an interruption of time, because this bird visits us for a certain part of the year, and for a short time becomes as it were our guest; but leaves us for the greater part of the year and is not seen by us.

SYMBOL 23

Wear not a ring.

EXPLANATION

We should understand this Symbol as an exhortation to the Pythagoric doctrines as follows: A ring embraces those that wear it after the manner of a bond; and the peculiarity of it is neither to pinch nor pain the wearer, but in a certain respect to be accommodated and adapted to him. But the body is a bond of this kind to the soul. The precept, therefore, *Wear not a ring*, is equivalent to, *Philosophize truly, and separate your soul from it's surrounding bond.* For philosophy is the meditation of death and the separation of the soul from the body. Betake yourself, therefore, with great earnestness to the Pythagoric philosophy, which through intellect separates itself from all corporeal natures, and is conversant through speculative disciplines with things intelligible and immaterial. Liberate yourself also from sin and from those occupations of the flesh which draw you aside from, and impede the philosophic energy; likewise from superabundant nourishment and unseasonable repletion, which confine the soul like a bond, and incessantly introduce a crowd of diseases, and interruptions of leisure.

SYMBOL 24

Inscribe not the image of God in a ring.

EXPLANATION

This Symbol, conformably to the foregoing conception, employs the following exhortation: Philosophize, and before every thing consider the Gods as having an incorporeal subsistence. For this is the most principal root of the Pythagoric dogmas, from which nearly all of them are suspended, and by which they are strengthened even to the end. Do not therefore think that the Gods use such forms as are corporeal, or that they are received by a material subject, and by body as a material bond, like other animals. But the engravings in rings exhibit the bond which subsists through the ring, its corporeal nature and sensible form, and the view as it were of some partial animal, which becomes apparent through the engraving; from which especially we should separate the genus of the Gods, as being eternal and intelligible, and always subsisting according to the same and in a similar manner, as we have particularly, most fully, and scientifically shown in our treatise concerning the Gods.[23]

SYMBOL 25

Behold not yourself in a mirror by the light of a lamp.

EXPLANATION

This Symbol advises us in a more Pythagoric manner to philosophize, not betaking ourselves to the imaginations belonging to the senses, which produce indeed a certain light about our apprehensions of things; but this light resembles that of a lamp, and is neither natural nor true. It admonishes us, therefore, rather to betake ourselves to scientific conceptions about intellectual objects, from which a most splendid and stable purity is produced about the eye of the soul, resulting from all intellectual conceptions and intelligibles, and the contemplation about these, and not from corporeal and sensible natures. For we have frequently shown that these are in a continual flux and mutation, and do not in any manner subsist stably and similar to themselves, so as to sustain a firm and scientific apprehension and knowledge in the same manner as the objects of intellectual vision.

SYMBOL 26

Be not addicted to immoderate laughter.

EXPLANATION

This Symbol shows that the passions are to be subdued. Recall therefore into your memory right reason, and be not inflated with prosperity nor abject in calamity; being persuaded that no change worthy of attention takes place in either of these. But the Symbol mentions laughter above all the passions, because this alone is most conspicuous, being as it were a certain efflorescence and inflammation of the disposition proceeding as far as to the face. Perhaps too it admonishes us to abstain from immoderate laughter, because laughter is the peculiarity of man with respect to other animals; and, hence he is defined to be a risible animal. It is shown therefore, by this precept, that we should not firmly adhere to the human nature, but acquire by philosophizing an imitation of Divinity to the utmost of our power; and withdrawing ourselves from this peculiarity of man, prefer the rational to the risible in the distinction and difference which we make of him with respect to other animals.

SYMBOL 27

Cut not your nails at a sacrifice.

EXPLANATION

The exhortation of this Symbol pertains to friendship. For of our relations and those allied to us by blood, the nearest of kin are brothers, children, and parents, who resemble those parts of our body which when taken away produce pain and mutilation by no means trifling; such as fingers, hands, ears, nostrils, and the like. But others who are distantly related to, us, such as the daughters of cousins, or the sons in law of uncles, or others of this kind, resemble those parts of our body from the cutting off of which no pain is produced; such as hair, nails, and the like. The Symbol, therefore, wishing to indicate those relations who have been for a time neglected by us through the distance of their alliance, employs the word *nails*, and says, Do not entirely cast off these; but if at sacrifices, or any other time, you have neglected them, draw them to you, and renew your familiarity with them.

SYMBOL 28

Offer not your right hand easily to every one.

EXPLANATION

The meaning of this Symbol is, Do not draw up, nor endeavour to raise, by extending your right hand, the unadapted and uninitiated. It also signifies that the right hand is not to be given easily even to those who have for a long time proved themselves worthy of it through disciplines and doctrines, and the participation of continence, the quinquennial silence,[24] and other probationary trials.

SYMBOL 29

When rising from the bed-clothes, roll them together, and obliterate the impression of the body.

EXPLANATION

This Symbol exhorts that, having applied yourself to philosophy, in the next place you should familiarize yourself with intelligible and incorporeal natures. Rising therefore from the sleep and nocturnal darkness of ignorance, draw up with you nothing corporeal to the day-light of philosophy, but purify and obliterate from your memory all the vestiges of that sleep of ignorance.

SYMBOL 30

Eat not the heart.

EXPLANATION

This Symbol signifies that it is not proper to divulse the union and consent of the universe. And still further, it signifies this, Be not envious, but philanthropic, and communicative: and from this it exhorts us to philosophize. For philosophy alone among the sciences and arts, is neither pained with the goods of others, nor rejoices in the evils of neighbours, these being allied and familiar by nature, subject to the like passions, and exposed to one common fortune. It likewise evinces that the future is equally unlooked for by all men. Hence, it exhorts us to sympathy and mutual love, and to be truly communicative, as it becomes rational animals.

SYMBOL 31

Eat not the brain.

EXPLANATION

This Symbol also resembles the former: for the brain is the ruling instrument of intellectual prudence. The Symbol, therefore, obscurely signifies that we ought not to dilacerate nor mangle things and dogmas, which have been the objects of judicious deliberation. But these will be such as have been the subject of intellectual consideration, becoming thus equal to objects of a scientific nature. For things of this kind are to be surveyed, not through the instruments of the irrational form of the soul, such as the heart and the liver; but through the pure rational nature. Hence, to dilacerate these by opposition, is inconsiderate folly; but the Symbol rather exhorts us to venerate the fountain of intelligence, and the most proximate organ of intellectual perception, through which we shall possess contemplation, science, and wisdom; and by which we shall truly philosophize, and neither confound nor obscure the vestiges which philosophy produces.

SYMBOL 32

Indignantly turn from your excrements and the parings of your nails.

EXPLANATION

The meaning of this Symbol is as follows: Despise things which are connascent with you, and which in a certain respect are more destitute of soul, since things which are more animated are more honourable. Thus also when you apply yourself to philosophy, honour the things which are demonstrated through soul and intellect without sensible instruments, and through contemplative science; but despise and reject things which are opined merely through the connascent instruments of sense without intellectual light, and which are by no means able to acquire the perpetuity of intellect.

SYMBOL 33

Receive not Erythinus.[25]

EXPLANATION

This Symbol seems to be merely referred to the etymology of the name. Receive not an unblushing and impudent man; nor on the contrary one stupidly astonished, and who in every thing blushes, and is humble in the extreme, through the imbecility of his intellect and reasoning (dianoetic)[26] power. Hence this also is understood, Be not yourself such a one.

SYMBOL 34

Obliterate the mark of the pot from the ashes.

EXPLANATION

This Symbol signifies, that he who applies himself to philosophy should consign to oblivion the confusion and grossness which subsist in corporeal and sensible demonstrations, and that he should rather use such as are conversant with intelligible objects. But ashes are here assumed instead of the dust in the tables, in which the Pythagoreans completed their demonstrations.[27]

SYMBOL 35

Draw not near to that which has gold, in order to produce children.

EXPLANATION

The Symbol does not here speak of a woman, but of that sect and philosophy which has much of the corporeal in it, and a gravitating tendency downwards. For gold is the heaviest of all things in the earth, and pursues a tendency to the middle, which is the peculiarity of corporeal weight; but the term to *draw near* not only signifies to be connected with, but always to approach towards, and be seated near another.

SYMBOL 36

Honour a figure and a step before a figure and a triobolus.

EXPLANATION

The exhortation of this Symbol ts as follows: Philosophize and diligently betake yourself to disciplines, and through these, as through steps, proceed to the thing proposed; but reject the progression through those things which are honoured and venerated by the many. Prefer also the Italic philosophy,[28] which contemplates things essentially incorporeal, to the Ionic,[29] which makes bodies the principal objects of consideration.

SYMBOL 37

Abstain from beans.

EXPLANATION

This Symbol admonishes us to beware of every thing which is corruptive of our converse with the Gods and divine prophecy.

SYMBOL 38

Transplant mallows indeed in your garden; but eat them not.

EXPLANATION

This Symbol obscurely signifies that plants of this kind turn with the sun, and it thinks fit that this should be noticed by us. It also adds, *transplant*, that is to say, observe its nature, its tendency towards, and sympathy with, the sun; but rest not satisfied, nor dwell upon this, but transfer, and as it were transplant your conception to kindred plants and pot-herbs, and also to animals which are not kindred, to stones and rivers, and, in short, to natures of every kind. For you will find them to be prolific and multiform, and admirably abundant; and this to one who begins from the mallows, as from a root and principle, is significant of the union and consent of the world. Not only, therefore, do not destroy or obliterate observations of this kind; but increase and multiply them as if they were transplanted.

SYMBOL 39

Abstain from animals.

EXPLANATION

This Symbol exhorts to justice, to all the honour of kindred, to the reception of similar life, and to many other things of a like kind. From all this, therefore, the exhortatory type through Symbols becomes apparent, which contains much in it of the ancient and Pythagoric mode of writing.

Notes to Appendices

1. The original is αγνοηθεις, but it should doubtless be αγνευθεις, agreeable to our translation.

2. Because virtue is the perfection of life, and the proper perfection of any being is the felicity of that being.

3. And this is the case with intellectual goods.

4. The handle of a vessel was called an ear by the Greeks.

5. The original is χελιδονες, which is literally swallows; but as no bird of that species is known among us to be loquacious, I have introduced one that is proverbially so.

6. Self-sufficiency must not be considered in the vulgar sense, as consummate arrogance; but as the internal possession of every thing requisite to felicity.

7. Long garments or robes, both by ancients and moderns, have always been worn as marks of distinction; consequently, like riches, they are among the objects of desire; and although not so extensively pernicious, yet the philosopher very properly places them among things that are by no means free from danger; and which are neither to be embraced by every one, nor without the greatest caution.

8. The sense requires that instead of εν τοις αγαθιος, as in the original, we should read εν ταις ευτυχιαις.

9. Cleobulus, one of the seven wise men.

10. Σκηνους, literally, of a tent or moveable habitation, to which the body, as the receptacle of the soul, may be very properly compared.

11. That is, it is the extremity of insolence on the part of the woman, and of unmanliness on the part of the man. This assertion, however true generally speaking, has nevertheless many splendid exceptions.

12. According to Ælian and Suidas also, *melanurus* is a fish; but as the word signifies that which has a *black termination*, it is very appropriately used as a symbol of a material nature.

13. Iamblichus most likely alludes here to a more copious work on this subject, which is lost.

14. *viz.* Those Gods that are characterized by the *intelligible*, and *intellect*. See Taylor's translation of Proclus, On the Theology of Plato, and his introduction to and notes on the Parmenides of Plato.

15. The justice to which we are exhorted, in this Symbol, belongs to the *theoretic* virtues, concerning which see Mr . Taylor's notes on the Phædo of Plato.

16. In the original ξυνωδιας; but it should evidently be as in the translation ζωωδιας.

17. The *crangæ* are fish belonging to the genus *cancer*.

18. Aristotle has discussed with his usual accuracy every thing pertaining to the nature of justice in the fifth book of his Nicomachean Ethics.

19. By this it appears that the philosophy which is wholly busied in the investigation of sensibies, similar to that which has been so industriously studied in a neighbouring country, and propagated in this, was very prevalent in the time of Iamblichus.

20. Σωματων is erroneously printed in the original for ασωματων.

21. The Platonic philosophy makes a just and beautiful distinction between το αΐδιον, *the perpetual*, and το αιωνιον, the eternal.

"For the eternal," says Olympiodorus (in Arist. Meteor. p. 32), "is a total *now* exempt from the past, and future circulations of time, and totally subsisting in a present abiding *now; but the perpetual* subsists, indeed, always, but is beheld in the three parts of time, the past, present, and future: hence we call GOD *eternal* on account of his being unconnected with time; but we do not denominate him *perpetual*, because he does not subsist in time."—Note to Mr. Taylor's Translation of *Sallust on the Gods and the World*, p. 64.

The elegant and accurate Boethius also very properly makes the distinction between that which is *eternal*, and that which is *perpetual*, or subsisting in time. He says:

"Deum igitur *æternum* esse, cunctorum ratione degentium commune judicium est. Quid sit igitur *æternitas*, consideremus. Hæc enim naturam nobis pariter divinam, scientiamque patefecerit. Æternitas igitur est, interminabilis vitæ tota simul et perfecta possessio, quod ex collatione temporalium clarius liquet. Nam quidquid vivit in tempore, id præsens a præteritis in futura procedil: nihilqne est in tempore constitutum, quod totum vitæ suæ spatium pariter possit amplecti. Sed crastinum quidem nondum apprehendit: hesternum vero jam perdidit. In hodierna quoque vita non amplius vivitis, quam in illo mobili transitorioque momento. Quod igitur temporis patitur conditionem, licet illud, sicut de mundo censuit Aristoteles, nec creperit umquam esse, nec desinat, vitaque ejus cum temporis infinitate tendatur, nondum tamen tale est, ut *æternum* esse jure credatur. Non enim totum simul, infinitæ licet vitæ spatium comprehendit, atqne complectitur: sed futura nondum traosacta jam non habet. Quod igitur interminabulis vitæ plenitudinem totam pariter comprehendit, ac possidet, cui neque futuri quidquam absit, nec præteriti fluxerit, id *æternum* esse jure perhibetur: idque necesse est, et sui compos præsens sibi semper assistere, et infinitatem mobilis temporis habere præsentem."

i.e. that "GOD is *eternal*, is the common judgment of all reasonable creatures. Let us, therefore, consider what *eternity* is, since this will at once discover to us the divine nature, and divine knowledge. *Eternity*, therefore, is the at once total and perfect possession of interminable life; and this will clearly appear from a comparison with things temporal. For whatever lives in time, *that* having a present subsistence, proceeds from the past to the future, and nothing is constituted in time which can uniformly embrace the whole space of its life. For it does not yet apprehend the morrow, and it has already lost yesterday. In daily life also you live only in a variable and transitory moment. That, therefore, which is subject to a temporal condition, although it may never have begun, nor cease to be, as Aristotle thought of the world, (see his first book De Cœlo); and although its life may be extended with the infinity of time, it nevertheless is not such that it can be rightly believed to be eternal. For notwithstanding it comprehends and embraces the space of infinite life, it does not comprehend and embrace the whole at once, since it is destitute of the future which has not yet arrived. That, therefore, which at once comprehends and possesses the whole fulness of interminable life, from which nothing future is absent, and nothing past has escaped, that alone can be rightly reckoned *eternal;* for it is necessary that *the eternal* should always abide present to, and be a partaker of, itself; and possess the infinity of flowing time present."— Boeth. de Consolat. Philosoph. lib. v.

22. There is also the same mistake here with respect to σωματων and ασωματων as noted above.

23. This work is unfortunately lost. (See Fabric. Biblioth. Græc. tom. iv. p. 293.)

24. This alludes to the silence of five years imposed by Pythagoras on a great part of his auditors.

25. This is said to be a fish of a red colour.

26. This is that power of the soul which reasons scientifically.

27. That is, by drawing diagrams.

28. That is, the philosophy of Pythagoras, which is called Italic, because it was first propagated in Italy.

29. Thales was the founder of this sect, and the most illustrious professors of it were Anaximander, Anaximenes, Anaxagoras, and Archelaus.

Made in the USA
Middletown, DE
21 November 2023

43196577R00149